Genders and Sexualities in the Social Sciences

Series Editors
Victoria Robinson
Centre for Women's Studies
University of York
York, UK

Diane Richardson
Sociology, Claremont Bridge Building
Newcastle University
Newcastle Upon Tyne, UK

The study of gender and sexuality has developed dramatically over recent years, with a changing theoretical landscape that has seen innovative work emerge on identity, the body and embodiment, queer theory, technology, space, and the concept of gender itself. There has been an increasing focus on sexuality and new theorizing on masculinities. This exciting series will take account of these developments, emphasizing new, original work that engages both theoretically and empirically with the themes of gender, sexuality, and, crucially, their intersections, to set a new, vibrant and contemporary international agenda for research in this area.

More information about this series at
http://www.palgrave.com/gp/series/15001

Julieta Vartabedian

Brazilian *Travesti* Migrations

Gender, Sexualities and Embodiment Experiences

Julieta Vartabedian
Department of Sociology
University of Cambridge
Cambridge, UK

Genders and Sexualities in the Social Sciences
ISBN 978-3-319-77100-7   ISBN 978-3-319-77101-4   (eBook)
https://doi.org/10.1007/978-3-319-77101-4

Library of Congress Control Number: 2018935123

© The Editor(s) (if applicable) and The Author(s) 2018
This work is subject to copyright. All rights are solely and exclusively licensed by the Publisher, whether the whole or part of the material is concerned, specifically the rights of translation, reprinting, reuse of illustrations, recitation, broadcasting, reproduction on microfilms or in any other physical way, and transmission or information storage and retrieval, electronic adaptation, computer software, or by similar or dissimilar methodology now known or hereafter developed.
The use of general descriptive names, registered names, trademarks, service marks, etc. in this publication does not imply, even in the absence of a specific statement, that such names are exempt from the relevant protective laws and regulations and therefore free for general use.
The publisher, the authors and the editors are safe to assume that the advice and information in this book are believed to be true and accurate at the date of publication. Neither the publisher nor the authors or the editors give a warranty, express or implied, with respect to the material contained herein or for any errors or omissions that may have been made. The publisher remains neutral with regard to jurisdictional claims in published maps and institutional affiliations.

Cover image © Frans Lanting Studio / Alamy Stock Photo

Printed on acid-free paper

This Palgrave Macmillan imprint is published by the registered company Springer International Publishing AG part of Springer Nature.
The registered company address is: Gewerbestrasse 11, 6330 Cham, Switzerland

To my mother

Acknowledgements

I write these lines with a deep emotion while remembering all the people who helped and supported me to transit this long journey. First of all, this research would not have been possible without the generosity of all the participants who shared with me their time and experiences. I am particularly indebted with Reyna, who so kindly opened up for me her world in Lapa (rest in peace, queen of the queens, I will never forget you). Two projects of Rio de Janeiro City Council (*Projeto Damas* and the 'Program to combat child sexual exploitation') were very generous in allowing my participation. Also, *Stop Sida* and *Àmbit Dona* were two organisations in Barcelona which provided me with much support during the research. The scholarship for a research stay outside of Catalonia, Agency for Management of University and Research Grants (AGAUR) allowed me to go to Brazil.

My family, friends, and colleagues from Argentina, Spain, Brazil, the United Kingdom, and Portugal were so important for me, not only alongside my vital trajectory but also through their interest and support in my work throughout these years. Thank you so much for so much love. I am very grateful to Mónica Moreno Figueroa, who provided me with incredible support as my mentor while I was a postdoctoral fellow in the UK and helped me to refine my work on beauty. I am also indebted to Janice McLaughlin and Sally Hines for their warm interest in my research and support whenever necessary. As a special mention, I have no words with which to thank Michael Langan, Maddie Breeze, Dagmar Baumunk, Alvaro Jarrín, and Caroline Burns for their help in reviewing my English phrasing and also the content of the book. You cannot imagine how important your support was; thank you so much!

I am so thankful to Diane Richardson and Victoria Robinson, the editors of the series, who trusted in my research and gave me the opportunity to publish my work. I am also grateful to the editorial team at Palgrave Macmillan, particularly to Beth Farrow, for their help and support during the production of this book.

Last but not least, I want to thank Vincent for his beautiful maps, great patience, support, and love. Without him, this book would not have been possible.

Contents

1	Introducing *Brazilian Travesti Migrations*	1
2	Disrupting Dichotomous Boundaries of Gender and Sexuality	21
3	Brazilian *Travestis* and the Beginning of Our Encounters	45
4	On Bodies, Beauty, and *Travesti* Femininity	67
5	On Clients, *Maridos*, and *Travestis'* Sexualities	113
6	*Travesti* Sex Workers' Bodily Experiences and the Politics of Life and Death	139
7	Trans Migrations: Brazilian *Travestis'* Spatial and Embodied Journeys	163
8	*Travestis'* Paradoxes in the Contemporary World	225
Glossary		239
Index		241

List of Maps

Map 7.1	Lapa and Glória	185
Map 7.2	São Cristóvão	187
Map 7.3	Copacabana	190
Map 7.4	Barra da Tijuca	192
Map 7.5	Les Corts	206
Map 7.6	Ciutat Vella	208
Map 7.7	Sant Martí	209

1

Introducing *Brazilian Travesti Migrations*

Brazilian Travesti Migrations is a multi-sited ethnography with Brazilian *travesti* sex workers carried out in Rio de Janeiro and Barcelona. In 2005, I participated in a research project together with the female (non-trans) sex workers in Barcelona. Although trans women sex workers were outside the scope of the research, they were very visible. Trans sex workers used to go to the local non-governmental organisation (NGO) *Àmbit Dona*, which collaborated with female and trans sex workers in the neighbourhood of the Raval, and where we also conducted the research interviews. We had the opportunity to meet many trans women sex workers with different nationalities, experiences, concerns, and ways of embodying femininity. Two years later, I participated in another research project with transsexual women activists in the emblematic *Colectivo de Transexuales de Catalunya* in Barcelona. I was interested in how they were positioned regarding the medical discourse and practices and how they related to the more global trans movement. Most of the participants were Spanish and presented a corporeal aesthetic quite different from the trans sex workers I met some years before and who, most of them, came from Latin America and self-identified as *travestis*.

© The Author(s) 2018
J. Vartabedian, *Brazilian* Travesti *Migrations*, Genders and Sexualities in the Social Sciences, https://doi.org/10.1007/978-3-319-77101-4_1

Considering that there is no a single way of representing our gender identities and that trans experiences are diverse and can be very flexible, I became interested in the different ways transsexuals and *travestis*, migrant and local, sex workers and non-sex workers were producing and performing femininity. I then perceived trans embodiments as a privileged place for understanding how different cultural contexts can value certain ways of embodying femininity and privilege some forms of embodiment over others. Although at first I wanted to focus on a comparative analysis of Spanish and Latin American trans women's aesthetics, during my first approaches to the field in Barcelona I noticed that the Brazilian *travestis* were considered—among the Spaniards and other Latin American *travestis*—as the most 'beautiful' and 'feminine' ones. In this way, the Brazilian *travestis* were embodying the corporeal myths also assigned to Brazilian women (Edmonds 2010; Jarrín 2017). I then wondered why did they stand out so much once in Spain. Why the Brazilians (and not the Ecuadorians, for example)? Was there any specificity in the ways Brazil was producing the so-called most beautiful *travestis* of the world? Was Brazil the 'paradise' of sexual diversity which encouraged *travesti* identity expressions? I finally decided to focus exclusively on the Brazilian *travestis* and go to Brazil to understand why and how they were constructed with so much fame.

I also realised very soon that since the 1970s, a significant number of Brazilian *travestis* have migrated to Europe, initially to France, to enter the sex work market. *Travestis'* flow between Brazil and Europe continues to this day, despite the fact that the 'conquered' territories and the modalities of sex work have been reconfigured. However, little is known about them. They are considered as 'men' who generally enter European territory to engage in prostitution.[1] It is also common to identify *travestis* as 'transvestite gays,' stressing precisely that it is their sexuality that defines exclusively their gender expressions, while—anecdotally—they cross-dress. Non-trans and trans activists often call them 'transgender,' 'trans,' or even 'transsexuals,' invisibilising *travestis'* particularities. The confusions and ignorance around *travestis'* identities are common and rooted in a long sexological and medical tradition that has pathologised sexual and gender expressions outside heteronormativity.[2]

The German sexologist Magnus Hirschfeld (1992 [1910]) used the term 'transvestite' for the first time in 1910 to refer to a new clinical category that names people who feel the compulsion to wear clothes of the 'opposite' sex. It was thus claimed that 'transvestism' was a variant of homosexuality, that is, it was understood as a 'gender inversion' until the nineteenth century. Some years later, the 'transsexual' medical category was developed in the United States to refer to clinical cases that required sex reassignment surgeries to adapt the body to the mind (Cauldwell 1949). The influential Harry Benjamin (1966) differentiated 'transvestism'—where the sexual organs were a source of pleasure—from 'transsexualism'—where the genitals became a source of disgust. In this way, transsexuality was constructed as a 'problem' of (gender) identity, while 'transvestism' was constructed as a sexual perversion. The medical paradigm then influenced the way to define and 'treat' not only transsexuality but also pathologised transvestism. Currently, the Diagnostic and Statistical Manual of Mental Disorders (DSM-5)[3] defines transsexuality as a gender dysphoria and the 'transvestic disorder' as part of the paraphilias, that is, sexual deviations.

However, Brazilian *travestis* seem to be outside any medical classification. They do not only cross-dress as most of them modify their bodies in a permanent way to live all day *as* women. Moreover, they do not consider themselves transsexuals either because *travestis* do not believe they were born in the *wrong* body nor do they seek surgical transition to fully adapt their bodies to the desired gender, as is more conventionally expected. The term *travesti* originally derived from the verb *transvestir* (that is, cross-dress) but is currently employed (mostly in Latin America) to refer to people who want to look and feel, as they say, *like* women, without giving up some of their male characteristics, such as their genitals. Within this premise, they are aware that they do not want to *be* women, but they mainly seek to resemble women through the construction of a constantly negotiated femininity. In other words, *travestis* are neither transsexuals nor transvestites, but *travestis*, the term they self-identify with and is used throughout the manuscript.[4] Moreover, *travestis* also show that the transvestite/transsexual medical dichotomy fails since the boundaries between these categories are very fluid and cannot represent the great diversity of the gender expressions found in reality.

In spite of this gender diversity and fluidity, *travestis'* identities are generally included and invisibilised under the category 'transsexual' in research conducted in Spain (García and Oñate 2010; Fernández Dávila and Morales 2011), since it is perceived politically more correct to name them as such. Nowadays in Spain, fruit of the powerful medical institutionalisation around transsexuality, to be called *travesti* is an act that discredits by its close link with prostitution. Though, more than 40 years ago, the Spanish term *travestí* (accentuating the last syllable) was popularly used to refer to a variety of people who were born with a body assigned as male but, temporarily or permanently, lived as women. In fact, the few Spaniards who self-defined as 'transsexuals,' who had undergone surgery abroad, were not widely accepted as they were seen as 'castrated persons' by the *travestís*. During the Spanish transition to democracy, and after many years of obscurantism during the dictatorship, the *travestís* were able to be more visible as never before—as artists in many cabarets of the big cities. When these shows began to go out of style, prostitution became the main economic means of life for the vast majority.

Between the late 1980s and early 1990s, and once the medical discourse on transsexuality was already hegemonic in Spain, transsexuals (no longer *travestís*) began to organise by creating political collectives. They argued for the institutionalisation of transsexuality in the health system in order to be able to modify their bodies with more guarantees and facilities to be integrated into society. They also wanted to break the stereotypes that associated them with HIV/AIDS and demanded the respect of their rights as citizens to move away from the environment of prostitution and supposed marginality. Yet, transsexuals (mainly, transsexual women) kept a distance from the *travestís*—renewed with the arrival of Latin American *travestis*, who reflected everything that the transsexuals wanted to avoid.

After an intense political struggle, and having achieved its main objectives, new generations of transsexuals, more politicised and developing new terminologies and identities such as 'trans,' 'transgender,' or 'transfeminist,' began to demand the depathologisation of transsexuality. At present, a large number of these groups critique liberal politics of inclusion and assimilation and reject any medical mandate that determines how their bodies *should be*. They demand that transsexuality is not understood as a disease because the problem is not with their bodies, but with society, which wants them to fit—paying the price of pathologisation—into the normative gender binary moulds called 'man' and 'woman' (Coll-Planas and Missé 2010; Missé 2013).

As in Spain, in Brazil, when the first legal sex reassignment surgery was performed in 1998 and the US medical discourse on transsexuality slowly emerged in the local medical scene, there were already trans subcultures with their own trajectories and historical specificity (Jarrín 2016). During the 1960s, the term *travesti* referred to homosexual 'female impersonators' (later known as *transformistas*) who had the opportunity to move from the Carnival—where they were accepted—to some of the most important theatre shows in the big cities as stars. However, the Brazilian military dictatorship (1964–1985) declared *travestis* as enemies of 'Brazilian family morals' (Hutta and Balzer 2013, 75) and prohibited the theatre shows, while it started an era of great persecution and violence against those who embodied a more feminine appearance. Prostitution became their main source of living and the place where they could express their femininity (though they were harshly persecuted). Concurrently, at the beginning of the 1970s, some *travestis* travelled to France to work in the recognised cabarets of Paris. They obtained fame and the possibility to feminise their bodies as never before, and to live permanently *as travestis*. Some years later, a great number of *travestis* continued going to Europe to work profitably as sex workers. Meanwhile, those who remained in Brazil, and after 20 years of military dictatorship, were no longer seen as artists but as 'criminal' sex workers, as drug addicts, and, later, as living with the HIV infection (Balzer 2010). At the beginning of the 1990s, the first *travesti* organisations appeared to prevent HIV/AIDS among the *travesti* population and struggle against police violence. Therefore, it is in this context where until today the *travesti* sex workers are perceived as 'criminals,' while concurrently, from the late 1990s, medical discourse constructs transsexuality as a disorder requiring medical intervention. Hence, as Berenice Bento asserts (2008, 12), 'it seems that being transsexual still sounds like something that confers more legitimacy and power, once the *travesti* is constructed as the radical other.'[5] However, Brazilian scholars have widely worked with *travestis* and produced important research on these so popular and relevant gender expressions (Benedetti 2005; Duque 2011; Pelúcio 2005, 2009; Silva 1993, 2007; Silva and Ornat 2014; Teixeira 2008; among others).

In addition, and although in Brazil the category 'transsexual' is gaining legitimacy, it does not represent—nor is it used by—the great majority of the participants of this research. Even though, once in Europe, some Brazilian *travestis* appropriate more 'politically correct' words such as 'trans' or 'transsexual' to avoid a sharper social stigma. Throughout the manuscript, I employ *travesti*, as it is the term which the participants self-identify with, and also in order to recognise *travestis'* political struggle in Brazil to be visible within the movement for sexual diversity (Silva 2013). At the same time, my aim is to avoid the 'U.S. hegemonic block on canon-making scholarship' (Noble 2011, 263) and I do not adopt terms such as 'transgender,' which has no sense for the *travestis*, comes from a different social and linguistic context, and is not interchangeable with *travestis* (Lewis 2010). This book stands against the 'global metropole' knowledge on trans issues (Connell 2012, 858), which ends up colonising trans experiences and then overshadows local understandings of the *travesti* subculture. I use Latin American and Spanish scholars to decentre hegemonic and ethnocentric characterisations of trans experiences coming, mainly, from an English-speaking, white, and middle-class milieu. Finally, to name those who do not self-identify exclusively as *travestis*, I employ 'trans' as an umbrella term to refer to people who have or express a gender identity different from the one they were assigned at birth. This category then includes a wide variety of gender expressions such as transgender, transsexuals, cross-dressers, and genderqueers.

An Embodied Ethnography

As it is further explored in Chap. 2, feminist scholars, allied with postmodernism and queer theory, have shown that there is no an accurate and fixed correspondence between the sexed body and the gendered identity, challenging the relationship between sex and gender through an understanding of sex as a social and cultural construction (Butler 1990; Foucault 1990; Laqueur 1990; Sedgwick 1990). Queer theory's emphasis on the performativity of gender criticises dominant social classifications based on the male/female and the hetero/homo binaries. In this way, trans people are positioned as the vanguard in this crusade to denaturalise and destabilise hegemonic assumptions about gender and sexuality. However, queer theory has been also criticised for its radical deconstruction of identity categories and a tendency to overemphasise the potential transgression of trans people (Connell 2012; Felski 1996; Hines 2006, 2009, 2010; Namaste 1996, 2000; Prosser 1998). It seems that it is compulsory to subvert, transgress, dismantle, and deconstruct any power relationship in any way possible, usually thus neglecting trans people's lived experiences. It is precisely in this critique of the dematerialisation of trans experiences that I situate this research.

Brazilian Travesti Migrations is an embodied ethnography in which Brazilian *travestis'* bodies become a key element in understanding *travestis'* identity formations. Gender, sexuality, and space are the three main axes from where to read *travestis'* embodiments as means to become intelligible subjects and, at least temporarily, interpellate a social structure which renders them as abject beings—people whose humanity is being denied constantly (Butler 1993). Therefore, feeling beautiful and desired for *travestis* cannot be thought of as a 'mere' superficiality in their understandings of femininity. Rather, the pursuit of beauty and femininity allows *travestis* to construct themselves as social subjects who feel desired and empowered.[6] In this way, the book's main aim is to understand Brazilian *travesti* sex workers' negotiations of gender and sexualities through their (trans)national displacements: while moving, *travestis* are reinforcing their sense of self in search of a safer place from where to position themselves, live, and face society. Moreover, *travestis'* bodily transformations do not seek to achieve the 'right body,' in case such a body exists as Halberstam (1998) questioned—as if the body were a stable and safe destination to reach a 'coherent sense of home' (Prosser 1998). On the contrary, and although most of the *travestis* follow very well-defined aesthetic practices in their hierarchical career of beautification, their body modifications are framed in a continual process of negotiation in which their identities are reconfigured constantly. In other words, *travestis'* search for a 'perfect' body, as they say, is part of an endless and costly process that, ultimately, is the main way *travestis* find to 'make their lives liveable' (Alsop et al. 2002, 211). In assuming to live as *travestis*, and although discrimination is greater once they feminise and modify their bodies to live all day *as* women, their bodies situate them—though sometimes precariously—in the world.

In sum, bodies and embodiment are at the core of this research, as it is through *travesti* embodiments that they negotiate gender, sexuality, and space in their search of becoming intelligible (and desired) subjects. As a researcher, my own body was also used as a way to get closer to the participants: I was analysed and criticised for my 'lack of' femininity. As it is examined in Chap. 3, my body—between laughter and taunts—allowed the *travestis* to position me unfavourably on their own scale of beauty, and from that point, I began to build relationships with them.

A Multi-sited Ethnography

The transits between Rio de Janeiro and Barcelona are frequent throughout the book. However, this is not a comparative study as I centred mostly in Brazil to analyse *travestis'* main practices, conceptions, and categories that operate in their contexts of origin. Nevertheless, Barcelona, as a representative of any other big European city in the *travesti* circuit of commercial sex, gives prestige to those who 'successfully' can travel to Europe. Rio de Janeiro and Barcelona are then important places for their becoming *travestis*, as their processes of gender transformation are contoured through *travestis'* spatial and bodily mobilisations. In this way, the category 'trans migrations' is useful to understand trans mobilities as acts of survival (Doan 2016) that display both the capacity and agency of trans people as sexualised and gendered subjects, as well as the economic processes in which migrants are inserted. Rio de Janeiro and Barcelona can be read as two cities through which *travestis* are constructed. I did not have the opportunity to accompany the migration processes of the participants following the Rio—Barcelona route. The vast majority of the *travestis* I met in Rio travelled to different cities in Italy to work as sex workers. Although I contacted Brazilians who lived in Barcelona, I could not establish a continuous observation of the migration project of the same *travesti* on both sides of the Atlantic. Such a task, which was

Introducing *Brazilian Travesti Migrations* 9

ethnographically very rich, would have required more time for fieldwork and meant only working with *travestis* in Rio who planned to migrate to Barcelona during the fieldwork period. Therefore, the probabilities of this follow-up were actually very low.

The Research and My Positionality

The fieldwork was divided into two parts. In the first part, I stayed in Rio de Janeiro for six consecutive months in 2008. The second part of my fieldwork also lasted six months and took place in the city of Barcelona, intermittently, between 2009 and 2011. In both cities, I carried out participant observation and 26 in-depth, semi-structured interviews with Brazilian *travestis*, plastic surgeons, and NGO agents who had links with *travesti* sex workers. My entry into the field was adapted to the mode in which I structured my fieldwork in each city (see Chap. 3 for a further explanation of the participant/researcher embodied relationship). For instance, in Rio de Janeiro, beyond the number of *travestis* interviewed, I could interact with many other *travestis* in different political events or with those who daily visited the old house (the *casarão*), where between 10 and 15 *travestis* lived and where the majority of my fieldwork in Rio was carried out. The *casarão*, in the neighbourhood of Lapa, was like a 'social centre' in which the affairs of the *travesti* sex workers of the area were organised and resolved. The *casarão* was run by Reyna,[7] a *travesti* leader and sex worker in Lapa, who allowed me to get close to the *travesti* subculture in Rio de Janeiro.

Parallel to my insertion in the *casarão*, I had the opportunity to participate in two projects of the City Council of Rio de Janeiro, where I knew other *travestis*. The 'Ladies Project' (*Projeto Damas*) was created to provide professional training to *travestis* so they could access the formal labour market. Organised twice a year, it trained a group of no more than 15 *travestis* for three months to acquire the basic tools to seek and obtain work outside the realm of prostitution. For example, they were taught to write a CV, introduce themselves to their work colleagues, use the 'correct' clothing in a work environment, the importance of meeting a schedule and being punctual, among other aspects. The participation to these courses was compulsory and they received financial support for the travelling expenses to stimulate their participation. After completing the training, for a month and a half, they had to do internships in different agencies and public offices that collaborated with this project.

I was not able to fully evaluate the outcomes of this project as I could not do a systematic and comparative monitoring of, at least, the two courses offered per year. I entered the project once the training had started and it was attended by eight *travestis*, consequently, it can be deduced that almost half of their colleagues did not finish the training. In addition, I learned that very few attendees managed to obtain a formal contract of employment in the places where they carried out their internships.[8] For the vast majority of *travestis*, prostitution and, to a lesser extent, domestic service and hairdressing will remain their main sources of income.[9]

The second project was part of the 'Program to combat child sexual exploitation.' A team of three social educators and social workers, and the driver of a van, handed condoms and lubricants to female (non-trans) sex workers and *travestis* in various prostitution areas in Rio de Janeiro two days a week in order to detect cases of sexual exploitation. They worked during the night and the van stopped in different prostitution venues along the three or four hours required for the journey. I participated once a week when the van's route was travelling exclusively to *travesti* prostitution venues.

The advantage of being able to join this team was that I could access places inaccessible to me individually. This was not only due to the difficulties of entering into new and somehow dangerous territories as a woman who is alone in Rio, but because of the possible mistrust that my presence could cause in the sex workers when introducing myself in unknown *travesti* prostitution venues of the city. Therefore, this program allowed me to meet many other *travesti* sex workers in areas which seemed to be inaccessible to me as a foreign researcher. Moreover, the careful collaboration of the members of the team who were working-class *cariocas*, that is, originally from Rio de Janeiro, helped me to understand some of the codes of the different prostitution venues in the city.

In Barcelona, since 2008, I have been strengthening the relationships with Pia, a *travesti* from Rio de Janeiro, who was about 50 years old, a sex worker and former political activist who has lived in Barcelona for more than 18 years. I regularly visited Pia at her self-managed flat, where she lived and worked. For me, Pia was the nexus of union par excellence between Rio and Barcelona. In fact, I had met her in Barcelona before I started the fieldwork in Rio and she was the one who provided me with some contacts in her hometown. Her deep knowledge of some of the *travestis* with whom I interacted in Rio, coupled with her understanding of the situation of Brazilian *travestis* on both sides of the Atlantic, made Pia an important participant in my research.

At the same time, I visited the surroundings of the Camp Nou, the home stadium of the Barcelona football team. This area is one of the main *travesti* prostitution venues in the city. I accompanied a *travesti* worker of the NGO Stop SIDA in her weekly delivery of preventive material to the sex workers who worked there. We went walking and with a very limited infrastructure (compared to the project I participated in Rio). However, I met several Brazilian *travestis* who promised me future encounters but, which eventually, did not materialise. I was not even able to apply the 'snowball' technique with the few *travestis* I did interview. I arranged interviews with many *travestis*, only for them to end up cancelled or a no-show. It is also true that the constant displacements of the *travestis* across Europe and Spain made it more difficult to locate and identify a more or less fixed number of Brazilian *travestis* in Barcelona. Generally, older *travestis* who were already settled in the city—as they did not seek new territories to work—were somehow easier to meet.

The lack of openness of the younger *travestis* towards strangers (as was my case) was justified by the distrust possibly generated by being 'without papers,' that is to say, being in an irregular legal situation as immigrants. Thus, many of them lived in fear of being deported because their tourist visa had expired. Some of them were also working in private apartments with very little or no free time to dedicate to me. With their main focus on working, earning money, and avoiding being expelled from the country, I could understand that talking to me was not high on their agenda. Silva and Ornat (2014) also remarked the difficulties in achieving trust and legitimation as researchers among Brazilian *travestis* who were 'illegally' working as sex workers in Spain (Madrid) because they could be read as a 'threat.'

12   J. Vartabedian

After accepting that in Barcelona I could not meet the number of Brazilian *travestis* that I would have liked, I found another explanation that made sense of the easy access I had to the participants in Brazil. The answer was Reyna, as she was my 'key informant' in Rio (Bogdan and Taylor 1975). The hierarchical and pyramidal organisation of the *travestis* of Lapa facilitated that as soon as their leader, Reyna, accepted me, I could go on to approach the rest and interact with them in the *casarão*. In Barcelona, although I could not deny that there were pimps or *madrinhas*,[10] they were invisible to me. In other words, I did not seek to carry out a comparative study between Rio de Janeiro and Barcelona. As I already said, Barcelona is another scale, among other cities, of the process of beautification and social, symbolic, and economic empowerment of new generations of *travesti* sex workers. Rather than thinking in terms of two cities with opposing realities, I prefer to imagine a continuum between them to understand *travestis*' identity formations and the impact (trans) national displacements have on their lives.

The age of the *travestis* I interviewed ranged from 23 to 65. Most of them were young *travestis* who had a very low level of education, came from the lower social class of the country, were *morenas* (mixed race) or black street sex workers, had almost no family ties, and were at different levels in their processes of body modification. I employ the term 'first generation' of *travestis* to name those who were older than 50 years, middle class, white, completed secondary education, and some of them currently preferred to be called 'transsexual' or '*transformista*' to differentiate themselves from the younger *travesti* sex workers. Most of them had travelled to Europe in the 1970s and faced greater constraints on the public exposure of their identities under the Brazilian military regime, but had the opportunity to study before their bodily transformations. Almost all of them were *cariocas*, from Rio, in sharp contrast to the younger generations which, in greater proportion, came from the North and Northeast regions of Brazil.

The majority of the *travesti* interviewees were current and former sex workers, with a smaller number of actresses, dancers, and hairdressers (from the 'first generation'). Although I met some *travesti* activists—though current or former sex workers—and very few non-sex workers, I interacted mostly with *travesti* sex workers, and this manuscript focuses on their experiences. As I worked with a small sample, it is not my aim, nor it is possible, to consider this research as representative of the *travesti* population. There are many ways of living and experiencing *travesti*/trans subculture, and I do not seek to homogenise its rich diversity.

A primary ethical concern as a non-trans person working with trans people is the issue of appropriation, structural transphobia, and misrepresentation. It was one of my priorities to consider working and researching 'with' trans participants rather than 'on' them. Jacob Hale's (1997) guidelines for non-trans people writing on these issues, and the debate it inspires, was absolutely useful for me. In this way, *Brazilian Travesti Migrations* does not aim to 'give voice' to the *travestis* (a rather colonising project) but to open a space from where the participants' voices can be heard. It was the *travestis* who outlined the research, and I sought to understand their social worlds from within. Moreover, although photographs were important throughout the research process, I do not use any of them to 'illustrate' the book. It is then a political and ethical decision not to show them to avoid any possible frivolity that the images may generate. As I describe in Chap. 3, I use photography more as a way to approach the *travestis* rather than an end in itself.

In addition, it is also very important to recognise my own privileges as a white passing, middle-class, educated, and heterosexual 'ciswoman.' Throughout the book, I use 'women' instead of 'ciswomen' because—although it is not my intention to leave 'women' as an unquestioned and unmarked category—stressing constantly on the 'cis' aspect would run the risk of emphasising the differences between women, instead of creating community among them (Allen 2014). In sum, in this manuscript, I display myself as an anthropologist marked by my social class, gender, sexuality, education, and nationality to reflect how we interacted during the research process.

Outline of the Book

Brazilian Travesti Migrations emerges from the junction of ethnographic research, feminist and trans studies, queer theory (and its critiques), social and queer geography research, sex work, and trans migration studies. In the next chapters, I question how one is to become a 'beautiful' and 'feminine' *travesti* in a social milieu that dehumanises them and whose 'illegitimate' bodies are left to die. Following Brazilian *travesti* embodiments, the intersection of gender, sexuality, and space allow us to better understand *travestis*' own ways of becoming intelligible subjects. Many *travestis* can find a place, though ephemeral, where they can feel beautiful and desired sex workers. In this way, their (trans)national migrations are part of their embodied experiences which allow them to transit through the spatial geographies necessary to becoming *travestis*.

Chapter 2 is a review of the main theoretical frameworks used to question the sex/gender binary system. I show how anthropologists and feminist scholars have contributed to destabilising the male/female binary and visualise the fictional character of sex. The deconstructionist turn, particularly through queer theory and politics, has used trans issues as the paradigm of disruption and transgression. However, queer theory has also been criticised for its radical indeterminacy and detachment of materiality and trans people's lived experiences. I discuss that *travestis*' embodiments, and even though there is not a political will of transgression, interpellate heteronormativity. Concurrently, I explain how they also reinforce a normalised heterosexuality while strengthening the male/female binary through their sexual practices. Finally, I focus on the critiques of dematerialisation within queer theory to understand the meaning of the material in this research.

Chapter 3 is an introduction to the context in which *travestis* appeared publicly in the mid-twentieth century in Brazil and the meaning of living as a *travesti* today. It also describes the way most *travesti* sex workers organise themselves through hierarchical relationships which situate other *travesti* leaders on the top (*mães/madrinhas*). The chapter presents their main aesthetic practices for becoming *travestis* and examines the embodied relationships established between the participants and myself during the fieldwork to, finally, focus on the importance of the photographs within the research.

Chapter 4 starts contextualising the theoretical scenario from which *travesti* beauty is understood by examining various feminist and ethnographic analyses on feminine and trans beauty. The chapter explores the

Brazilian racial classification system to better understand the importance of beauty and cosmetic surgery in a country where the bodies and the skin tone matter. It also describes cosmetic surgeries as an example of a very popular and national practice which, ultimately, reinforces Brazilian social and racial inequalities. As *travestis* reflect national concerns about beauty, their body modifications performed in order to feel beautiful situate them in a scale of success and failure among the group and allow them to 'produce' themselves as intelligible and desired subjects while giving sense to their existence.

Feminist discussions on the intersection of sexuality and gender provide the theoretical framework to Chap. 5, which analyses the ways in which *travestis* interact socially and sexually with their clients and *maridos* (husbands). It also examines one of the main hierarchical and popular classificatory system of homosexuality in which the 'active'/'passive' relationships contribute to an understanding of how the notions of masculinity and femininity are structured in Brazil, to then better comprehend *travestis*' own sexual performances and social interactions.

Chapter 6 describes the different meanings that sex work has for the *travestis* and how this activity shapes their social interactions, bodies, and lives. It situates this discussion using some scholars' readings of Mbembe's concept of *necropolitics* to understand the structural exclusions that dehumanise *travestis*. As abject-others without value as citizens in a neoliberal scenario, prostitution becomes the main opportunity *travestis* have to survive but also is the space of construction and learning of femininity, and of reaffirmation of their bodily transformations. The chapter also examines *travesti* embodiments of their 'Brazilianness' as an identity that gives them value in the transnational and competitive sex market.

In Chap. 7, I describe some social geographers and queer scholars' analyses of normative spaces and the difficulties non-heteronormative sexualities and genders have in finding safe places in contemporary cities. I problematise the metaphor of 'home' as a tool to examine trans people's gender and spatial mobilisations. The chapter also introduces the so-called sexual migration and queer migration to then describe the specificity of trans migrations. It, finally, examines Brazilian *travesti* national and transnational displacements and how they influence ways of becoming *travestis*.

It particularly focuses on the different prostitution venues *travestis* transit in Rio de Janeiro and Barcelona to understand their embodiments in the ongoing process of the *travesti* identity formations.

Finally, in Chap. 8, I stress the many paradoxes Brazilian *travestis* have embodied throughout *Brazilian Travesti Migrations*. I focus on how practices of beautification and mobilisation are acts of survival that display *travestis'* agency as sexualised and gendered subjects to change and improve their lives in a heteronormative society which proclaims that their 'non-domesticised' bodies *must* be left to die.

Notes

1. Throughout *Brazilian Travesti Migrations*, I use both 'sex work' and 'prostitution' to refer to an income-generating form of labour. I do not adhere to an abolitionist stance when employing 'prostitution,' as it denotes the activity in which sexual services are offered in exchange for money. Although I do not deny that there are many cases of sex trafficking which oppress, mainly, women and their autonomy, this book does not consider *all* sex work in terms of exploitation and (trans) women sex workers cannot be seen as 'victims' of an activity that, in the vast majority of cases, they freely decide to exercise. I also exclusively refer to 'sex workers' to avoid the stigma associated with the category 'prostitute' and support sex workers' mobilisations for human rights (Kempadoo and Doezema 1998; Williams 2014). However, it is worth noting that some sex workers political organisations and scholars in Latin America use 'prostitute' in 'an attempt to redefine this term' (Silva and Ornat 2016, 331).
2. Heteronormativity is based on the assumptions that render heterosexuality as natural, normal, and superior. In this way, the concept works as a tool to analyse 'systems of oppression and contributes to an understanding of how more general gender structures and hierarchies are constructed in society' (Herz and Johansson 2015, 1011).
3. Fifth edition, American Psychiatric Association, 2013.
4. For *travesti* and other terms, I retain the original Portuguese words to emphasise, precisely, their contextual and emic meanings.
5. All the translations from the Portuguese and Spanish are mine.

6. I follow Kabeer's (1999, 437) notion of empowerment that 'is inescapably bound up with the condition of disempowerment and refers to the processes by which those who have been denied the ability to make choices acquire such an ability.'
7. All the names of the research participants have been changed to keep their anonymity.
8. In 2013, the website *Transempregos* was created, a non-profit project that aims to be a bridge between employers and trans employees to seek their insertion in the labour market.
9. See Posso and La Furcia (2016) to understand how the 'whore/hairdresser' dyad is displayed among Colombian trans women.
10. As it is explained in Chap. 3, *madrinhas* (godmothers) is the term *travestis* employ to name those with more experience and economic means who protect, guide, and advise younger *travestis* in exchange for respect and money.

References

Allen, Samantha. 2014. Language Tips for Cis Feminists Speaking on Trans Issues. http://frufruscrub.tumblr.com/post/91765505896/language-tips-for-cis-feminists-speaking-on-trans. Accessed 8 Aug 2017.

Alsop, Rachel, Annette Fitzsimons, and Kathleen Lennon. 2002. *Theorizing Gender*. Cambridge: Polity Press.

Balzer, Carsten. 2010. «Eu acho transexual é aquele que disse: 'Eu sou transexual!'». Reflexiones etnológicas sobre la medicalización globalizada de las identidades trans a través del ejemplo de Brasil. In *El género desordenado. Críticas en torno a la patologización de la transexualidad*, ed. Miquel Missé and Gerard Coll-Planas, 81–96. Barcelona/Madrid: Egales.

Benedetti, Marcos. 2005. *Toda feita: o corpo e o gênero das travestis*. Rio de Janeiro: Garamond.

Benjamin, Harry. 1966. *The Transsexual Phenomenon: A Scientific Report on Transsexualism and Sex Conversion in the Human Male and Female*. New York: Julian Press.

Bento, Berenice. 2008. *O que é transexualidade*. São Paulo: Editora Brasiliense.

Bogdan, Robert, and Steven Taylor. 1975. *Introduction to Qualitative Research Methods: A Phenomenological Approach to the Social Sciences*. New York: Wiley.

Butler, Judith. 1990. *Gender Trouble: Feminism and the Subversion of Identity.* New York: Routledge.

————. 1993. *Bodies That Matter: On the Discursive Limits of 'Sex.'* New York: Routledge.

Cauldwell, David. 1949. Psychopathia Transexualis. *Sexology* 16: 274–280.

Coll-Planas, Gerard, and Miquel Missé, eds. 2010. *El género desordenado. Críticas en torno a la patologización de la transexualidad.* Barcelona/Madrid: Egales.

Connell, Raewyn. 2012. Transsexual Women and Feminist Thought: Toward New Understandings and New Politics. *Signs: Journal of Women in Culture and Society* 37 (4): 857–881.

Doan, Petra. 2016. You've Come a Long Way, Baby: Unpacking the Metaphor of Transgender Mobility. In *The Routledge Research Companion to Geographies of Sex and Sexualities*, ed. Gavin Brown and Kath Browne, 237–246. Abingdon/New York: Routledge.

Duque, Tiago. 2011. *Montagens e Desmontagens: desejo, estigma e vergonha entre travestis adolescentes.* São Paulo: Annablume.

Edmonds, Alexander. 2010. *Pretty Modern: Beauty, Sex, and Plastic Surgery in Brazil.* Durham: Duke University Press.

Felski, Rita. 1996. Fin de siècle, fin de sexe: Transsexuality, postmodernism and the death of history. *New Literary History* 27 (2): 137–153.

Fernández Dávila, Percy, and Adriana Morales. 2011. *Estudio TranSex 2010. Conductas de riesgo y detección de necesidades para la prevención del VIH/ITS en mujeres transexuales trabajadoras sexuales.* Barcelona: Stop SIDA. [Unpublished Technical Report].

Foucault, Michel. 1990. *The History of Sexuality*, An Introduction. Vol. 1. London: Penguin.

García, Antonio G., and Sara Oñate Martínez. 2010. De viajes y cuerpos: proyectos migratorios e itinerarios corporales de mujeres transexuales ecuatorianas en Murcia. In *Tránsitos migratorios: Contextos transnacionales y proyectos familiares en las migraciones actuales*, ed. García Antonio, M. Elena Gadea, and Andrés Pedreño, 361–403. Murcia: Universidad de Murcia.

Halberstam, Jack. 1998. *Female Masculinity.* Durham: Duke University Press.

Hale, Jacob. 1997. *Suggested Rules for Non-Transsexuals Writing About Transsexuals, Transsexuality, Transsexualism, or Trans.* https://sandystone.com/hale.rules.html. Accessed 23 Feb 2008.

Herz, Marcus, and Thomas Johansson. 2015. The Normativity of the Concept of Heteronormativity. *Journal of Homosexuality* 62 (8): 1009–1020.

Hines, Sally. 2006. What's the Difference? Bringing Particularity to Queer Studies of Transgender. *Journal of Gender Studies* 15 (1): 49–66.

———. 2009. A Pathway to Diversity?: Human Rights, Citizenship and the Politics of Transgender. *Contemporary Politics* 15 (1): 87–102.

———. 2010. Queerly Situated? Exploring Negotiations of Trans Queer Subjectivities at Work and Within Community Spaces in the UK. *Gender, Place and Culture* 17 (5): 597–613.

Hirschfeld, Magnus. 1992 [1910]. *Transvestites: The Erotic Drive to Cross Dress*. Buffalo: Prometheus Books.

Hutta, Jan, and Carsten Balzer. 2013. Identities and Citizenship Under Construction: Historicising the 'T' in LGBT Anti-Violence Politics in Brazil. In *Queer Presences and Absences*, ed. Yvette Taylor and Michelle Addison, 69–90. Basingstoke: Palgrave Macmillan.

Jarrín, Alvaro. 2016. Untranslatable Subjects. Travesti Access to Public Health Care in Brazil. *Transgender Studies Quarterly* 3 (3–4): 357–375.

———. 2017. *The Biopolitics of Beauty: Cosmetic Citizenship and Affective Capital in Brazil*. Oakland: University of California Press.

Kabeer, Naila. 1999. Resources, Agency, Achievements: Reflections on the Measurement of Women's Empowerment. *Development and Change* 30: 435–464.

Kempadoo, Kamala, and Jo Doezema, eds. 1998. *Global Sex Workers: Rights, Resistance, and Redefinition*. London: Psychology Press.

Laqueur, Thomas. 1990. *Making Sex: Body and Gender from the Greeks to Freud*. Cambridge, MA: Harvard University Press.

Lewis, Vek. 2010. *Crossing Sex and Gender in Latin America*. New York: Palgrave Macmillan.

Missé, Miquel. 2013. *Transexualidades. Otras miradas posibles*. Barcelona/Madrid: Egales.

Namaste, Viviane. 1996. 'Tragic Misreadings.' Queer Theory's Erasure of Transgender Subjectivity. In *Queer Studies. A Lesbian, Gay, Bisexual and Transgender Anthology*, ed. Brett Beemyn and Mickey Eliason, 183–203. New York/London: New York University Press.

———. 2000. *Invisible Lives. The Erasure of Transsexual and Transgendered People*. Chicago: University of Chicago Press.

Noble, Bobby. 2011. 'My Own Set of Keys': Mediations on Transgender, Scholarship, Belonging. *Feminist Studies* 37 (2): 254–269.

Pelúcio, Larissa. 2005. 'Toda Quebrada na Plástica.' Corporalidade e construção de gênero entre travestis paulistas. *Campos* 6 (1–2): 97–112.

─────. 2009. *Abjeção e Desejo: uma etnografia travesti sobre o modelo preventivo de aids*. São Paulo: Annablume, Fapesp.

Posso, Jeanny, and Angie La Furcia. 2016. El fantasma de la puta-peluquera: Género, trabajo y estilistas trans en Cali y San Andrés Isla, Colombia. *Sexualidad, Salud y Sociedad – Revista Latinoamericana* 24: 172–214. https://doi.org/10.1590/1984-6487.sess.2016.24.08.a. Accessed 14 June 2017.

Prosser, Jay. 1998. *Second Skins: The Body Narratives of Transsexuality*. New York: Columbia University Press.

Sedgwick, Eve. 1990. *Epistemology of the Closet*. Berkeley: University Of California Press.

Silva, Hélio. 1993. *Travesti: a invenção do femenino*. Rio de Janeiro: Relume Dumará.

─────. 2007. *Travestis: entre o espelho e a rua*. Rio de Janeiro: Rocco.

Silva, Joseli Maria. 2013. Espaço interdito e a experiência urbana travesti. In *Geografias malditas: corpos, sexualidades e espaços*, ed. Joseli Silva, Marcio Ornat, and Alides Chimin Jr., 143–182. Ponta Grossa: Todapalavra.

Silva, Joseli M., and Marcio J. Ornat. 2014. Intersectionality and Transnational Mobility Between Brazil and Spain in *Travesti* Prostitution Networks. *Gender, Place and Culture* 22 (8): 1073–1088.

─────. 2016. Sexualities, Tropicalizations and the Transnational Sex Trade: Brazilian Women in Spain. In *The Routledge Research Companion to Geographies of Sex and Sexualities*, ed. Gavin Brown and Kath Browne, 331–340. Abingdon/New York: Routledge.

Teixeira, Flávia do B. 2008. L'Italia dei Divieti: entre o sonho de ser *européia* e o *babado* da prostituição. *Cadernos Pagu* 31: 275–308.

Williams, Erica. 2014. Sex Work and Exclusion in the Tourist Districts of Salvador, Brazil. *Gender, Place and Culture* 21 (4): 453–470.

2

Disrupting Dichotomous Boundaries of Gender and Sexuality

In 1949, Simone de Beauvoir's *The Second Sex* claimed that women's social subordination was not due to biological factors. On the contrary, it was the patriarchal system that placed women in the position of the 'second sex' to perpetuate male dominance. Margaret Mead (1935), with her ethnographic studies in Samoa and New Guinea, discussed the idea of the variability of the human species, that is, that sexual roles and people's behaviours were modified according to socio-historical contexts and were not fixed by nature. These first contributions, among others, began to open the way to denaturalise gender identities by distancing them from a sexed body that was used to justify women's oppression.

Alongside the denaturalisation of the category 'woman,' from the late 1960s and during the 1970s, feminist theorists developed the concepts of sex and gender to give them a different nuance than those implied by their use in the medical field until then. These early efforts succeeded in turning the concept of gender into a sociological category, distancing it from the psychological bias provided by the medical discourse (Stolcke 2003). In the 1950s, mainly in the United States, cases of intersexual and transsexual people drew the attention of physicians, endocrinologists, and psychologists to explain the breakdowns between the biological sex and the desired sexual identity. The term gender referred to the social sex,

© The Author(s) 2018

J. Vartabedian, *Brazilian* Travesti *Migrations*, Genders and Sexualities
in the Social Sciences, https://doi.org/10.1007/978-3-319-77101-4_2

21

that is, it was a socially prescribed 'role' acquired through experience. This category was used not only to explain these cases that, although they were not new, were subject to incredible media attention and 'scientific' interest (for example, in the case of the famous transsexual Christine Jorgensen, see Aizura 2012), but also to justify the surgical interventions that were performed on bodies which were considered 'wrong' and did not adjust to the 'real' self. Harry Benjamin (1966), Robert Stoller (1968), and Richard Green and John Money (1969) contributed to developing the idea that these people had malleable bodies, and it was necessary to 'adequate' their sex to the 'correct' gender through surgical interventions.

Yet, feminist scholars primarily used gender as a social and political category. The sex/gender binary was thus actively employed to position sex as 'the biological differences between females and males defined in terms of the anatomy and physiology of the body; with gender as the social meanings and value attached to being female or male in a given society' (Richardson 2008, 5). However, while trying to minimise the biological differences and provide them with different meanings and cultural values in claims for women's equality, this political and theoretical crusade focused mainly on analysing gender and, on the contrary, leaving intact and unquestionable that of sex (Millett 1970; Ortner and Whitehead 1981; Rubin 1975). As Haraway (1991, 134) stressed:

> Fatally, in this constrained political climate, these early critiques did not focus on historicizing and culturally relativizing the 'passive' categories of sex or nature. Thus, formulations of an essential identity as a woman or a man were left analytically untouched and politically dangerous.

Since the 1980s, and especially in the 1990s, the questioning of the sex/gender distinction was emphatic. The impact of postmodernism and the destabilisation of the categories sex, gender, and sexuality, coupled with the theoretical and critical rethinking of feminist studies, queer theory, and, to a lesser extent, anthropological studies, fostered a propitious field for this debate. In this chapter, I consider this theoretical turn in order to (1) describe some cases of the so-called third gender used in anthropology to show that the binary gender system is neither universal nor innate and how this, apparently, destabilises hegemonic and dualistic notions of female/male; (2) examine some feminist contributions that destabilise more deeply the sex/gender distinction; (3) analyse queer theory and its great theoretical and political impact in regard to trans issues; (4) question queer theory's deconstruction of identity categories and its overemphasis on transgression; and, finally, (5) propose the necessity of an embodied ethnography to bring *travestis'* own particularities and corporeal experiences into analytical focus.

Anthropological Approaches and Critiques of the 'Third Gender' Category

Towards the end of the 1980s, the consensus on the biological (sex) as a passive and empty surface that provided the basis for the cultural (gender) was coming into question. Sex could no longer be understood as acultural and prelinguistic, nor gender as a subsequently constructed category. A new conceptual framework arose to transcend and undermine the sex/gender distinction and the dichotomies associated with it. Feminist anthropologists Martin and Voorhies (1975) were among the first to argue that there are more than two physical sexes in some societies. They used the term 'supernumerary sexes' to refer to the possibility of finding ethnographic examples that evade the hegemonic sexual dichotomy of our society. Nevertheless, in most anthropological studies, the idea of the multiplicity of sexes did not have as much impact as that of multiple gender roles to highlight, precisely, variations in gender relations according to different cultures. But Martin and Voorhies clearly refused to accept as universal and hegemonic the duality of sex and gender. Among the Navajo, in the Southwestern coast of the United States, *nadle* is the term used to identify intersexed-born children, a third possibility of sex/gender.

Rosalind Morris (1995) discusses 'decomposing difference' in literature that 'emphasizes moments of collapsed, blurred, or subverted difference; instances of secondary ambiguity; and so-called 'third gender's' (579). The term 'third gender' is used to highlight the impossibility of employing dichotomous gender categories as a framework for the ethnographic evidence found in some non-Western societies (Towle and Morgan 2002). The sexual and gender binarism of the West has a history and cannot be seen as universal because there are examples of less rigid and restricted sex/gender systems worldwide. Gilbert Herdt (1996) understands that it is precisely the consideration of sexual dimorphism as one of the hegemonic principles of social structure that has marginalised the study of sexual and gender variations. According to him, classic studies on sex and gender within anthropology 'have assumed a two-sex system as the "normal and natural" structure of "human nature"' (34).

Ethnographic literature on *two-spirited people* (formerly known as *berdache*) gender identities among Native North Americans (Blackwood 1984; Callender and Kochems 1983; Goulet 1996; Jacobs 1983; Roscoe 1996), the *xaniths* of the coast of Oman, in the Arabian peninsula (Shaw 2007; Wikan 1991), the *hijras* in India (Nanda 1990), the *kathoeys* in Thailand (Totman 2003; Ünaldi 2011), or the *muxes* of the Isthmus of Tehuantepec in Mexico (Subero 2013) seems to challenge the sexual and gender dichotomy of Western society through gender and, to a lesser extent, sexual variety. Most of the people studied are assigned male gender at birth (or are intersex) and dress, behave, and perform the tasks ascribed to women. However, instead of being considered 'women,' they are constructed as an intermediate gender, a 'third' one, as men and women simultaneously.

The scope of the term 'third gender' was not ignored by a significant number of anthropologists who encountered various limitations to it. It was employed more as an alternative to dualistic theories than as an appropriate category. Towle and Morgan (2002) elaborated one of the most systematic critiques to the concept. They considered that it is a Western concept that must be questioned when thinking on 'how "our" narratives about "them" (cultural others) reflect our own society's contradictory agendas concerning sexuality, gender, and power' (476). There is a danger of believing that adhering to the triadic gender system would imply greater freedom and less oppression than in the binary system. It is usually reinforced in the distinction between Western (as oppressive) and non-Western (as potentially liberating) gender systems. This distinction leads to essentialising other cultures and 'distorts the complexity and reality of other peoples' lives' (490). The 'third gender' system can also be very rigid and intolerant. Moreover, the belief that intercultural evidence about gender variation in 'other' cultural contexts can inform radical changes 'at home' is a fallacy. Morris (1995) considers that it is necessary to analyse these examples in relation to the social, economic, and political dynamics of each cultural context and go beyond the 'third gender' category because, frequently, those who are identified in this way are so in relation to an earlier socialisation which is not always based on admiration and respect.

Some ethnographic examples of gender variability may strengthen, rather than dismantle, the ideology of the dichotomous gender system. Don Kulick (1998), in his ethnographic study of Brazilian *travestis* in Salvador, asserts that the 'third gender' theorists naturalise and reinforce traditional conceptions of sexual dimorphism by suggesting that people who do not fit into the male/female binary opposition are left out of the binomial or transcend it, instead of reconfiguring and altering it. Carolyn Epple (1998) also examines how the supposed discovery of a third, fourth, or more gender roles reifies and leaves the male/female binary system intact, rather than disrupting it. According to the author, understanding the *nadle* Navajos as an alternative gender 'keeps the meanings of "man" and "woman" safe from its disruptive influences, and thus forecloses the opportunity for truly radical reformulations of gender' (273).

There is also a tendency while employing the 'third gender' category for each type of gender variation to be so aligned according to a nation or culture. For example, India has its *hijras*, the Arabian peninsula its *xaniths*, Thailand its *kathoeys*, Native America its *two-spirits*, and Mexico its *muxes*. Although the categories are useful to understand the social world, they also establish an unalterable model of interpretation. Finally, Towle and Morgan express their discomfort with how non-Western examples are employed in certain popular trans literature in the United States. Often, it is understood that the presence of the category 'third gender' assumes the existence of difference and freedom. Equating the *hijras* or *two-spirits* with contemporary Western trans politics and identity is, according to the authors, an incongruous move. They consider that it is a mistake to import and appropriate these categories, idealise them, and imagine their adaptation to other (Western) cultural contexts.

Therefore, the 'third gender' category can leave intact an essentialising male/female binary opposition. These ethnographic examples are usually decontextualised by Western anthropologists in attempts to understand 'our' gender system and, simultaneously, eventually establish ethnocentric presuppositions about 'other' cultures. Although anthropological examples of gender variant systems contribute to widening gendered social expressions—as they show that there is no an accurate and fixed correspondence between the sexed body and the gendered identity—anthropologists have not succeeded in dismantling the female/male distinction or questioning the supposed biological component of sex. In the next section, I focus on how feminist scholars, allied with postmodernism and queer theory, do question and challenge the relationship between sex and gender by arguing that sex is also a social and cultural construction.

Disturbing the Sex/Gender Binary and the Emergence of Queer Theory

In one of the most influential studies on the history of the construction of sexual difference, Thomas Laqueur (1990) argues that 'sex' is the product of concrete cultural and historical events. For centuries, both male and female bodies were interpreted hierarchically and along a vertical axis according to the same sex category: the vagina was considered the internal version of the penis. The prevailing belief was in the existence of a single sex, but of two genders, independent of biology. From the end of the eighteenth century, the conception of sexual difference changes radically, due to political and epistemological shifts rather than scientific advances. The 'two-sex model' emerged, which emphasised physical differences between men and women. The two sexes were not only different but also immutable, two opposite sexes ordered horizontally according to the presence or absence of the phallus. A radical dimorphism of biological divergence between male and female bodies was progressively established.

Disrupting Dichotomous Boundaries of Gender and Sexuality   27

Laqueur's great contribution shows us how the social meanings of an era have shaped understandings of sex. Thus, the association of XX-chromosomes, ovaries, or female genitalia with an *exclusively* biologically female body is rather a new invention in history. Similarly, Fausto-Sterling (2000) argues that labelling someone as male or female depends on a social decision, that is, our conception of gender is what defines sex, and not the other way around. As she states, the 'more we look for a simple physical basis for "sex," the more it becomes clear that "sex" is not a pure physical category. What bodily signals and functions we define as male or female come already entangled in our ideas about gender' (4). Evidence of intersexed bodies 'that evidently mix together anatomical components conventionally attributed to both males and females' (31) challenges the certainty of the 'true' sex of a person. The two-sex model has been naturalised and constructed as truth cared and continuously reiterated by science. Children who are born with sexual indeterminacy 'usually disappear from view because doctors "correct" them right away with surgery' (31).

Judith Butler, in her very influential book *Gender Trouble* (1990), has shown that feminist understandings of the binary sex/gender distinction have limited the wider possibilities of different masculinities and femininities when analysing sex as independent of gender. Butler does not only question the sex/gender distinction but reverses the relationship established so far between the two, arguing that gender creates sex. In her well-known quote, Butler asserts:

> If the immutable character of sex is contested, perhaps this construct called 'sex' is as culturally constructed as gender; indeed, perhaps it was always already gender, with the consequence that the distinction between sex and gender turns out to be no distinction at all. (1990, 7)

For Butler, gender is performatively enacted. The solid and 'natural' appearance of gender is instituted and reinforced through a 'stylized repetition of acts' (140).[1] She uses the idea of 'gender parody' when referring to practices of drag and cross-dressing to analyse how we are all performing gender as a kind of parody or impersonation. Our beliefs that we are 'really' women or men are, in fact, an illusion. Thus, there is neither a 'real' gender nor an 'original' identity on which gender is moulded. Gender reality 'is created through sustained social performances' (141) in a continual process that produces the effect of a stable gender identity. For Butler, performances are performative 'in that they bring into being gendered subjects' (Richardson 2008, 12). Moreover, 'sex' is an effect of discourse as discourses construct meaning. When a doctor proclaims a newborn 'girl' or 'boy,' she/he is making a normative and performative claim while producing a concrete action. For Butler, performative acts are forms of speech that authorise, that is, the statements generate an action.

Butler's work, alongside other great influences as Foucault (1990), Rubin (1984), or Sedgwick (1990), lays the grounds for the development of queer theory. Queer studies emerged in the late 1980s as a theoretical and political strategy to denature heteronormative understandings of sex, gender, sexuality, and their interrelation (Sullivan 2003). Before becoming a theory and political movement, the use of the concept 'queer' was—in an English-speaking context—a homophobic slur; a way of insulting directed at homosexuals and all those whose behaviour, appearance, and lifestyle 'escaped' from the dominant rules of human *nature*. The appropriation of 'queer' reflects an ensemble of practices and discourses which transgress (or aim to transgress) essentialisms related to the institutionalisation of heterosexuality. Queer activism—which emerged from a reaction to the ethnocentrism and androcentricity of gay activism (Coll-Planas 2012)—and its heterogeneous theoretical corpus are based on a critique of the male/female and the hetero/homo binaries and the criticism of any essence and naturalisation of gender and sexuality. In other words, queer analysis and politics represent 'a deconstructive *raison d'etre* that aims to "denaturalize" dominant social classifications and, in turn, destabilize the social order' (Green 2007, 28).

With queer theory's emphasis on the performativity of gender, trans people have become 'the vanguard in the war against a binary/heterosexist construction of gendered identity' (Alsop et al. 2002, 204). Trans bodies contradict hegemonic gender expectations, and thus, trans people *ideally* represent gender disruption. According to Sandy Stone (1991, 296), trans people are 'a set of embodied texts' with the potential to challenge fixed male/female identifications based on dichotomous categories of gender and sexuality. Queer theory then understands trans people's experiences as a 'deconstructive tool' (Hines 2006, 51) that contributes to queer theory's main objectives towards, first, a 'radical deconstructionism' that interrogates our gender and sexual orientation categories, making evident they are not exhaustive; and, second, a 'radical subversion,' which means that 'queer theory seeks to disrupt the normalizing tendencies of the sexual [and gender] order, locating nonheteronormative practices and subjects as crucial sites of resistance' (Green 2007, 28). Yet, based on poststructuralist and postmodern deconstructions of identity categories, one of the main criticisms of queer theory lies in its radical deconstruction of identity categories and 'a tendency to over-state the relationship between trans and transgression' (Hines 2010a, 608). In the next section, I examine the most contested aspects of queer theory and politics.

The Limits of Queer Analysis: Beyond Transgression

The indeterminacy and radical constructiveness of queer theory have been questioned from different angles. One of the issues that seems to be more problematic is, following Sally Hines, that 'queer theory presents the dilemma of how to deconstruct identity categories and positively account for difference, without losing sight of the experiences that constitute difference' (2008, 26). Queer theory has been criticised for not paying enough attention to the issues of structure and materiality, neglecting trans people's lived experiences (Connell 2012; Felski 1996; Hines 2006, 2009, 2010a; MacDonald 1998; Namaste 1996, 2000; Prosser 1998). For example, Viviane Namaste (1996) understands the centrality of trans people in queer theory to dismantle the strict binarism of gender and sexuality. However, she questions why queerness becomes detached and completely ignores the suffering and precarious situation of black transsexual women who are sex workers, suffer transphobic violence daily, and do not seek to disrupt any pattern because they are focusing on surviving. Also, transsexual scholars have argued that queer analysis neglects the importance of the body within transsexuality while refuting transsexual people's narratives based on authenticity and identity (Prosser 1998). Connell (2012, 864) discusses the tendency in deconstructionist theory to 'degender the groups spoken of, whether by emphasizing only their nonnormative or transgressive status; by claiming that gender identity is fluid, plastic, malleable, shifting, unstable, mobile, and so on; or by simply ignoring gender location.'

Thus, there is a tendency in queer analysis to overemphasise the transgressive potential of trans identities in destabilising sexual and gender binaries. The fight against any kind of heteronormativity becomes final: it is compulsory to subvert, transgress, dismantle, denaturalise, deconstruct and defy any power relationship in any way possible. Clearly, not all experiences can be read as transgressive, nor should they be seen and understood solely within this perspective and with this end. Butler (1990) discusses the subversive capacity of drag when referring specifically to the documentary *Paris is Burning* where the gay and trans community of Latin and Afro-American origin organise fashion shows and dance competitions in New York in the mid-1980s. She considers drag as a subversive practice, which makes evident the parodic nature of the gender identities. Nevertheless, in *Bodies that Matter* (1993), Butler recognises that not all drag performances are necessarily subversive. Although transvestite practices can be read as subversive because they evidence the performativity of gender, this impersonation is not enough to undermine the roots of heterosexuality. Doing drag can repeat, imitate, and parody gender norms, but does not necessarily challenge such norms. As Butler states, 'heterosexuality can augment its hegemony *through* its denaturalization, as when we see denaturalizing parodies that reidealize heterosexual norms *without* calling them into question' (1993, 231, emphasis in original).

Since the 1990s, trans/queer activists have faced different accusations when they reassert that they are not conformist and they do not intend to *fit* in any identitary model. For instance, Leslie Feinberg (1996) rejects any kind of association between gender identity and a specific bodily expression. On the contrary, she/he proposes to transit through male and female identities constantly and that the requirement of *passing* is the result of oppression. Kate Bornstein (1994) argues that transsexuals cannot become men or women, not due to the fact that they are not 'authentic,' but because those who refuse to identify themselves as 'men' or 'women' radically deconstruct the sex/gender binary system.

Myra Hird's (2000) critical contribution is that queer theory combines existing gender practices while performing gender. The supposed queer subversion does not imply transgression because '*all* modern expressions of sexual and gender identity depend on the current system of the two-sex system for their expression' (Hird 2000, 359, emphasis in original). For Hird, there is transgression precisely when sex and the sexual difference can be transcended. According to Van Lenning (2004), the bodies themselves can never be subversive by definition, but they depend on the meanings assimilated into them. Van Lenning suggests broadening the categories of femininity and masculinity and considering that the lives of those people who subvert the limits of sex should not be romanticised because not all of them intend to transgress and, rather, they are surrounded by suffering and pain. In this way, Aizura (2012) proposes that the *idea* of the gender variant is one which should be theorised as a threat to the dominating order, instead of transsexual and transgender people themselves. In fact, rather than 'disrupt the social order, the complexities of transgendered histories and bodies may disrupt the lives of trans people' (Davis 2009, 98).

In sum, these theoretical discussions have often positioned trans/queer issues 'as a site of either gender rebellion or gender conformism' (Hines 2010a, 600). In order to avoid the polarities and the dichotomies associated with it (oppression/empowerment, stable/fluid, hegemonic/subversive), Erin Davis (2009) proposes understanding trans experiences in an intermediate way because 'while transsexed bodies, histories, and identities may "exceed" the limits of intelligibility, trans individuals are engaged in meaning making—creating coherence both for themselves and for others' (99). Queer theory's emphasis on the fluidity and subversion of identities cannot represent the complex and lived experiences of trans people, many of whom seek social recognition in their everyday interactions and, therefore, aspire to become intelligible subjects. In other words, and as Davis clearly states, 'gender identity is not static, but it is also not unbounded' (99–100).

32   J. Vartabedian

There are also two other aspects of queer theory which deserve to be considered critically. Firstly, queer theory is used as the *most legitimate* referential framework to analyse issues related to sex, gender, and sexuality in academia. It sets itself up as a universalist proposal which becomes the most 'correct' way to get closer to the trans' experiences. Acknowledging the great value queer analysis and politics have in dismantling the hegemony of psycho-medical knowledge on the regulation of bodies, genders, and sexualities, queerness may assume the risk to become 'the norm' and exclude those identified as non-queer for being 'old-fashioned' or 'conservative.' At the same time, and secondly, I understand that this focus may become ethnocentric by being constituted as the milieu (above all, English-speaking, white, and middle class) entitled to examine *other* sex or gender non-normative variants. In effect, when reading all these variants from the exclusively queer point of view, we run the risk of homogenising experiences and conceptions which should be explained according to their own political, social and cultural context.

As I describe next when referring to Brazilian *travestis*, although their bodies interpellate the sex/gender binary system, *travestis'* experiences cannot be thought of *exclusively* in terms of transgression. I examine how they understand their becoming *travestis* by focusing on their actual lives, desires, and feelings. In addition, I question queer theory's tendency towards the disembodiment of identities (Salamon 2010) as the body becomes a key element to understand *travestis'* experiences. Throughout *Brazilian Travesti Migrations*, *travestis'* identity constructions are experienced in/through their bodies. In this way, I align with a 'move towards materiality within deconstructive approaches to gender and sexuality' (Hines 2010b, 13).

On the Subversive Potential of *Travestis* and Its Limits

The bodily, social, and sexual trajectories of *travestis* contribute to avoid thinking about their practices in either/or terms of transgression/submission. It was not my aim (nor my task) to grant *travestis'* experiences a political scope that *should* be understood according to an academic/queer language. I preferred to be attentive to how they defined themselves and explain what it means to be a *travesti* sex worker in Brazil and Spain today. To start with, most of the research participants in Rio de Janeiro but also in Barcelona did not consider themselves as 'transgressors,' many of them did not even know the meaning of the term (as was the case with the concept 'transgender'). Although Samanta did not understand my question if she had ever felt that she was transgressing any norm, she claimed that 'since she became a *travesti* she feels more powerful' (Field notes, 23 July 2008, Rio de Janeiro). Reyna also stated:

> In order to be transgressive, it is necessary to go against a rule. I am not against any rule, I am not normal but I am not against anything! (Personal interview, 6 May 2008, Rio de Janeiro)

Rather, most of the *travestis* with whom I interacted preferred to give sense to their gender in terms of their bodies, that is, they considered the conjunction of female and male characteristics as: 'fascinating,' 'mysterious,' 'pretty,' 'odd,' and 'different.' They were proud of their bodies, especially those recognised among the group as 'beautiful' and 'successful' *travestis*.[2] Many of them were also fulfilled with their penises, an element that made them feel 'different':

> For men, my body is like a fantasy, a fetish. More on my day-to-day I see [myself] a woman with something different, do you understand? But in my work [sex work] I know that I am a fantasy. (Priscila, personal interview, 22 May 2008, Rio de Janeiro)

> I love my penis, I love looking at myself naked in front of a mirror and looking at my feminine body with a penis in between my legs. Ah, that's very gratifying to me. (Samanta, personal interview, 8 September 2008, Rio de Janeiro)

As we see throughout the book, the 'mystery' and 'fascination' that their bodies generate are aspects that *travestis* relate to beauty and their *particularity* for which they are sought out, admired, and desired—mainly—by men. Most of them recognise themselves as feminine and 'beautiful' *travestis* which can also have the ability to penetrate and give pleasure to other bodies.

Concurrently, although most of the participants did not actively claim to disrupt any sexual and gender binarisms, *travestis* are not passive subjects unaware of the meanings attached to their bodies. As we see in the next chapter, since childhood, they have suffered rejection and violence by a transphobic society that is not ready to respect gender differences. However, in spite of the great adversities, most of them decide (to continue) living *as travestis*. Evidently, reaffirming what they want to *be* is an empowered decision with concrete and sometimes lethal effects over their lives. *Travestis* strategically combine performing and embodying their own ways of understanding femininity with the desire to claim the sexual pleasure of being penetrated and, at the same time, penetrating, creating in this way a 'game' where the symbols of masculinity and femininity are appropriated, sometimes rejected, and sometimes accepted in certain contexts of social and sexual interaction. Furthermore, their penises destabilise the assumption—a foundation of heteronormativity—that female bodies have a vagina ('cultural vagina,' according to Garfinkel 1967). *Travestis* repeatedly declare that they are sought out and desired due to their penises, that thing that makes them 'fascinating' and determines—in the field of sexuality—how they will behave and negotiate the gender roles they will perform. However, and whatever the level of 'reaction' to their bodies, and even though there is no a political will of transgression on the part of *travestis*, it can be said that their bodies interpellate and mobilise the male/female dichotomy.

Thinking about *travestis* as an 'alternative' or a 'third gender' would imply recognising that the male/female binary is 'overcome' or 'transgressed.' In effect, any attempt to overcome or transgress the binary, in reality, does not modify it but leaves it intact, because, as suggested by Hird (2000), the supposed transgression of gender and sex identities depends on the current dichotomous system for its expression. For example, one person can defy gender rules by dressing and acting one day as a 'man' and another as a 'woman.' This way, that person breaks up the association of a body with a specific gender identity. However, although it is acknowledged that such an action destabilises the sex/gender system and blurs its boundaries, the meanings of 'man' and 'woman' remain unchanged because it is 'transgressed' within known parameters of gender. Transgression implies a radical reformulation of gender, transcending any sexual difference.

Nonetheless, *travestis* also reinforce a normalised heterosexuality. *Travestis'* gender constructions are intimately related to how they experience and live their bodies and sexualities. In this way, they attach to the bodies and sexual practices a quite 'conservative' meaning that, ambiguously, strengthens the male/female binarism. For instance, Roberta, a self-identified transsexual who underwent a sex reassignment surgery, told me that, before the surgery, she loved penetrating men. However, she always ended up regretting the penetration because her feminine appearance was problematic for her when feeling so much pleasure. Roberta also asserted that, unlike *travestis* who liked drawing men and women's attention, she wanted to use less silicone prosthesis 'because I had the [sex reassignment] surgery and I became a woman' (personal interview, 7 August 2008, Rio de Janeiro). Therefore, Roberta assumed that women are more 'discrete' in their way of performing femininity and since she was operated upon she had to behave in that way. Cristina recounted that if *travestis* imitated women it was because they really liked women, she thought that 'women's feminine body shapes are beautiful, their sensitivity, when the women are sensitive for being mothers' (personal interview, 12 September 2008, Rio de Janeiro). Similar to Roberta, Cristina also associated 'sensitivity' to womanhood, something that many *travestis* admire and aim to imitate (though, without getting rid of their male attributes). Finally, following the same ideas, Rosanne told me that 'I think a *travesti* does not want to be ugly, it's a combination of aesthetics with the psychological. To be a *travesti* is not only to think about being like a woman but to know how to be beautiful, to be attractive … that is common in a woman' (personal interview, 27 August 2009, Barcelona). These statements reinforce hegemonic gender norms based on stereotyped conceptions on how to be a 'woman.' As it is examined in Chap. 5, *travestis* also usually seek a boyfriend or *marido* (husband) who assumes the 'macho' role in sexual intercourse and social behaviours, thus reinforcing *travestis'* own femininity and strategic 'submissive' position. According to Larissa Pelúcio (2009), in *travestis'* gender constructions, 'they subvert the gender and, paradoxically, also emphasise the character of submissiveness behind the contemporary cult to standards of normality, health and beauty' (184).

Therefore, *travestis'* gendered experiences cannot 'satisfy' more radical queer assumptions about gender disruption because, as Davis (2009, 102) expressed, 'unintelligibility may disrupt individual lives.' *Travestis'* particularity lies in the fact that they are capable of performing the gender assigned to men and women, without being men or women. In this way, they can follow normative gender conceptions which provide meaning to their bodies and sexual practices in order to become intelligible subjects without giving up some features that also make them 'different' and 'fascinating.' It is in the intersection of gender and sexuality that *travestis* will transit simultaneously among the margins of femininity and masculinity. Consequently, their experiences, bodies, and sexual practices are what provide sense to their gender identities. In fact, it is precisely this chameleon-like ability which can reinforce heteronormative gender norms and, at the same time, that can be very disturbing, which outlines most of the *travesti* gender expressions. Although for my research participants, such particularity may be called neither 'transgression' nor 'submission,' it definitively mobilises and interpellates the structures on which the learnt notions on sex, gender, and sexuality lie. In the next and final section, I focus on the critiques of dematerialisation within queer theory to understand the meaning of the material in this research project.

Looking for the Material

We have already advanced the great importance bodies have throughout *Brazilian Travesti Migrations*. As we explain further in the next chapter, this research is based on an embodied ethnography delineated by the corporeal experiences of the participants and myself (Vartabedian 2015). Whilst bodies are key elements to understand *travestis'* gender constructions, as an anthropologist, I also used my own body to get into participants' universe and become an intelligible subject/researcher. In this way, this embodied research aims to show the body that suffers, enjoys, is transformed, beautified, or injured, taking also into account the 'sociality of matter' (Clough 2000), that is to say, the materiality of the bodies is the springboard to examine the social practices and discourses which, ultimately, constitute that matter.

Rahman and Witz (2003) explore how feminists have used the concept of the 'material.' In the 1970s, feminist materialists addressed women's oppression as the historical result of the social relations rooted in capitalism. Also, feminist sociological constructionists' accounts of the concept 'gender' allowed them to overcome the reductionist presumptions based on the biological difference between men and women. Material feminists like Delphy or Hartmann aimed to 'develop a materialist foundation for a theory of patriarchy' (Rahman and Witz 2003, 247) in which patriarchy was considered a 'mode of production' where men controlled the labour of women in the private and public spheres. In the 1990s, feminists expanded the concept of the material to go beyond the economic. Butler's (1998) problematisation of the distinction between the material and cultural emphasised that the social is under-theorised within Marxist materialism and, thus, it was necessary to include the cultural, privileging poststructuralism as the more proper theory to analyse 'the *effectivity* of the discursive (that is cultural) rather than the *determinism* of the material (namely, the economic)' (Rahman and Witz 2003, 249, emphasis in original).

As we have discussed earlier, Butler (1993) asserts that we cannot consider the matter (that is, the body) as prior to discourse because 'is fully sedimented with discourses on sex and sexuality' (29). For Butler, the matter is always materialised in the way that has 'to be thought in relation to the productive and, indeed, materializing effects of regulatory power in the Foucauldian sense' (9–10). Therefore, she reshapes the matter into materiality to denote 'the process of materialization that stabilizes over time to produce the effect of boundary, fixity, and surface we call matter' (9). In this way, Butler's cultural materialism is criticised by the idea that 'bodies can only ever come to matter through discourse and culture' (Rahman and Witz 2003, 255). In other words, while querying any ontological stability of gender and sexuality's construction, Butler evokes materiality as the 'materialized effects' of the discursive formation of gender. Although she asseverates that 'to call a presupposition into question is not the same as doing away with it' (Butler 1993, 30), materialist feminists consider problematic that poststructuralist and deconstructionist analyses have contributed to an uncertain and ephemeral way to account for a social ontology of gender and sexuality.

Finally, as Rahman and Witz suggest, other feminists have recuperated the body from the term 'materiality.' For example, Bordo (1993, 1998), Rothfield (1996), or Young (1994) analyse the embodied practices of gendered and sexualised beings in order to recognise that we *are* bodies and cannot avoid the physical locatedness in time and space, in a specific socio-cultural context from where we interact with the world. However, this bodily and lived experience cannot be detached from social practice and discourse. The materiality is linked not only with *being* but also with a 'similarly practical "doing" of the gendered social—that sense of "materiality" as actual practices and actions' (Rahman and Witz 2003, 256). Similarly, Hines (2009) refers to an emerging 'material queer turn' that aims to address 'the ways in which gender and sexuality are constructed through cultural meanings and practices, and the ways in which gender and sexuality are lived through the body' (97). In other words, it is necessary to examine the material and cultural together and analyse how discourse, structure, and embodied experiences converge as multiple layers to acknowledge how power relations are produced and resisted. Likewise, Connell (2012) is not satisfied with the exclusive explanation of gender as performative and citational. Rather, she characterises gender as ontoformative because 'social practice continuously brings social reality into being, and that social reality becomes the ground of new practice, through time' (866). *Brazilian Travesti Migrations*, thus, brings the body to the foreground to examine how the material, the discursive, and the embodied are entangled to develop an account of *travestis'* gender and sexuality constructions.

This chapter has presented a review of the main theoretical frameworks used to question the sex/gender binary system. Anthropologists and feminist scholars have contributed to destabilising—with disparate efficiency—the male/female binary and visualise the fictional character of sex, that is, there is no correspondence between the sex assigned at birth and the performed gender. The deconstructionist turn, particularly through queer theory and politics, has used trans issues as the paradigm of disruption and transgression. However, queer theory has also been criticised for its radical indeterminacy and detachment of materiality and trans people's lived experiences. As we see throughout the next chapters, I bring Brazilian *travestis'* own particularities and bodily experiences to explore gender, sexuality, and space as structuring axes in *travestis'* lives.

Notes

1. Before Butler and queer analysis, ethnomethodologists Garfinkel (1967), and Kessler and McKenna (1978) analysed transsexuality as an example that provides 'key evidence about how gender categories are sustained in everyday practices of speech, styles of interaction, and divisions of labor' (Connell 2012, 860).
2. Although these categories are explained further in Chap. 4, *travestis* create symbolic and corporeal hierarchies that organise them as 'successful' or not according to—mostly—the degree of beauty achieved.

References

Aizura, Aren. 2012. The Persistence of Transgender Travel Narratives. In *Transgender Migrations. The Bodies, Borders, and Politics of Transition*, ed. Trystan Cotton, 139–156. New York/London: Routledge.

Alsop, Rachel, Annette Fitzsimons, and Kathleen Lennon. 2002. *Theorizing Gender*. Cambridge: Polity Press.

Benjamin, Harry. 1966. *The Transsexual Phenomenon: A Scientific Report on Transsexualism and Sex Conversion in the Human Male and Female*. New York: Julian Press.

Blackwood, Evelyn. 1984. Sexuality and Gender in Certain Native American Tribes: The Case of Cross-Gender Females. *Signs: Journal of Women in Culture and Society* 10 (1): 27–42.

Bordo, Susan. 1993. *Unbearable Weight. Feminism, Western Culture and the Body*. Berkeley: University of California Press.

———. 1998. Bringing Body to Theory. In *Body and Flesh: A Philosophical Reader*, ed. Donn Welton, 84–97. Oxford: Blackwell.

Bornstein, Kate. 1994. *Gender Outlaw: On Men, Women, and the Rest of Us*. New York: Routledge.

40   J. Vartabedian

Butler, Judith. 1990. *Gender Trouble: Feminism and the Subversion of Identity*. New York: Routledge.

———. 1993. *Bodies That Matter: On the Discursive Limits of 'Sex.'* New York: Routledge.

———. 1998. Merely Cultural. *New Left Review* 227: 33–44.

Callender, Charles, and Lee Kochems. 1983. The North American Berdache. *Current Anthropology* 24 (4): 443–470.

Clough, Patricia. 2000. Judith Butler. In *The Blackwell Companion to Major Social Theorists*, ed. George Ritzer, 754–773. Oxford: Blackwell.

Coll-Planas, Gerard. 2012. *La carn i la metàfora. Una reflexió sobre el cos a la teoria queer*. Barcelona: Editorial UOC.

Connell, Raewyn. 2012. Transsexual Women and Feminist Thought: Toward New Understandings and New Politics. *Signs: Journal of Women in Culture and Society* 37 (4): 857–881.

Davis, Erin. 2009. Situating 'Fluidity.' (Trans)Gender Identification and the Regulation of Gender Diversity. *GLQ: A Journal of Lesbian and Gay Studies* 15 (1): 97–130.

de Beauvoir, Simone. 1989 [1949]. *The Second Sex*. New York: Vintage Books.

Epple, Carolyn. 1998. Coming to Terms with Navajo *nádleehí*: A Critique of *berdache*, 'Gay,' 'Alternate Gender,' and 'Two-Spirit'. *American Ethnologist* 25 (2): 267–290.

Fausto-Sterling, Anne. 2000. *Sexing the Body. Gender Politics and the Construction of Sexuality*. New York: Basic Books.

Feinberg, Leslie. 1996. *Transgender Warriors: Making History from Joan of Arc to Dennis Rodman*. Boston: Beacon Books.

Felski, Rita. 1996. Fin de siècle, fin de sexe: Transsexuality, Postmodernism and the Death of History. *New Literary History* 27 (2): 137–153.

Foucault, Michel. 1990. *The History of Sexuality*, An Introduction. Vol. 1. London: Penguin.

Garfinkel, Harold. 1967. *Studies in Ethnomethodology*. Englewood Cliffs: Prentice-Hall.

Goulet, Jean-Guy. 1996. The 'Berdache'/'Two-Spirit': A Comparison of Anthropological and Native Constructions of Gendered Identities Among the Northern Athapaskans. *The Journal of the Royal Anthropological Institute* 2 (4): 683–701.

Green, Adam. 2007. Queer Theory and Sociology: Locating the Subject and the Self in Sexuality Studies. *Sociological Theory* 25 (1): 26–45.

Green, Richard, and John Money, eds. 1969. *Transsexualism and Sex Reassignment*. Baltimore: Johns Hopkins University Press.

Disrupting Dichotomous Boundaries of Gender and Sexuality 41

Haraway, Donna. 1991. *Simians, Cyborgs, and Women. The Reinvention of Nature*. New York: Routledge.

Herdt, Gilbert. 1996. Introduction. Third Sexes and Third Genders. In *Third Sex, Third Gender. Beyond Sexual Dimorphism in Culture and History*, ed. Gilbert Herdt, 21–81. New York: Zone Books.

Hines, Sally. 2006. What's the Difference? Bringing Particularity to Queer Studies of Transgender. *Journal of Gender Studies* 15 (1): 49–66.

———. 2008. Feminist Theories. In *Introducing Gender and Women's Studies*, ed. Diane Richardson and Victoria Robinson, 3rd ed., 20–34. Basingstoke: Palgrave.

———. 2009. A Pathway to Diversity?: Human Rights, Citizenship and the Politics of Transgender. *Contemporary Politics* 15 (1): 87–102.

———. 2010a. Queerly Situated? Exploring Negotiations of Trans Queer Subjectivities at Work and Within Community Spaces in the UK. *Gender, Place and Culture* 17 (5): 597–613.

———. 2010b. Introduction. In *Transgender Identities: Towards a Social Analysis of Gender Diversity*, ed. Sally Hines and Tam Sanger, 1–22. New York/Abingdon: Routledge.

Hird, Myra. 2000. Gender's Nature. Intersexuality, Transsexualism and the 'Sex/Gender' Binary. *Feminist Theory* 1 (3): 347–364.

Jacobs, Sue-Ellen. 1983. Comments on 'The North American Berdache' by Charles Callender and Lee Kochems. *Current Anthropology* 24 (4): 459–460.

Kessler, Suzanne, and Wendy McKenna. 1978. *Gender: An Ethnomethodological Approach*. Chicago: University of Chicago Press.

Kulick, Don. 1998. *Travesti: Sex, Gender and Culture among Brazilian Transgendered Prostitutes*. Chicago: University of Chicago Press.

Laqueur, Thomas. 1990. *Making Sex: Body and Gender from the Greeks to Freud*. Cambridge, MA: Harvard University Press.

MacDonald, Eleanor. 1998. Critical Identities: Rethinking Feminism Through Transgender Politics. *Atlantis* 23 (1): 3–12.

Martin, Kay, and Barbara Voorhies. 1975. Supernumerary Sexes. In *Female of the Species*, 84–107. New York/London: Columbia University Press.

Mead, Margaret. 1935. *Sex and Temperament in Three Primitive Societies*. New York: William Morrow and Company.

Millett, Kate. 1970. *Sexual Politics*. Garden City: Doubleday.

Morris, Rosalind. 1995. All Made Up: Performance Theory and the New Anthropology of Sex and Gender. *Annual Review of Anthropology* 24: 567–592.

Namaste, Viviane. 1996. 'Tragic Misreadings.' Queer Theory's Erasure of Transgender Subjectivity. In *Queer Studies. A Lesbian, Gay, Bisexual and Transgender Anthology*, ed. Brett Beemyn and Mickey Eliason, 183–203. New York/London: New York University Press.

———. 2000. *Invisible Lives. The Erasure of Transsexual and Transgendered People*. Chicago: University of Chicago Press.

Nanda, Serena. 1990. *Neither Man Nor Woman. The Hijras of India*. Belmont: Wadsworth.

Ortner, Sherry, and Harriet Whitehead, eds. 1981. *Sexual Meanings: The Cultural Construction of Sexuality*. Cambridge: Cambridge University Press.

Pelúcio, Larissa. 2009. *Abjeção e Desejo: uma etnografia travesti sobre o modelo preventivo de aids*. São Paulo: Annablume, Fapesp.

Prosser, Jay. 1998. *Second Skins: The Body Narratives of Transsexuality*. New York: Columbia University Press.

Rahman, Momin, and Anne Witz. 2003. What Really Matters? The Elusive Quality of the Material in Feminist Thought. *Feminist Theory* 4 (3): 243–261.

Richardson, Diane. 2008. Conceptualizing Gender. In *Introducing Gender and Women's Studies*, ed. Diane Richardson and Victoria Robinson, 3rd ed., 3–19. Basingstoke: Palgrave.

Roscoe, Will. 1996. How to Become a Berdache: Toward a Unified Analysis of Gender Diversity. In *Third Sex, Third Gender. Beyond Sexual Dimorphism in Culture and History*, ed. Gilbert Herdt, 329–371. New York: Zone Books.

Rothfield, Philipa. 1996. Menopausal Embodiment. In *Reinterpreting Menopause: Cultural and Philosophical Issues*, ed. Paul Komesaroff, Philipa Rothfield, and Jeanne Daly, 32–53. London: Routledge.

Rubin, Gayle. 1975. The Traffic in Women: Notes on the 'Political Economy' of Sex. In *Toward an Anthropology of Women*, ed. Rayna Reiter, 157–210. New York: Monthly Review Press.

———. 1984. Thinking Sex: Notes for a Radical Theory of the Politics of Sexuality. In *Pleasure and Danger: Exploring Female Sexuality*, ed. Carole Vance, 267–319. London: Routledge.

Salamon, Gayle. 2010. *Assuming a Body. Transgender and Rhetorics of Materiality*. New York: Columbia University Press.

Sedgwick, Eve. 1990. *Epistemology of the Closet*. Berkeley: University Of California Press.

Shaw, Alison. 2007. Changing Sex and Bending Gender: An Introduction. In *Changing Sex and Bending Gender*, ed. Alison Shaw and Shirley Ardener, 1–19. Oxford: Berghahn Books.

Stolcke, Verena. 2003. La mujer es puro cuento: la cultura del género. *Quaderns de l'Institut Cátala d'Antropologia* 19: 69–95.

Stoller, Robert. 1968. *Sex and Gender: The Development of Masculinity and Feminity*. Vol. 1. London: Maresfield Reprints.

Stone, Sandy. 1991. The Empire Strikes Back: A Posttranssexual Manifesto. In *Body Guards: The Cultural Politics of Gender Ambiguity*, ed. Kristina Straub and Julia Epstein, 280–304. New York: Routledge.

Subero, Gustavo. 2013. *Muxeninity* and the Institutionalization of a Third Gender Identity in Alejandra Islas's *Muxes: auténticas, intrépidas, buscadoras de peligro. Hispanic Research Journal. Iberian and Latin American Studies* 14 (2): 175–193.

Sullivan, Nikki. 2003. *A Critical Introduction to Queer Theory*. Edinburgh: Edinburgh University Press.

Totman, Richard. 2003. *The Third Sex: Kathoey, Thailand's Ladyboys*. London: London Souvenir Press.

Towle, Evan, and Lynn Morgan. 2002. Romancing the Transgender Native. Rethinking the Use of the 'Third Gender' Concept. *GLQ: A Journal of Lesbian and Gay Studies* 8 (4): 469–497.

Ünaldi, Serhat. 2011. Back in the Spotlight: The Cinematic Regime of Representation of *Kathoeys* and Gay Men in Thailand. In *Queer Bangkok: Twenty-First-Century Markets, Media, and Rights*, ed. Peter Jackson, 59–78. Hong Kong: Hong Kong University Press.

Van Lenning, Alkeline. 2004. The Body as Crowbar. Transcending or Stretching Sex? *Feminist Theory* 5 (1): 25–47.

Vartabedian, Julieta. 2015. Towards a Carnal Anthropology. Reflections of an 'Imperfect' Anthropologist. *Qualitative Research* 15 (5): 568–582.

Wikan, Unni. 1991. The Xanith: A Third Gender Role? In *Behind the Veil in Arabia: Women in Oman*, 168–186. Chicago: University of Chicago Press.

Young, Iris Marion. 1994. Gender as Seriality: Thinking About Women as a Social Collective. *Signs* 19 (3): 713–738.

3

Brazilian *Travestis* and the Beginning of Our Encounters

Travestis exist throughout Latin America and the world, but those from Brazil are particularly well known as 'they occupy a strikingly visible place in both social space and the cultural imaginary' (Kulick 1998, 6). Although some succeed in achieving public fame and admiration, their success hardly represents the experiences of the vast majority of *travestis*. Thus, most of the research participants came from economically rather poor backgrounds, had low levels of education—especially the younger generation—were stigmatised, and suffered violence from the police, their clients (in the case of the sex workers), and society in general. Being a *travesti* in Brazilian society is a difficult proposition, as it is both intolerant and ambivalent towards sexual and gender diversity (Green 1999). The supposed freedom and permissiveness Brazil projects through its Carnival festivities contrasts with the presence of a rigid gender system and patriarchal tradition (Parker 1991).

According to DaMatta (1997), the interpretation of the Carnival as an event in which gender roles are reversed and social differences fade is an illusion. Numerous studies (Bastide 1959; Green 1999; Scheper-

---

Part of this chapter is based on earlier versions of published work (see Vartabedian 2015, 2016).

© The Author(s) 2018

J. Vartabedian, *Brazilian* Travesti *Migrations*, Genders and Sexualities in the Social Sciences, https://doi.org/10.1007/978-3-319-77101-4_3

45

Hughes 1992) claim that heterosexual men who temporarily become transvestites—that is, men who dress up as women during Carnival—rather than reversing gender roles, are in fact collectively reaffirming their masculinity through a parody or farce, 'showing how far they can go beyond their own heteronormative limits' (Figari 2009, 134). Nevertheless, during the era of the military dictatorship (1964–1985), Carnival became the place *par excellence* for *travestis* to display themselves publicly without fear of repression.

In this chapter, I introduce the context in which *travestis* appeared publicly in the mid-twentieth century in Brazil and what it means to live as a *travesti* today. I also describe the way *travesti* sex workers organise their social relationships in order to survive in a harsh milieu of competitiveness and violence. Additionally, I present their main aesthetic practices for becoming *travestis* while advancing how their migratory displacements play a crucial role in achieving it. Finally, I describe how I started the research in Rio while examining my own bodily experiences and new role as a 'photographer' during this ethnographic encounter.

The Emergence of *Travestis*: From Theatre Shows to the Streets

The origin of the term *travesti* dates back to the early twentieth century in Brazil. In the 1940s, the so-called Transvestites' Balls emerged as privileged places for those who wanted to display publicly other forms of gender expressions. Although the street Carnival supporters could also transvestite there, Transvestites' Balls were the main places where the rule was the non-regulation, and the masculine and feminine norms could be transgressed without worrying about any social hostility or punishment. However, from the 1950s, the Brazilian press made a clear distinction between the Carnival events where heterosexual men cross-dressed for a temporary gender transgression and those effeminate men who wore feminine clothes to express their 'real' identity (Green 1999, 213). A moralistic tone against any homosexual participation in Carnival started to appear in magazines and newspapers of that period.

Although the word *travesti* existed, it did not have the same meaning as it is given today. Until the mid-1970s the term was used as a synonym of transvestite or *transformista*, that is, homosexual female impersonators. The word *travesti* was also used to refer to *all* homosexuals. This does not mean that there were no people who wanted to live their femininity permanently. Yet, their public exposure in the streets was forbidden during the military dictatorship. Cross-dressing was only accepted during Carnival, in specific balls, or on stages—where some *travesti* artists obtained fame and recognition. As Figari (2009) described, femininity could only be represented indoors. Those who wanted to live as women had to hide and protect themselves in the darkness of the night. According to the Penal Code, it was forbidden to change the gender distinction in public places and, therefore, *travestis* 'could only find one place, the prison, if they were off stage or out of bed' (Figari 2009, 133).

Balzer (2010) also points out how, in democratic Brazil, after the Second World War, trans people were able to move away from the space of the Carnival to the theatre stages of the big cities where they obtained a greater social acceptance. It was the military coup of 1964 that forced these new national celebrities to leave the stage due to censorship and persecution. In the public opinion, they were constructed as corrupting the morality of the Brazilian family. After 20 years of military dictatorship, 'in the view of most part[s] of Brazilian society, *travestis* were no longer admired and respected celebrities, but they were considered criminals associated with "prostitution," drugs, and later, HIV/AIDS' (Balzer 2010, 89). In fact, prostitution became their main economic resource for survival: the increase in the number of *travesti* sex workers was closely linked to the repression of the dictatorship (Hutta and Balzer 2013). However, within this space of illegality, discourses and practices constructed around their identities began to emerge. *Travestis* started to go out massively to the street to fight for a space for the female (non-trans) sex workers. Nevertheless, obtaining this visibility was not easy in a social and political context where 'everything was prohibited,' as Reyna stated. *Travesti* Fernanda Farias de Albuquerque recounts in her biography that 'in Rio, we were killed as if we were chickens. Three or four *travestis* per week' (Albuquerque and Jannelli 1996, 79).

It was not difficult to notice experiences of the violence of past decades inflicted on *travestis'* lives and bodies while I was in Rio de Janeiro. The expression 'survivors' referred to older *travesti* sex workers (approximately 50 years and older), who had had to struggle for survival during the hardest period of *travesti* persecution in Brazil. On some of the older research participants' bodies, scars, mainly on the arms and necks, were visible. I was informed that they used to cut themselves with a hidden razor blade on different parts of the body during arbitrary arrests ('Gillette in the flesh,' to use the phrase of Mott and Assunção 1987) in order to claim their release. If they wanted to be released, they had only their own bodies to protest with and the ability to threaten the police with their possibly infected blood.[1]

After the military dictatorship, the first generations of *travestis* who dared to exhibit themselves in the streets opened the path to forge an identity. At the beginning of the 1990s, the first NGO organised by *travestis*, ASTRAL (*Associação de Travestis e Liberados*), was founded in Rio de Janeiro. Its main aims were to denounce police violence, campaign for justice and prevent HIV/AIDS among the *travesti* population (Hutta and Balzer 2013). The professionalisation of *travesti* self-organisation was an important first step in their campaign for rights.

Brazilian *Travestis* Today

It is undeniable that the situation today has improved compared to 40 or 50 years ago: both the intensity and magnitude of violence have decreased. New generations of *travestis* recognise that they have more opportunities to live their lives as *travestis* (Duque 2011) and their political movements are much stronger and numerous. *Travestis* can more easily access basic rights such as health or education and more public policies are being implemented to improve trans people's lives.

In 2011, the campaign *Rio Sem Homophobia* (Rio Without Homophobia) was launched in the state of Rio de Janeiro to combat discrimination against LGBTI people, assist them, and promote citizenship among this population. Since 2010, it is possible to use trans people's social names in state administrations of various regions of the country which encourage them, among other issues, to continue their studies

Brazilian *Travestis* and the Beginning of Our Encounters

while they feel less discriminated and more respected. There is, for the first time, a trans woman in the volleyball league (Botta 2017) and trans people (both men and women) are becoming more visible as the main characters of the very influential and mass consumption soap operas in the Brazilian popular culture (although these characters are sometimes reinforcing stereotypes of trans people). Some recent online publications bear headlines such as '"I want to show that it is possible," says a *travesti* listed as rector [at the university] in Ceará' (Carneiro 2015), '"I am a *travesti* and I do not prostitute myself," says a public school teacher in São Paulo' (Freitas 2016), 'Meet Paula Beatriz, the first trans director at the state education network' (Secretary of Education 2017) or 'For the first time, a black *travesti* gets her PhD degree' (Superintendence of Social Communication 2017). Nevertheless, they are still very few and presented as 'exceptional' examples, and most of them are middle-class academics/professionals who are not representative of the limited options available to more vulnerable *travestis*.

Actually, only a few Brazilian *travestis* have won local fame and recognition as actresses or models in periods of less trans visibility. Roberta Close is one example. In the mid-1980s, she was claimed as one of the 'most beautiful women in Brazil,' becoming a model of beauty for both *travestis* and women. She became a very popular character throughout the country. Roberta Close participated in various television shows and, in 1984, was on the cover of *Playboy*, where she posed nude, together with an article entitled 'The greater sexual enigma of Brazil: Roberta Close.' Likewise, the popular Rogéria was an actress from Rio de Janeiro and recognised in Brazil for her long trajectory in the national Globo TV and theatre shows. She was one of the first to arrive in Paris, at the end of the 1960s, to work as an artist in *Le Carrousel* of Paris. A more recent case is the Brazilian trans model Lea T, who gained great media recognition when, in 2010, she became one of the stars of the *Givenchy* campaign and posed naked for an edition of *Vogue* magazine. Daughter of a former Brazilian soccer player Lea T was already living in Milan, where she began studying veterinary medicine and did her first work as a model. In 2015 she was hailed by *Forbes* magazine as one of 12 influential women who changed Italian fashion. In 2016 Lea T participated in the Rio Olympics, leading the Brazilian team into the stadium. It was the first time an openly trans person took part in the opening ceremony of the Olympics.

Despite these great exceptions and acknowledging that in the last years there have been positive changes towards trans people's rights, the reality of the vast majority of *travestis* is another one: marginality, violence, transphobia, and discrimination determine their day-to-day lives, balancing a fine line between life and death. *Travestis* are still far from being considered full citizens. Murders continue to take place, insults and street assaults are very common, and prejudice against them is still powerful.

In February 2017, *travesti* Dandara dos Santos was brutally tortured and killed by a group of men in Northeast Brazil (Phillips 2017). The case gained international attention because the crime was registered through a mobile phone video that circulated on the Internet. Dandara was considered an 'abject' being, somebody who did not enjoy the status of subject because she had embodied 'those "unlivable" and "uninhabitable" zones of social life' (Butler 1993, 3). As *travestis* are outside any intelligibility because they do not follow a 'coherent' linearity between sex, gender, and desire, their humanity is being denied constantly. They are considered by a rigid heteronormative society as *viados* ('fags') (Kulick 1998) who *offend* 'real' men by making their bodies feminine while desiring other men and keeping their male genitalia. In this way, *travestis must* be submitted, punished, corrected, or even eliminated (Cabral et al. 2013).

According to the Transgender Europe's Trans Murder Monitoring Project, Brazil—with 1071 cases—has the highest rate of reported killings of trans and gender-diverse people in 71 countries worldwide from 1 January 2008 to 30 September 2017 (total: 2609 reported murdered) (TGEU, Transgender Europe 2017). Also, the risk of a *travesti* to be murdered is 14 times greater than that of a gay person (GGB, Gay Group of Bahia 2016). *Travestis* are, within the diverse spectrum of LGBTI people, the most rejected and endangered in Brazil. For others, the ability to 'pass' and to be accepted in the gender presented can determine staying alive in a rigidly heteronormative society as the Brazilian one. Compared to gays, lesbians, and even trans men who seem to be less rejected, *travestis'* gender embodiments are generally more visible, and the combination of feminine shapes and male genitalia causes much discomfort. *Travestis* repudiate the performance of a hegemonic masculinity, which is highly valued in Brazil. According to a recent study, during 2017, there were

Brazilian *Travestis* and the Beginning of Our Encounters   **51**

185 reported killings of trans people in Brazil, of which 95% were trans women (Nogueira and Cabral 2018). Trans men have less social visibility, and their small community has been organised politically only since 2010 (Ávila 2014). Generally, as trans men's bodily changes can *better* satisfy heteronormative social expectations on how to look/be a 'man,' many of them take advantage of their capacity to 'pass' in order to 'favour personal comfort and individual access to rights' (Almeida 2012, 519). In this way, the invisibility of trans men's experiences, which is a violence in and of itself, contributes to reinforce a phallocentric gaze in society that ignores the expression of other (subordinated and marginalised) masculinities (Ávila 2014) and, ultimately, punishes more severely those who do not *properly* conform to social and gender expectations. Furthermore, Brazilian misogynist society, together with racism and classism, contribute to exposing feminine bodies to high levels of violence. Trans and non-trans people (effeminate gays included) who embody different ways of understanding femininity are considered valueless, more vulnerable subjects in a society which praises masculinity.

Moreover, Almeida and Heilborn (2008, 240) consider that butch lesbians and *travestis* are similar in that both present a 'dissident bodily grammar.' Butches can also be repressed as they *offend* a society when disrupting more radically the sexual and gender norms. As a sad example of lesbophobia, the black and butch lesbian Luana Barbosa dos Reis was brutally killed by the police in the suburbs of São Paulo in 2016, when she was aggressively mistaken as a 'suspicious' (for being black and poor) man. Although Luana warned the police she was a 'woman,' her defensive behaviour in front of the three police officers was an excuse for beating her to death. Luana was not only the target of a Brazilian social order which is racist and criminalises poverty, but her gender performativity was 'outside' a social binary gender script that accused her of behaving *as* a man, without *being* a 'real' one (Torres and Jesus 2017). In this way, Luana was interpellating a hegemonic masculinity and, therefore, should be punished.

Similarly, *travestis* with a lower level of education, who are poorer or black, and have less social resources to overcome structural inequalities, have more chances to suffer stigma, be marginalised, and attacked. Sex work is the territory which *travestis* associate most with death, although, as we discuss in Chap. 6, it is also paradoxically 'their possibility of existence in a transphobic society' such as the Brazilian one (Cabral et al. 2013, 302). Some of the research participants say:

> The Brazilian is not used to *travestis* outside the streets. The same as with black people, they want them to go to the kitchen. *Travesti* is for the streets, for prostitution. Do you understand? Prejudice and hypocrisy. (Martine, personal interview, 5 August 2008, Rio de Janeiro)

> Society does not give work, so they [young *travestis*] have to resort to prostitution because they do not have another option. Even if they are trained for a type of work, people still have that bias and do not provide a job. (Bibi, personal interview, 12 September 2008, Rio de Janeiro)

It is precisely this hypocrisy that determines that the person who publicly attacks a *travesti* will often be the one who pays for their sexual services. *Travestis* are aware of it; for example, Samanta recounts that 'there are a lot of risks in this profession, we go out with men who are armed, without knowing where they are going to take us. But I always try to take care of myself, I do not get into the car of every man who stops for me' (personal interview, 8 September 2008, Rio de Janeiro). The society also keeps a relationship of love/hate towards *travestis* (Kulick and Klein 2003) that makes them simultaneously 'fascinating and dangerous, seductive and polluters' (Pelúcio 2008, 6).

Becoming *Travestis*[2]

Aspiring *travestis* have to embark on a complicated, dangerous, and expensive career in order to become *a travesti*. It is an ongoing process because they are always looking for 'perfection,' that is to say, to feel *like* women, but women who are beautiful and desirable according to their own standards. The use of the term 'becoming' shows that it is a process in permanent construction; nobody becomes *completely* a *travesti* as there is a constant mobility and work behind it (Butler 1990, 1993). According to Reyna:

The *travesti*'s mission is impossible, the pursuit of perfection is an impossible mission. Nobody is perfect, neither man nor woman are perfect. But we are pretty close to perfection because we can turn into women that do not exist; they exist in the fantasy of the people. (Personal interview, 6 May 2008, Rio de Janeiro)

As we see in depth in Chap. 4, their sense of 'perfection' is achieved by modifying their bodies and using different techniques to beautify themselves. *Travesti* femininity is expressed not only in the bodily forms, but also in the way of dressing, make-up, walking, moving their long hair, fixing their finger and toenails, and so on. They will embark on a long and never-ending career in order to obtain the dreamed and idealised aesthetic appearance.

This process is performed through several stages. Following Pelúcio (2005), the first stage begins when they are *gayzinhos*, an emic classification referring to young gays, who have assumed their sexual orientation but are not yet dressing up as women or taking hormones. The second stage consists in what we could call the 'production'; it is a common expression *travestis* use to refer to *montagem*, namely, when they begin to make up and to dress up with women's clothes only occasionally for some leisurely events. The third stage is the beginning of a more permanent way of expressing femininity: they start with body hair removal, dressing more frequently *like* women, or taking feminine hormones. Finally, the last stage corresponds to their self-identification as *travestis*, when they wear—all the time—clothes assigned to women and are already planning to inject industrial and liquid silicone into their buttocks and hips. In further steps, those who have the resources will undergo cosmetic surgeries to 'improve' their appearances.

As is described in Chap. 7, a relevant argument alongside this manuscript is the recognition that these first modifications, and those that will follow, are directly related to the geographical-spatial mobilisations that *travestis* usually experience throughout their lives. The movements, both across space and gender, are constitutive of *travestis'* gender identities. As Pelúcio describes: '*Travestis* do not fix [in one place]. The body changes, the gender oscillates, the addresses change, the mobile phones are changed constantly. ... *Travestis'* circulation, although intense, is done through the margins' (Pelúcio 2009, 74–5).

54   J. Vartabedian

Most of the *travestis* who I met were thrown out of their homes or ran away at a very early age. Their families—the great majority coming from the working classes—did not accept their first expressions of femininity. Consequently, they had to migrate to other Brazilian cities, both to escape from family violence and local prejudices, and to find a new space where they could transform themselves freely and with greater tolerance than in their places of origin.

Large cities like São Paulo or Rio de Janeiro are authentic schools in *travestis'* lives. The vast majority of them used to arrive as *gayzinhos* and only a few of them start to ingest feminine hormones while still living in small towns. As Reyna summed it up, when they first arrive in the city, newcomers are 'very primitive, like a diamond in the rough' (personal interview, 19 August 2008, Rio de Janeiro).[3] As she was presented in Chap. 1, Reyna was a *madrinha*, a powerful *travesti* who introduced young *gayzinhos* or newcomer *travestis* to their new lives in Rio de Janeiro. In the next section, I explore the way they organise themselves and how their social relations are developed.

Mães and *Madrinhas*

It is very difficult to become a *travesti* without an already established network of social relationships. A *gayzinho* who wants to become a *travesti* must be linked to a complex and hierarchical system of relationships that will introduce her into the *travesti* subculture. In big cities like Rio, they will learn how to dress, do their make-up, and perform a specific type of idealised womanhood. They will also meet other *travestis* and those who will start to modify their bodies with silicone injections. They will learn the codes and rules of sex work, the streets, and the night. They will also get money lent by their *mães* or *madrinhas* to travel and work in Europe, one of their greatest goals.

Mães (mothers) and *madrinhas* (godmothers), *travestis* with more experience and economic means, are their teachers. They protect, guide, and advise those *travestis* who have just arrived into the big city, in exchange for which the *filhas* (daughters) or *afilhadas* (god-daughters) show respect but also pay them money periodically. Hence, an exchange of symbolic and economic goods is required to enter into this subculture.[4]

Brazilian *Travestis* and the Beginning of Our Encounters 55

During my fieldwork in Rio de Janeiro, I befriended a *mãe* (Alessandra) and a *madrinha* (Reyna), two powerful and highly respected business partners in the area of Lapa. Each of them had several *filhas* or *afilhadas*. As it is a hierarchical society, Alessandra should be higher-ranking than Reyna. However, in other areas of Rio, there are *mães* with less power and influence than the *madrinha* of Lapa. Reyna, then, was as powerful as Alessandra. However, these denominations are symbolic. The bonds between the *mãe/madrinha* and the *filha/afilhada* are based on social, economic, and power relations. The initiate receives protection by her *mãe/madrinha*, that is, she offers her entire network of contacts in case of possible conflicts or needs: from corrupt police to drug dealers. The *mãe/madrinha* will also offer beauty advice to the newcomer (when and where to change their bodies) and teach them how to behave. The *filha/afilhada* not only owes respect and admiration to her *mãe/madrinha* but also regularly makes payments for this 'protection' and training. Also, they have to pay their daily accommodation (in case her *mãe/madrinha* is the owner or rents the house where the *filhas/afilhadas* live) or the right to use the space on the street to work.

At the same time, a *mãe/madrinha* will receive regular money for the debts contracted by the young *gayzinhos/travesti* to reach Rio de Janeiro or Europe. Powerful *mães/madrinhas* are the ones who finance these trips to Europe. Thus, they play an important part in maintaining the prostitution networks in Brazil and abroad. Finally, *mães/madrinhas* will charge fines if their *filhas/afilhadas* failed to meet certain standards of behaviour. For example, the *mães/madrinhas* of Lapa established that it was prohibited to work on the streets after sunrise or to rob clients. *Travestis* could even be physically punished if they did not obey. Reyna, very proudly, showed me the baseball bat she used to 'correct' those *travestis* who 'needed' it.

To sum up, respect, fear, violence, admiration, commitment, money, and debts converge in a bond that, after a time one comes to discover, has little to do with 'maternal love' and more with the needs, of some of them, to access supportive networks and the desire, of the others, to obtain great economic advantages from providing these. In any case, it cannot be denied that some *travestis* consider their *mães/madrinhas* as real maternal figures and maintain strong emotional ties to them. The metaphor of motherhood is used as a characteristic attributed for femininity and the

56   J. Vartabedian

ability to care for and nurture a new person (Pelúcio 2009). Generally, the newcomers are also 'baptised' by their *mães/madrinhas*, that is, they often choose the names that will accompany *filhas/afilhadas* in this new 'birth.'

However, we cannot analyse this bond without taking into account the economic relations that are sustaining it. Another reading of their symbolic and affective value would describe *mães/madrinhas* as 'pimps.' The most powerful, those who control the sex market and mobilise a large number of *travestis* to reach Europe, are aware that they can be accused of trafficking, as pimping is punished by the criminal code because it is considered a practice of sexual exploitation. Exploring this subject further in Chap. 7, *travestis* do not usually consider the 'help,' as they put it, received to travel, as abusive, because the debts they contract to reach Europe are not seen as exploitation (Piscitelli 2008; Teixeira 2008). The more *filhas/afilhadas* are sent to Europe, the greater recognition *mães/madrinhas* will have among the *travestis*. For example, the powerful Reyna recounted that she had more than 2000 *afilhadas* she was *looking after*. Power, money, and prestige synthesise the maintenance and reproduction of these *mães/madrinhas*. Therefore, the 'production' of new *travestis* is crucial to sustaining this organisation that generates great profits for those who are, above all, controlling the desired flow of bodies and money.

The Beginning of the Research in Rio

In Chap. 1, I described how fieldwork was carried out in Rio de Janeiro and in Barcelona. In this section, I focus more deeply on the participant/researcher-embodied relationship established during our ethnographic encounter in Rio, where fieldwork was more intensely experienced. To start with, it is important to acknowledge that although the doors of the *casarão* were open for me to conduct and develop my research once the leader and respected *madrinha* Reyna accepted my presence in Lapa, I remained completely invisible in the eyes of *travestis* at the beginning— they were simply not interested in my presence in the *casarão*, the old house where the majority of my fieldwork in Rio was carried out. I did not incite much curiosity in them. I had decided to introduce myself as Argentinian, although I had been living in Spain for years. I had thought, mistakenly, that our possible Latin American connection would be something we had in common. I believed that any type of association with Europe could create a great distance between us, due to the post-colonial influence, and the idealisation of the Old World as more opulent and powerful. Although I played down the importance of Spain in my life and tried to minimise the impact of my arrival in the *casarão*, the differences between us were more than obvious and could not be hidden. In fact, my accent in speaking Portuguese made them identify me with a country (Argentina) to which they had no particular devotion. It became clear that my Latin roots were not a very effective identity resource.

Gradually, instead of trying to hide the unhideable (my level of education, the place where I lived, or my social class) I decided to begin to negotiate and accept the position in which they had begun to place me, precisely, because of our differences. My visits every day to the *casarão* allowed them to gradually become accustomed to my presence. My presentation as a 'harmless' woman made it possible for them to consider me as a friendly person. They found it very funny when I used expressions from the African Yoruba language that they commonly used and taught me,[5] because it would seem so incongruous that, given my background, I would use the language of a very marginal, Brazilian gay-*travesti* context. Slowly, my *docility* encouraged them to ask me to do shopping and errands in the neighbourhood. As a result, I felt more visible to *travestis*, but still not taken seriously.

My Body Analysed

As a woman, for *travestis*, I was far from being a 'good' exponent of femininity. They considered me too 'unsophisticated' taking into account the type of woman they aspire to be. My aesthetic 'imperfection' put me in an unfavourable position before *travestis* because they did not admire me and, in fact, they laughed at my style, which was so far from their own canons of femininity. However, I slowly learned to take advantage of my 'defects' to strike up a dialogue with them and so obtain information about their own experiences, particularly the aesthetic values associated with their way of understanding femininity. It was through my body that I took the place of the 'other' to be analysed and criticised.

It was Natalia, with her extrovert, fun personality, who was most determined to expose my physical 'weaknesses.' One of my major 'defects' was the small size of my breasts. At least ten *travestis* during my fieldwork suggested that I had breast implants because I would look better. My (small) breasts became a perfect target for Natalia's 'attacks.' One day, with the greatest audacity and impudence, she broke the ultimate barrier between our interacting bodies (Goffman 1959) and, putting her hand into my T-shirt, pulled out and exposed one of my breasts. It was in a room in the *casarão* together with other *travestis* in a leisurely, joking atmosphere when Natalia made reference to my 'hormone tits.' The hormones that *travestis* take to begin the process of feminisation produce an augmentation of their mammary glands. Nevertheless, these small breasts that they acquire, thanks to hormones, form part of the initiation process of their physical transformation. In consequence, they are only accepted while they have recently started the transition process. Years later, those who still have these breasts based on hormone treatment are the object of derision and reprobation by the rest of the group. The augmentation of the breasts using silicone breast implants is a highly valued and costly ideal associated with becoming a 'true' *travesti*. Therefore, my 'hormone tits' turned me into a 'defective' woman, or using the imagination, they equipped me to be a *travesti* who has recently started the process of bodily transformation. This comparison prompted me to think about the dissociation and de-naturalisation of women/femininity put forward by *travestis*. If, according to their own perceptions, femininity presents itself as an attribute obtained by strength, dedication, and money, then they can liken my own femininity to a new *travesti*, still in the process of transformation. My lack of willpower, in their eyes, to 'improve' my appearance and have, for example, breast implants, exposed me to the jokes and taunts that would have been made to a *travesti* who had not satisfied the aesthetic ideals of the group.

Natalia's assaults promoted a very embarrassing 'game' for me amongst us. She provoked me physically in a way I was totally unprepared for, lifting my skirt or my T-shirt to expose my breasts in the middle of the street at dusk, with passers-by and buses full of people returning to their houses after work. I responded by making myself firm and unmovable in the face of these public 'attacks.' In fact, I never felt I was being sexually harassed, instead, it was a provocation on the part of Natalia to test my own limits and provoke me. Obviously, these incidents only lasted seconds in which I tried to face up to her with my body, to show her tacitly that I could resist her 'attacks,' and that this *amapô* (which means 'woman' in the Yoruba language) would not be as easily shamed as Natalia hoped. Her humour and irreverence in front of everyone turned me into one of many daily events for her to have fun. It was evident that my docility encouraged these provocations. However, beyond my involuntary bodily exhibitions, this type of behaviour that Natalia displayed allowed me to reaffirm my presence in the *casarão*, and, although I was changed into a subject for observation and criticised for my 'small amount' of femininity, I began to be a physically visible researcher. My own body served as a bridge for the *travesti* participants to get closer to me as well as analyse and criticise me as a 'defective' woman. My body, between laughter and taunts, allowed them to position me unfavourably on the scale of *travesti* beauty, and from that point, I began to build relationships with them. I was never an erotic-sexual competitor for them and perhaps accepting this caricature of myself enabled me to continue my work in the field.

Becoming a 'Photographer'

One day the *travestis* informed me that there was going to be a beauty contest in a popular discotheque in a neighbourhood north of Rio, where *travestis* often met. A few *travestis* of the *casarão* were going, and I did not want to miss this event. That Saturday the hairdresser worked several hours in the *casarão*. There was an atmosphere of nervous expectation amongst those that were going, and of teasing and relief at not having so much competition for work on the streets, amongst those who were staying.

Once at the discotheque, *travestis* finished getting dressed. Before they were ready to go out on stage, I decided to take individual and collective photos. The *travestis* showed great enthusiasm for the idea. They felt beautiful and desired enough to have these instances of glamour captured on my camera. A couple of days later, I offered copies of my photos as a gift to those who had participated in the beauty contest. They liked the idea. They observed their bodies and postures in minute detail. They made various comments, including criticism, praise, and laughter. From

60   J. Vartabedian

this time on, they started to want more photos. Before going to work, completely made-up, I began to take pictures of them in various clothes, hairstyles, and poses. Day after day, I would arrive at the *casarão* with copies of photos to deliver. My fame as a 'photographer' extended to *travestis* who did not live in the *casarão* and wanted their photos taken in the streets where they worked. They always chose the pose and location of where I would take the photo, although I was in charge of identifying which street lighting suited the quality of the picture, as almost all the photos were taken at night.

Very few *travestis* keep photos of the past, of when they were *gayzinhos*. Their bodily changes to become *travestis* imply, in the majority of cases, a radical break with the past, associated with the violence and incomprehension from their families. To be transformed into a *travesti* can be understood then as a rebirth, and to this end, it is necessary to eliminate all traces of a body associated with pain and rejection. However, a few *travestis* in the *casarão* showed me their photos of when they were still young in the towns of their birth. With these photos, they could place their present aesthetic body alongside that of the past. They were very pleased with themselves when their old photos were analysed and I could not recognise them. It transpired that the past (the 'before') is connected with 'ugliness.' On the other hand, the present (the 'after') signifies beauty, self-esteem and confidence, even though this beauty forms part of a process that is ephemeral and temporary, for they were constantly enhancing their bodies, looking for a permanent 'perfection.' In short, the photos I delivered were considered as a type of trophy,[6] where it was possible to manifest their daily efforts to feel more beautiful and feminine. This 'after' is the result of a hard process of embellishment and, thus, is an investment and a conscious work.

Returning to the *casarão,* through the photos that I had given them, I could, without feeling intrusive, access their rooms, sit with them on their beds, and listen to their opinions about the images I showed them, watch a soap opera on the television together, observe how they dressed and put on make-up, among other events. It was through the medium of the photographs that *travestis* allowed me to observe and get close to their world. My presence in the *casarão* as a 'photographer' found a legitimate space. I began to gain more respect or, at least, the view of me as a docile and 'imperfect' person changed considerably. As a 'photographer,' I started to interact with them from another angle, far from the laughter that I had generated in them at first. The images strengthened my place as a researcher in the field, as my presence was useful and sought after by *travestis*.

At the same time, the photos were a vehicle through which *travestis* performed a specific type of femininity in front of me; their sensual poses, their provocative glances, and the exposure of their buttocks in tiny dresses contributed to the construction of their own way of understanding femininity and *travesti* beauty. The photos became 'agent-objects' (Gell 1998) that influenced the way in which *travestis* and 'photographer' interacted, mediating our corporeal and subjective experience. But the photographs constituted much more than a means of experiencing an ethnographic encounter. As Moreno Figueroa points out, they 'are flexible and permeable platforms upon and through which it is possible to organise life experience and "knowledge" of the self' (2006, 105). What the photographs show is not as important as why they were created. What was meant by the *travestis* showing off their beauty? Why had they chosen to pose in this particular way? Were photographs a form of empowerment? Photos are, then, 'densely coded objects' (Wells 2000, 33) that have to be situated and *read* according to the social and cultural dynamics that favoured their creation. Every photo provides evidence of the existence of the subject/object photographed now, since 'the photograph's essence is to ratify what it represents' (Barthes 2000 [1980], 85). When the *travestis* posed in front of my camera, it started a process in which they themselves, in dialogue with my own gaze, came into being as subjects/objects that *exist*, in the phenomenological sense that Barthes gives, to the study of photography. It is through the photographs that they recognised themselves as beautiful *travestis* and made sense of their own bodily changes in search of a desired femininity.[7]

The *travestis* with whom I interacted constructed their own images to be represented, choosing me as 'photographer,' they always selected the poses and the moment to be photographed. However, I was not a passive observer without any control over the photographic reality that we were creating together. As Hall (1999) states, the relationship between who is seen and who sees forms part of a cultural practice where both subjects 'are seen as mutually constitutive. Each is implicated in the other; neither could exist without the other' (Hall 1999, 310). As Barthes (2000 [1980], 81) shows, there is a kind of umbilical cord that unites a body photographed with the gaze of the one who takes the photograph. In agreement with Hall, Phelan maintains that 'one needs always the eye of the other to recognise (and name) oneself' (Phelan 1993, 15). In these gaze exchanges, where to see and be seen, it is important to highlight that the act of looking is a cultural practice that has nothing to do with the 'natural.' On the contrary, the gaze depends on a series of conventions, knowledge, and social beliefs that organise what we are seeing and endow it with significance (Berger 1972; Phelan 1993; Lalvani 1996). My own gaze, thus, influenced the way in which *travestis* showed themselves to me. Finally, although the photographs were an important tool of interaction that strengthened the participant/researcher relationship, it was not my aim to expose them and use them 'picturesquely' in my research. Thus, the lack of photographs throughout *Brazilian Travesti Migrations* is due more a political decision to keep them as a medium and not as an end in itself and avoid any possible frivolity that the exposure of the *travestis'* images may generate.

This chapter was an introduction to the context in which the *travestis* emerged and what it means to live as a *travesti* today in Brazil within their own stratified subculture in which they develop different strategies and practices to become a 'real' and beautiful *travesti*. The chapter also focused on the participant/researcher-embodied relationship and the importance of photography during the research. In the next chapters, I follow some Brazilian *travesti* sex workers' main embodied and spatial journeys. We can go on.

Notes

1. See Ritterbusch (2016) for the use of this strategy among Colombian trans women sex workers.
2. Here (as in most part of *Brazilian Travesti Migrations*) I will refer to the *travesti* sex workers I met in Rio de Janeiro. New trans generations, aligned more with queer discourse and politics, might assume other corporeal trajectories. However, in 2008 when fieldwork in Brazil was done, they were still not visible in Rio de Janeiro.

3. Reyna was interviewed two times.
4. Jennie Livingston's documental *Paris is Burning* also showed how kinship relationships ('mothers') organised the ball contestants within the 'houses' during the 1980s in New York.
5. Classifying linguistic system that *travestis* particularly use to communicate amongst themselves. The majority of the expressions contain terms originating in Yoruba and used in Afro-Brazilian religious cults, which makes them incomprehensible to anyone who is not in the gay-*travesti* environment.
6. Many *travestis* placed these photos in albums or hung them on walls in their rooms. I especially remember one *travesti* who created a montage in an empty fish tank, together with little-coloured stones, with all the photos that I took.
7. See Baderoon (2011) to know African photographer Muholi and her empowering photographic work on black trans people in South Africa.

References

Albuquerque, Fernanda, and Maurizio Jannelli. 1996. *Princesa*. Barcelona: Anagrama.

Almeida, Guilherme. 2012. 'Homens trans': novos matizes na aquarela das masculinidades? *Estudos Feministas* 20 (2): 513–523.

Almeida, Gláucia, and Maria Luiza Heilborn. 2008. Não somos mulheres *gays*: Identidade lésbica na visão de ativistas brasileiras. *Niterói* 9 (1): 225–249.

Ávila, Simone. 2014. *FTM,* transhomem, homem trans, trans, homem: A emergência de transmasculinidades no Brasil contemporâneo. PhD dissertation, Federal University of Santa Catarina (Brazil).

Baderoon, Gabeba. 2011. 'Gender Within Gender': Zanele Muholi's Images of Trans Being and Becoming. *Feminist Studies* 37 (2): 390–416.

Balzer, Carsten. 2010. «Eu acho transexual é aquele que disse: 'Eu sou transexual!'». Reflexiones etnológicas sobre la medicalización globalizada de las identidades trans a través del ejemplo de Brasil. In *El género desordenado. Críticas en torno a la patologización de la transexualidad*, ed. Miquel Missé and Gerard Coll-Planas, 81–96. Barcelona/Madrid: Egales.

Barthes, Roland. 2000 (1980). *Camera Lucida. Reflections on Photography.* London: Vintage Books.

Bastide, Roger. 1959. O homem disfarçado em mulher. In *Sociologia do Folclore Brasileiro*, 60–65. São Paulo: Ed. Anhambi.

Berger, John. 1972. *Ways of Seeing*. London: BBC and Penguin Books.

Botta, Emilio. 2017. Primeira trans da Superliga sonha com seleção e diz que mãe confunde seu nome. *Globo Esporte*, December 20. https://globoesporte.globo.com/sp/tem-esporte/volei/noticia/primeira-trans-da-superliga-sonha-com-selecao-e-diz-que-mae-confunde-seu-nome.ghtml. Accessed 1 Jan 2018.

Butler, Judith. 1990. *Gender Trouble: Feminism and the Subversion of Identity*. New York: Routledge.

———. 1993. *Bodies That Matter: On the Discursive Limits of 'Sex.'* New York: Routledge.

Cabral, Vinicius, Joseli M. Silva, and Marcio J. Ornat. 2013. Espaço e morte nas representações sociais de travestis. In *Geografias malditas: corpos, sexualidades e espaços*, ed. Joseli Silva, Marcio Ornat, and Alides Chimin Jr., 273–307. Ponta Grossa: Todapalavra.

Carneiro, Júlia. 2015. 'Quero mostrar que é possível,' diz travesti cotada a reitora no Ceará. *BBC Brasil*, January 13. http://www.bbc.com/portuguese/noticias/2015/01/150112_travesti_reitoria_ceara_jc_cc. Accessed 4 June 2017.

DaMatta, Roberto. 1997. *Carnavais, malandros e heróis: para uma sociologia do dilema brasileiro*. Rio de Janeiro: Rocco.

Duque, Tiago. 2011. *Montagens e Desmontagens: desejo, estigma e vergonha entre travestis adolescentes*. São Paulo: Annablume.

Figari, Carlos. 2009. *Eróticas de la disidencia en América Latina: Brasil, siglos XVII al XX*. Buenos Aires: Fundación Centro de Integración, Comunicación, Cultura y Sociedad – CICCUS and CLACSO.

Freitas, Olívia. 2016. 'Sou travesti e não me prostituo,' diz professora de escola pública de SP. *Folha de São Paulo*, May 5. http://www1.folha.uol.com.br/empreendedorsocial/minhahistoria/2016/05/1767302-sou-travesti-e-nao-me-prostituo-diz-professora-de-escola-publica-de-sp.shtml?cmpid=twfolha. Accessed 2 June 2017.

Gell, Alfred. 1998. *Art and Agency: An Anthropological Theory*. Oxford: Clarendon.

GGB, Gay Group of Bahia. 2016. *Relatório: Assassinatos de LGBT no Brasil*. https://homofobiamata.files.wordpress.com/2017/01/relatc3b3rio-2016-ps.pdf. Accessed 25 July 2017.

Goffman, Erving. 1959. *The Presentation of Self in Everyday Life*. New York: Anchor Books.

Green, James. 1999. *Beyond Carnival: Male Homosexuality in Twentieth-Century Brazil*. Chicago: The University of Chicago Press.

Hall, Stuart. 1999. Introduction: Looking and Subjectivity. In *Visual Culture: The Reader*, ed. Jessica Evans and Stuart Hall, 309–314. London/Thousand Oaks/New Delhi: Sage/The Open University.

Hutta, Jan, and Carsten Balzer. 2013. Identities and Citizenship Under Construction: Historicising the 'T' in LGBT Anti-violence Politics in Brazil. In *Queer Presences and Absences*, ed. Yvette Taylor and Michelle Addison, 69–90. Basingstoke: Palgrave Macmillan.

Kulick, Don. 1998. *Travesti: Sex, Gender and Culture Among Brazilian Transgendered Prostitutes*. Chicago: University of Chicago Press.

Kulick, Don, and Charles Klein. 2003. Scandalous Acts: The Politics of Shame Among Brazilian *Travesti* Prostitutes. In *Recognition Struggles and Social Movements. Contested Identities, Agency and Power*, ed. Barbara Hobson, 215–238. Cambridge: Cambridge University Press.

Lalvani, Suren. 1996. *Photography, Vision and the Production of Modern Bodies*. New York: State University of New York Press.

Moreno Figueroa, Mónica. 2006. The Complexities of the Visible: Mexican Women's Experiences of Racism, Mestizaje and National Identity. PhD dissertation, University of London.

Mott, Luiz, and Aroldo Assunção. 1987. Gilete na carne: etnografia das automutilações dos travestis da Bahia. *Temas Imesc* 4 (1): 41–56.

Nogueira, Sayonara, and Euclides Cabral, eds. 2018. *A carne mais barata do mercado*. Uberlândia (MG): Observatório Trans. https://storage.googleapis.com/wzukusers/user-31335485/documents/5a4bd0e51c26cuBf611F/Dossie2018.pdf. Accessed 5 Jan 2018.

Parker, Richard. 1991. *Bodies, Pleasures and Passions: Sexual Culture in Contemporary Brazil*. Boston: Beacon Press.

Pelúcio, Larissa. 2005. 'Toda Quebrada na Plástica.' Corporalidade e construção de gênero entre travestis paulistas. *Campos* 6 (1–2): 97–112.

———. 2008. *Travestis brasileiras: singularidades nacionais, desejos transnacionais*. Paper Presented at the 26 Brazilian Anthropology Meeting, Porto Seguro, Brasil, June 1–4.

———. 2009. *Abjeção e Desejo: uma etnografia travesti sobre o modelo preventivo de aids*. São Paulo: Annablume, Fapesp.

Phelan, Peggy. 1993. *Unmarked. The Politics of Performance*. London/New York: Routledge.

Phillips, Dom. 2017. Torture and Killing of Transgender Woman Stun Brazil. *New York Times*, March 8. https://www.nytimes.com/2017/03/08/world/americas/brazil-transgender-killing-video.html?_r=0. Accessed 1 June 2017.

66 J. Vartabedian

Piscitelli, Adriana. 2008. Entre as 'máfias' e a 'ajuda': a construção de conhecimento sobre tráfico de pessoas. *Cadernos Pagu* 31: 29–63.

Ritterbusch, Amy. 2016. Mobilities at Gunpoint: The Geographies of (Im) mobility of Transgender Sex Workers in Colombia. *Annals of the American Association of Geographers* 106 (2): 422–433.

Scheper-Hughes, Nancy. 1992. *Death Without Weeping: The Violence of Everyday Life in Brazil*. Berkeley/Los Angeles: University of California Press.

Secretary of Education. 2017. Conheça Paula Beatriz, a primeira diretora trans da rede estadual de ensino. *São Paulo State Government*, March 8. http://www.educacao.sp.gov.br/noticias/conheca-paula-beatriz-a-primeira-diretora-trans-da-rede-estadual-de-ensino. Accessed 2 June 2017.

Superintendence of Social Communication. 2017. Pela primeira vez, travesti negra obtém título de doutora na UFPR. *Federal University of Parana*, March 30. http://www.ufpr.br/portalufpr/blog/noticias/pela-primeira-vez-travesti-negra-defende-tese-de-doutorado-na-ufpr/. Accessed 2 June 2017.

Teixeira, Flávia do B. 2008. L'Italia dei Divieti: entre o sonho de ser européia e o babado da prostituição. *Cadernos Pagu* 31: 275–308.

TGEU, Transgender Europe. 2017. Trans Day of Remembrance (TDoR) 2017. Trans Murder Monitoring (TMM) Research Project Update. *Transrespect Versus Transphobia Worldwide*, November 20. http://transrespect.org/en/tmm-update-trans-day-remembrance-2017/. Accessed 2 Jan 2018.

Torres, Igor de Santana, and Lilian Moura de Jesus. 2017. Uma análise interseccional da morte: Luana Barbosa e a insubordinação às estruturas. *Periódicus* 7 (1): 134–156.

Vartabedian, Julieta. 2015. Towards a Carnal Anthropology. Reflections of an 'Imperfect' Anthropologist. *Qualitative Research* 15 (5): 568–582.

———. 2016. Beauty That Matters: Brazilian *Travesti* Sex Workers Feeling Beautiful. *Sociologus: Journal for Social Anthropology* 66 (1): 73–96.

Wells, Liz. 2000. *Photography: A Critical Introduction*. London/New York: Routledge.

4

On Bodies, Beauty, and *Travesti* Femininity

Brazil is constructed as a symbol of beauty not only because of its women but also for its landscapes, beaches, and Carnival. Feeling beautiful and being in good shape are very important issues if you live in Brazil. In the last three decades, the 'beauty industry' has boomed in this country. In the city of Rio de Janeiro, the importance of the body in everyday life is quite visible. Bodies are displayed, compared, scrutinised, and exercised. The body is an important vehicle of social mobility in Brazil, and there is a common belief that beauty could erase social and racial inequalities. Brazilian *travestis* reflect national concerns about beauty, and the body is also central to understand the construction of their gender identities: *travestis*' experiences are primarily embodied experiences. It is precisely through their body modifications that most of the *travestis* with whom I interacted give sense to their existence and position themselves—although very precariously—in the world.

In this chapter, I contextualise the theoretical scenario from which *travesti* beauties are understood, by examining various feminist and ethnographic analyses on female and trans beauty, in order to later focus on

---

An earlier version of this chapter can be found in Vartabedian (2016).

© The Author(s) 2018

J. Vartabedian, *Brazilian* Travesti *Migrations*, Genders and Sexualities in the Social Sciences, https://doi.org/10.1007/978-3-319-77101-4_4

the Brazilian racial classification system and the great importance that beauty has in this country. I particularly analyse cosmetic surgeries as an example of a very popular practice that, ultimately, reinforces Brazilian social and racial inequalities. I finally explore the practices *travestis* use to modify and beautify their bodies to be closer to 'perfection,' as they proclaim.

Beauty and Power

Feminists have particularly questioned who is in charge of the definitions of the standards of beauty and the reasons for which it is mostly women who adhere to them (Colebrook 2006). During the second wave of feminism, the main feminist critique was that the bodies of women became passive objects for the consumption of the male gaze. Feminist debates emerged simultaneously with the anti-pornography movement, critiques against beauty contests, and the increasing commodification of beauty during the age of consumption. Women became 'victims' of the oppressive male ideology as they had to be thin but voluptuous and sensual, young but expert lovers, and white, appearing to be of a high social class (Davis 1991). Beauty, then, became a synonym for oppression. Naomi Wolf (1990) is one of the best-known representatives of this theoretical and political position. For Wolf, beauty—which is not a natural or universal category—is part of a myth and a hoax perpetrated by patriarchy through the fashion and aesthetic industry to divert and destabilise the struggle and liberation of women. Similarly, Wendy Chapkis (1986) believes that beauty is a way of keeping women controlled. She analyses female beauty practices to demonstrate the costly and painful rituals that women experience to follow the standards of what is considered 'acceptable' femininity. More recently, in a postfeminist and neoliberal era, new generations of scholars examine how beauty pressures are intensified and extensified in noxious ways without historical precedents. Digital technologies and social media create new ways of looking that 'we have never before been able to subject ourselves and others to this degree of forensic surveillance' (Elias et al. 2017, 26). The mandate to 'look good' is also extended to children, and new products are ready to be consumed that 'improve' every unimaginable part of the body. Moreover, it is not enough to discipline the body, but also women's psychic lives (Gill and Elias 2014). The 'love your body' discourses embrace the confidence of the self to, ultimately, regulate women's body in a more sophisticated way.

The conception of beauty as part of a hoax perpetrated by patriarchy and the beauty industry is criticised by a number of scholars who perceived beauty as more than a form of domination, as it is the means to gain recognition and power (Craig 2006; Davis 1991, 2003; Felski 2006; Holliday and Sanchez-Taylor 2006; Reischer and Koo 2004). This literature highlights the ideas of women's autonomy, agency, and responsibility, while at the same time problematising and discarding a victimising notion of women in the face of beauty. Elias et al. (2017, 21) call the 'affirmative turn' on beauty to the third-wave feminism which engages 'with beauty and fashion in terms of playfulness and pleasure rather than coercion.' The authors also employ the term 'aesthetic entrepreneurship' to name contemporary beauty narratives based on self-transformation that refer to 'not only the labour involved but also the agency and creativity with which people go about styling, adorning and transforming themselves' (Elias et al. 2017, 39). In this way, there are multiple readings on beauty, and it is possible to go beyond accounts of beauty related to women's 'passivity' or oppression.

In addition, for some scholars, beauty became an embodied concept 'that is not simply an articulation of dominant cultural values but also a negotiation of them' (Reischer and Koo 2004, 299). The concept of 'negotiation' is relevant because, in this process, women can actively negotiate the relationship they establish between their bodies and the elements they select to enhance their appearance (Davis 1991). However, as Craig (2006) asked, when women negotiate with beauty standards, do their elections constitute a resistance? Susan Bordo (1990, 1993) asserted that the agency of women regarding beauty practices was a weak approach. She noted that, influenced by Foucault, the aesthetic choices of each person could be shaped and determined by a disciplinary regime fomented by the beauty industry. For example, Bordo (1990) examined that the concerns with fatness, dieting, and thinness are part of one of the most powerful normalisation strategies of the twentieth century, ensuring the production of self-controlled and self-disciplined 'docile bodies.' Craig (2006) explained that Bordo's arguments did not satisfy scholars who questioned the analyses that refer to women as 'cultural dopes'[1] and emphasised the subjective experiences of women when analysing, for instance, cosmetic surgeries and the importance of women's discourses in recognising agency and the ability to intervene over their own bodies (Davis 1991; Gimlin 2007).

In an attempt to disentangle the agency-structure dichotomy, it is worthwhile to differentiate people's experiences of beauty and the practices promoted by the industry that profits from a wider context organised according to discriminatory and exclusionary beauty ideals. Coleman (2010) describes that the agency of women who seek to lose weight through a dieting website is 'produced through the interaction with the interface' (266). Agency is relational and created while women are 'engaging with,' rather than being intentional and conscious. Moreover, Holliday and Elfving-Hwang (2012) recount that, in the last years, very young women who undertake cosmetic surgery in the private health system are very demanding consumers who question the surgeon's authority on aesthetic judgments. These 'clients' are 'part of a "makeover culture" in which *becoming* has become significantly more important than the end result' (63, emphasis in original). Thus, exploring the 'doing' of people's daily routines and work on their appearance contribute to decentre the traditional victim/agent dichotomy regarding the consumption of aesthetic procedures. In fact, as Colebrook (2006) clearly posits, considering the challenging of feminist politics, the point is not if beauty is bad or good for women but how the pragmatics of beauty intersect with gender, race, class, ageing, while beauty is being experienced by the subjects. Thus, I follow Mónica Moreno Figueroa's (2013) approach on what beauty *does*, rather than what beauty *is*. Furthermore, we cannot delimitate what beauty *is* because it is not located in the qualities of the body. Instead, is '*produced* by the relationality of the individual and the social in particular gendered and racialised moments of interaction' (Moreno Figueroa 2013, 7, emphasis in original). Therefore, beauty can be thought as a *feeling* which exists in its *doing* and through a relational interaction.

Trans Beauty

Western trans people (particularly, those identified as transsexual women) are often accused of reinforcing gender norms rather than transgressing them. It is stated that, through male-to-female sex reassignment surgeries, cosmetic surgeries, and performances of a 'correct' form of femininity, many trans women succumb to the power of heterosexuality, *passively* adhering to the dichotomous model of masculinity/femininity (Kando 1973; MacKenzie 1994). However, as Sullivan (2003) suggests, instead of accusing them of being thoughtless subjects deceived by the heteronormative system of society, it can be productive to think of trans people, like all of us, as both agents and as reflecting the constraints of the world in which we live. For many trans people, 'passing,' that is, the ability to 'pass' and to be accepted in the gender presented, is a question of survival—of life and death. As Sullivan points out, this 'means not being denied a job, laughed at, beaten up, or even killed because one is "weird"' (2003, 106). In addition, Surya Monro (2005, 64) uses the term 'body fascism' to name the 'unequal treatment of people on the basis of appearance norms, and the stigmatisation of those deemed unattractive.' The pressures on trans people to 'pass' and fit social norms can be read as a sign of transphobia and can produce much suffering. Although for the medical establishment sex reassignment surgeries and/or (aesthetic) body modifications such as hormone therapies play a *normalising* and *corrective* role, those who are subjected to these practices should not be considered the passive victims of the gender system in society, because 'we transsexuals are something more, and something other, than the creatures our makers intended us to be' (Stryker 1994, quoted from Sullivan 2003, 107).

Several ethnographic works analyse beauty through the embodied experiences of trans people. The majority of them focus on trans beauty pageants as spaces where gender, Western beauty patterns, and the ideas of nation and modernity intersect. For example, Wong (2005) examines the importance of beauty contests for *kathoeys* in Thailand—who engage in several practices to whiten their skin, narrow their noses, and make their eyes more Western-looking. It is through the processes involved in creating beautiful *kathoey*s that they demand recognition, embodying ultra-feminine and Westernised beauty. Engaging in these practices of beautification is, for *kathoey*s, a way of being modern, that is, it signifies being middle-class, white, Western consumers (Aizura 2009). Although trans prejudices and marginalisation are not subverted—as they are popularly considered as 'second-class subjects' (Cameron 2006; Ünaldi 2011)—achieving a Westernised version of beauty enables *kathoey*s to construct themselves as modern and admired beautiful subjects.

Similarly, Ochoa (2014) studies how femininities are produced in Venezuela through the analysis of beauty pageants such as the national Miss Venezuela competition (for women) as well as local gay or *transformista* (trans woman) pageants. Ochoa reveals that to be 'a queen for a day' is a form of power which allows *transformistas* to gain momentary authority through beauty. Nevertheless, exposing their own femininity and gaining social legibility do not necessarily mean they become legitimate subjects; for example, they do not become more employable or marriageable.

Besnier (2002) examines how marginalised Tongan *leitī* (local trans women) seek to perform at the Miss Galaxy beauty pageant a nonlocal identity in order to embrace cosmopolitanism, modernity, and Westernness as a vehicle to ideally escape from poverty and local relationships which situate them unfavourably within the Tongan context. *Leitī* aim to embody a glamourised and exotic otherness which is particularly expressed through the use of English as a means of upward mobility. However, the contestant's attempt to perform an idealised and imagined nonlocal identity fails as *leitī* end up 'remaining in place in a geographical and social sense' (557).

As discussed with regard to *kathoeys, transformistas,* and *leitī*, beauty is a way for them to seek social legitimacy and modernity, even though they are still rejected and constructed as abject 'others' by society. While these examples expand our understandings of trans lives and bodies, they provide a partial view of the many ways in which trans people experience beauty. The beauty performances of trans subjects allowed the scholars mentioned above to discuss national logics around bodies, trans beauty pageants as (non)hegemonic ritual events, relationships between the local and the global/nonlocal, and ideas about modernity. However, I argue that beauty has real consequences for *travestis'* own way of constructing themselves. Beauty is analysed not as a mere representation or as the performance of a desired femininity or upward mobility, but as a pragmatic question with corporeal (and for many fatal) impacts over *travestis'* lives.

Constructing *Travestis'* Beauty and Femininity

Travestis seek to look *like* women and they then undertake the difficult task of modifying their bodies to feel like more beautiful and feminine *travestis*. They are aware that they have to modify the straight and muscular forms of a considered male body structure to soften and round it. This process requires great effort and a patient and costly work. However, as *travestis* say, it is something they have to suffer through, and that is the price they pay for beauty. One of the research participants states:

> as we are men, we come with a male body and it is easier for us to transform ourselves because we are doing one thing at a time. It is a hand-made body. The whole thing is to make a leg, the other one, you are doing little by little your butt, hips, waist. So that is why sometimes there are many *travestis* who have a body more beautiful than a woman's body. (Samanta, personal interview, 8 September 2008, Rio de Janeiro)

Another *travesti* refers to the *truques* (tricks)[2] they use to transform their bodies:

> There is the cute, beautiful *travesti*, but the woman is different, the woman is the woman. When the woman is born, she is beautiful, she is already beautiful. We say: 'Oh, what a beautiful *travesti*' but you see a few *truques*, some plastic [surgeries], something... she is cute but you know, you see that she has used some *truques*. (Priscila, personal interview, 22 May 2008, Rio de Janeiro)

In issues related to beauty and body, the *travestis'* references to women are constant. On the one hand, they recognise that women do not have to—*originally*—use some *truques* to be beautiful. As their beauty is 'natural,' they believe that women have to work far less to achieve it. At the same time, the *travestis* distinguish that society is more flexible with women when evaluating their bodies as 'feminine.' Some of the participants comment, with a great sense of humour, that

> Society is cruel, if a bearded woman has a face full of hairs, people will say that she has superfluous hairs, like various women that I have seen, have hormonal problems. If a *travesti* has fuzz on her face, people will say that she is bearded. (Reyna, personal interview, 6 May 2008, Rio de Janeiro)

> Although there are a lot of women who are not feminine and do not have a delicacy, sometimes people, men, demand a lot more of *travestis*. And the people [say]: 'Oh, you have to be feminine, look a lot like a woman.' And I see there are women who have nothing feminine and they are women, they are women. But because they are women, they forgive them. And people do not forgive us because we are not women; they think that we have to be perfect [laughs]. (Bibi, personal interview, 12 September 2008, Rio de Janeiro)

On the other hand, many *travesti* sex workers do not seek to resemble any woman except those who are considered as the most beautiful and glamorous. The glamour for *travestis* is related to both the splendour they could find on the remaining few stages where a few of them are presented as 'artists'[3] (Pelúcio 2011) and the economic success that allows them to access valued goods and services (clothes, perfumes, body care, cosmetic surgeries) and a well-designed body aesthetic. It is through beauty that many *travestis* aim to challenge the destiny of many other *travestis*, characterised by poverty and death in order to obtain a social, symbolic, and economic status that distinguishes them—although precariously—from the rest of their peers. The etic term 'successful' reflects precisely the *travestis* who are positioned at the peak of their career of body transformation and have achieved the material resources to feel like beautiful and admired *travestis*.

Travestis positively value both other *travestis* and glamorous women. They also consider that although women strive less to achieve beauty, it does not necessarily imply that they are more beautiful. In fact, there is a belief among them that they feel more beautiful than women because

On Bodies, Beauty, and *Travesti* Femininity   75

they take care of themselves much more and, according to Hélio Silva (2007), their femininity is more feminine than that of women, as it is a conscious, thoughtful, and meticulous construction. Also, as the recognised *mãe* and *bombadeira* Alessandra states: 'they want to obtain a body more perfect than a woman's one' (personal interview, 21 May 2008, Rio de Janeiro). *Travestis* aim to stand out, and their bodies are the main means to achieve it. However, in most cases, this pursuit of 'perfection,' as they call it, becomes an unattainable goal and makes them constantly unsatisfied with their bodies, and thus, they will always find some imperfections to 'correct.'

The references *travestis* employ to inspire and construct themselves change according to the aesthetic trends offer by large corporations such as the cinema, television, fashion, or the media, in a specific time. For Reyna, her main source of inspiration was Julie Newmar, the protagonist of Catwoman in the 1960s. As Reyna describes it, 'I admire and copy the body forms, of specifically powerful women, the heroines of the magazines' (Reyna, personal interview, 6 May 2008, Rio de Janeiro). Regina loves Marilyn Monroe and Julie Garland. For her part, Lina recounts that 'my ideal always had to be blonde, big chest, flashy as I am... Hollywood line, I have been always inspired by blondes, Marilyn, Jane Mayfield' (Lina, personal interview, 6 August 2008, Rio de Janeiro). Martine recognises that in her time, the women who influenced her were Sofia Loren, Gina Lollobrigida, and Marilyn Monroe. On the contrary, among the youngest generation of *travestis*, they emphasise the singer Cher because she is 'all plasticised' (that is, with many cosmetic surgeries), Gisele Bündchen, Angelina Jolie, Madonna, Beyoncé, or Brazilian TV presenter and model Daniela Cicarelli. From the Hollywood style of the big stars to models, actresses, and singers (and also other *travestis*), they admire those who not only are praised for their body contours, but by the fame and success that surrounds them. In a *travesti* subculture where appearance is closely related to one's own behaviour, it is not surprising that a *travesti* in the *casarão* chose Gisele Bündchen as her ideal of beauty 'because she earns a lot of money and was a successful model very fast' (Field notes, 21 August 2008).

We can see that—with the exception of Beyoncé—almost all the stars *travestis* mentioned are white and blond; darker skin tones are not an ideal of beauty for *travestis* in Brazil (Duque 2011). As the white ideal is

76   J. Vartabedian

unattainable for most *travestis*, as well as for Brazilian women who are brown or *morenas*, many employ practices to whiten their appearance: smoothing and brightening their hair, showing off the tan lines from their bikinis when they sunbathe so that people can see how 'white' they are, using blue or green contact lenses, as well as a lot of foundation and face powder to hide imperfections and look lighter. They may also adopt the names of actresses or singers who seem to be glamorous, rich, white, and blonde. Names like 'Liza Lawer' or 'Sabrina Sheldon,' chosen by Pelúcio's (2009) participants, are selected because they represent something *travestis* aspire to, realising the importance of the values associated with white culture.

Beauty and Race in Brazil

Alvaro Jarrín describes that Brazil introduced a 'positive' type of eugenics, based on a neo-Lamarckian tradition which emphasised 'the gradual disappearance of unfit populations through premarital certifications, increased sanitation, hygienic education, and fomenting white immigration from Europe' (2015, 538). These eugenic policies of whitening were undertaken in a national and European scientific context where the country's racial mixture was understood as a problem for Brazilian national development. Mulatto population was 'degenerating' the moral and physical health of the society according to the European ideals of white superiority (Gordon 2013). Thus, whitening was assumed as the solution to 'improve' race. However, at the end of the nineteenth century, the 'evidence' of a Brazilian black population threatened white elite and national aspirations to become a modern republic.

In the 1930s, Gilberto Freyre (1992) revaluated the racial panorama of the country to propose an optimistic way of understanding cultural and racial mixture. His classic work *Casa Grande & Senzala,* first published in 1933, described Brazil as a hybrid society where African, Indian, and European people live together 'harmoniously' in a society characterised by the exchange between genes and cultures. The myth of *mestiçagem* (miscegenation) particularly emphasised the influence of slave black women as a sexual and seductive symbol. Sexuality and eroticism were key elements in the proliferation of a new mixed population which was understood as beautiful. Brazil was constructed, then, as a 'racial democracy,' with the sensual *morena* or *mulata* (mixed race woman) as a decisive subject and one of the most powerful national identities (Edmonds 2010). Freyre's celebration of *mestiçagem* is thus materialised in the *mulata* erotic body which praises brownness as a synonym of beauty. She is usually portrayed as a very sensual and voluptuous samba dancer who embodies Brazilian culture and the tropical ethos. Jarrín (2015) describes how the eugenic discourse did not disappear after Freyre's thesis in the 1930s. Indeed, it was perfectly integrated into the growing science of plastic surgery. The eroticisation of brown people (mainly, women) was constructed as a result of Freyre's adaptation of eugenic discourse to 'improve' and whiten the population. To beautify meant to improve not only the self but the nation.

Paradoxically, Brazil's system of racial classification is organised as a 'fluid system' or colour continuum which is defined contextually and with slight gradations in skin colour, and, simultaneously, as a 'bipolar system,' where *mulatos/as* are considered as black and white is the norm (Pravaz 2003, 116–7). The widespread myth of origin based on miscegenation elevates brown or mixed corporeal type as one of the most powerful national pride which, eventually, blurs the category of race and minimises the black/white distinction that, with a lesser influence, also exists in Brazil. As Alexander Edmonds (2010, 134, emphasis in original) clearly states,

> 'triumphant miscegenation' reflects the persistence of eugenic thinking as well as informal color hierarchies that stigmatize blackness. Brown is beautiful partly because it avoids 'Africanoid exaggerations.'

A purely African appearance with no mixture of white characteristics is perceived as ugly in Brazil (Goldstein 2003; Wade 2009). Moreover, darker Brazilians are poorer than lighter skinned people, excluded from many social and work spheres, and experience racism on a daily basis (Sansone 2003; Telles 2004). In a context where phenotype and aesthetic appearance are more important than ancestry, one can *look* as white, black, or *moreno*. Instead of *being* of a particular race, 'colour is not fixed at birth' (Edmonds 2007a, 87) and is subjected to social change. In addition, other physical markers like hair texture and facial features decentre the importance that skin colour has in other racial contexts. For example, Brazilian black women are aware that they are aesthetically and socially in a disadvantaged position in relation to the desired *morenas* or *mulatas* who become the queen of the Carnival, and a few of them are recognised TV stars. Many black women identify simultaneously as black and *mulata* as a 'strategy of upward mobility' and personal empowerment (Pravaz 2003, 119). Embodying *mulatice* requires a hard performative work that, far from considering that black women are just duped by the myths of racial democracy, have productive effects over these women's lives as a strategy of economic survival and achieving social recognition. Therefore, self-identifying as *mulata* does not have to do with skin colour per se, but rather with a discourse and performance practice which enable darker women to gain more prestige.

Although brown is considered beautiful, whiteness continues to be the norm. Both discourses coexist even though there is a 'racial hierarchy of desirability' (Twine 1998) and, ultimately, white women are on the top.[4] The actress Vera Fischer, the children's TV presenter Xuxa, or the world's best-paid top model Gisele Bündchen are famous examples of the great success the 'North-European' style (Freyre 1987) has in the Brazilian media. A popular adage says 'A white woman to marry, a mulata to fornicate, a black woman to cook' (Caldwell 2004, 21). Traditionally, *boa aparência* (good appearance) implied that whiteness was a prerequisite to obtaining a job. Nowadays, it no longer appears in job advertisements, but having the 'right' appearance remains important.

In addition, cosmetic surgery[5] has 'masterfully' materialised the very carnal intersection of beauty and race to reflect the politics of the Brazilian racial system. The discourse of miscegenation is employed by cosmetic surgeons to explain Brazilian's female beauty 'particularity.' For example, Carolina, one of the aesthetic surgeons I interviewed in Rio de Janeiro, points out that:

> as we have a mixture of races and [we have] well-designed buttocks… the Brazilian woman has inherited some delicacy of European trait, some traces normally straight and black hair of the Indian, right? And the design of the hip, waist and hip that comes much from the black woman. So we did mix the races a lot, created a pattern that is very Brazilian… As if we had made a race completely different from all that gave birth to us, right? (Personal interview, 9 June 2008, Rio de Janeiro)

Some physical characteristics like hips, breasts or buttocks are assigned to a sexual category in Brazil (Caldwell 2007). Blackness is only valued for its curves and sensuality. Through the process of miscegenation, light-skinned women become 'darker' by approaching the eroticised body of the *mulata* through surgeries (Jarrín 2015, 543). Silicone buttocks implants promise a perfect *bumbum* (buttocks), as described by a surgeon I interviewed: 'although we [surgeons] are increasing our breasts, the national preference are the buttocks, this is the national preference' (Roberto, aesthetic surgeon, personal interview, 19 May 2008, Rio de Janeiro). Brazilian aesthetic procedures are used, therefore, to darken the (lower) body while lightening the face (Edmonds 2010; Jarrín 2015). The face represents the status of a person and is the basis of his/her racial classification. Therefore, it is desirable that the face's traits look lighter than the sexualised and eroticised lower body parts. For example, acquiring straight and long hair could make a black woman feel and look like a *mulata*. She would no longer embody *cabelo ruim* (bad hair) or *cabelo feio* (ugly hair), popular expressions to name African's women hair (Caldwell 2004; Gordon 2013).

Surgeons are aware they cannot 'change race,' as it is not the aim of the discipline, nor is ethical. However, they can 'correct' some traits (and make them 'lighter') as the mixture does not always produce beautiful and harmonious features. Surgeons believe that the so-called negroid nose needs a medical intervention. Actually, patients diagnosed with having the 'negroid nose' are frequently brown or white, that is, surgeons justify their corrective surgeries to replace the 'wrong' nose. As Jarrín concludes:

> The ideal patient to be 'harmonized' by plastic surgery is imagined as the one who has already benefited from miscegenation, and whose body can meet the plastic surgeon halfway in his biopolitical fantasy of whitening the nation through surgery. (2015, 544)

Beauty became, thus, a relevant political prism to examine race and racism in Brazil. The powerful discourse of miscegenation conceals any critical approach to race as it is supposed to be transcended by beauty. Furthermore, the responsibility is placed on the individual to become more beautiful, that is, lighter. However, the ideas of racial democracy are questioned through a more critical discourse which employs race (and avoids appearance identifications) to condemn the great inequalities black people experience in Brazil. The Black Movement is getting stronger, and race and identity politics are becoming central to current political discussions. There is a proliferation of black beauty practices that challenge dominant images of white beauty (Gomes 2006; Pinho 2004), and also, private corporations attract the black middle class to consume black beauty products and services while, concurrently, contributing to creating a black identity (Fry 2005).

The complex Brazilian racial system shows that there are multiple beauty standards, and it would be too simplistic to affirm that all Brazilian people want to be white. Being whiter is not always being better or more beautiful. Although whiteness is still very powerful and structures the aesthetic ideals of the country, the politics of *mestiçagem* reveal other discourses from where to read appearance in Brazil. Brazil is then an example of how local discourses question and complicate globalised practices based on the white standard of beauty worldwide (Holliday and Elfving-Hwang 2012; Menon 2017). There are many aesthetic procedures like skin lightening (Charles 2003; Tate 2016), eyelid surgery (Heyes 2009; Ouellette 2009), or rhinoplasty (Gulbas 2013) that have to be analysed locally. They emerge in a context where some physical characteristics which are considered an expression of race become more 'desirable' than others. These cosmetic procedures cannot be oversimplified by assuming that they follow 'a single standard of beauty' (Craig 2006, 167). In fact, there are competing standards which are constantly negotiated to gain agency.

The Brazilian Beauty Industry and the Promises of Social Mobility

The intersection of race and beauty is particularly promoted through a growing beauty industry which sustains the politics of beautification in Brazil with great profits. In the last three decades, the beauty industry has significantly increased in this country. Brazil has one of the biggest markets of perfume and cosmetic industry in the world. It is in the fourth position—behind the United States, China, and Japan—and represents 7.1%

of the world's consumption (ABIHPEC 2016). The personal hygiene, perfumery, and cosmetics industry presents until 2014 the most vigorous growth of the market. The number of beauty parlours has almost quadrupled in the last four years: from 155,000 in 2012 to 600,000 in 2016 (Bast 2016). Brazil also has the second largest market for gyms—in terms of the number of establishments—in the world (Bertão 2016). According to the International Society of Aesthetic Plastic Surgery (ISAPS), in 2015, Brazil had the second highest rate of plastic surgery in the world—behind the richer United States—and is at the top of the rankings for the total number of the face and head procedures (ISAPS 2016). Cosmetic surgery has grown from 50,000 in 1980 to 1,224,300 in 2015.

As it was advanced, the body is then an important vehicle of social mobility in Brazil (Goldenberg 2010) and there is a common belief that beauty could erase social inequalities. The great popularisation of cosmetic surgeries seems to be the application of medical solutions to problems related to social inequalities (Edmonds 2010).

There are examples of people who have challenged class position and—through their bodies—have moved up the social ladder. Few fashion models (Adelman and Ruggi 2008; Pereira 2008) or football players (Rial 2008) have acquired fame and international recognition. Their lives and socioeconomic status are admired by many people who would like to escape poverty and have better opportunities. NGOs promote courses in modelling at shantytowns in Rio (Jarrín 2017), and very humble boys aspire to become one day the next Ronaldinho or Neymar while they play football with great sacrifice in poor local clubs. The body also plays an important role in the market of marriage, where 'beautiful' *mulatas* seduce older and richer white men to improve socially (Goldstein 2003). However, Brazil is composed of a strictly hierarchical society that leaves a very small margin for transgression and social ascension. It is difficult to think in a kind of 'corporeal democracy' in which class differences remain invisible. On the contrary, social hierarchies become even more evident through bodies.

Novaes (2010) recounts that for Brazilian rich women beauty is equated to the model's thinness; conversely, poor women consider a beautiful body a curvy one, a body which characterised the *pagode* dancers. When analysing the importance of the bodies in the city of Rio,

Malysse (1998) considers that the body is a privileged place to examine the class antagonisms of the *carioca* society, since the 'natural' body became synonymous with a poor and popular social body. A 'natural' body means one which is not exercised or modified by any aesthetic procedure. For middle-class Brazilians, a 'natural' body is a fat one. *The body*, as if it was an autonomous and independent entity (Goldenberg 2010), is transformed and sculpted to obtain well-defined and 'healthy' shapes. Beauty practices transform the 'natural' body into a distinctive one (Bourdieu 1984), a body which distinguishes the different social groups: for the middle-class Brazilians, it provides distinction and success, while for the working class, it is a way of an aspired social mobility that, roughly, can be obtained. However, Jarrín (2017, 84) considers that '[t]he signs that provide bodily value cannot be said to reside within a particular class or to belong to a group that others then seek to imitate.' The experiences of beauty are also related to a field of social relations in which some bodies are more valuable than others, and reducing this to a mere imitation of the aesthetics of the upper class would limit how beauty is produced and reinterpreted among the different social strata.

In addition, the growth of cosmetic surgery and the boom of the beauty industry cannot be understood solely as a result of economic prosperity. There are structural reasons entangled with Brazilian's particular racial, cultural, and social configuration. Edmonds (2007b) considers that appearance became a key factor in the increasing number of women in the working marketplace: they have to compete and avoid discrimination. Moreover, the sexual and dating market demands more and more young, athletic, and embellished bodies, regardless of their gender. At the same time, Brazilian surgeons—beyond their high expertise and recognised techniques—used to consider the climatic conditions and people's bodily exhibitions (especially, in coastal cities such as Rio de Janeiro) to explain the importance of cosmetic surgery in Brazil:

> Here in Brazil, I think it is a place where people are very exposed, a country with a warmer climate, people are dressed in fewer clothes, they expose themselves more, expose their belly, their legs, and they value more the aesthetics. (Roberto, aesthetic surgeon, personal interview, 19 May 2008, Rio de Janeiro)

To conclude, cosmetic procedures give poor people the illusion of social mobility in a neo-liberal context of consumption where to feel beautiful is 're-interpreted as access to goods and the antidote to social exclusion is imagined as market participation' (Edmonds 2007b, 371). We live in 'an equilibrium of antagonisms' (Goldenberg 2010, 230), where *all* Brazilians can access beauty in a supposedly unclassed and liberated career of improvement and beautification to compete 'freely' in the sexual and labour markets. Next, we move on to focus on *travestis'* body modifications to become beautiful *travestis* and understand the importance that beauty has in their lives.

Travestis' Beautification Practices

As was already described, beauty relates to a way of feeling and of becoming *travestis*, that is, feeling beautiful is not a banal and hedonistic aim; on the contrary, it is through the body and ideas about beauty that *travestis* 'produce' themselves as subjects situated within a hierarchical scale of success or failure. While focusing on the *doing* of beauty, I stress the way in which beauty structures *travestis'* individual and social interactions in a milieu in which their gender, sexualities, and bodies matter. *Travestis* seek to materialise in their bodies a gender that is defined, mainly, by the fact of feeling *like* (white) women. They are aware that they cannot and do not want to *be* women, but they mainly seek to resemble them through the construction of a constantly negotiated femininity. But this imitation is not based on any type of woman. They are inspired by women whom they consider powerful, beautiful, and successful, those who are fully aware of their bodies and intervene only to increase certain bodily volumes. *Travestis* even consider that they are often more 'perfect' than women because they do not only have an element (their penises) that fascinates men, but—as it was already said—they embody their own way of understanding femininity in a more careful and studied style.

Mainly among the *travesti* sex workers, the materialisation of their gender expression is carried out through a long, costly, and painful process of bodily transformation. Although these bodily changes are experienced in different ways, they often follow certain procedures that are related to

84   J. Vartabedian

their becoming *travestis*. Thus, it is important to understand that in this process, they are not only transforming their bodies but also their own identities while producing new social subjects (Benedetti 2005). For example, Samanta expresses it clearly when she describes her 'birth' as a *travesti* when talking about her corporal modifications:

> Then I met Reyna [her *madrinha*] and the *travesti* was emerging, I was gradually transformed. But it was also very fast, I made a great effort for it. First, the silicone, then the nose, then the [mammary] prosthesis, then another litre of silicone and so on. (Samanta, personal interview, 8 September 2008, Rio de Janeiro)

Next, I examine this bodily process of becoming *travesti*, which begins at a more external level and has a more temporary effect (clothing, make-up, gestures) than those that modify their bodies in a more definitive way (hormones, liquid silicone, cosmetic surgeries). This is an endless process as *travestis'* identities are in permanent formation. Compared to the 'first generations' of *travestis* that have had to contend with very rudimentary technologies to feminise their bodies, today seems to be technologically easier.

The Beginning

The first performances of femininity appear when they consider themselves as *gayzinhos*. Once they face their sexual orientation towards the family and society, they start to pluck their eyebrows, delineating their eyes, wearing tight shorts, or walking in a way that is socially perceived as 'feminine.' The next step comes with what we have called the 'production' (*montagem*), that is, when they begin to openly make up and dress in clothes assumed as feminine only on very specific occasions. From time to time, they start their first performances, embodying body aesthetics that mimic those assigned to women. The make-up not only allows them to beautify some parts of the face but also hide the imminent beard and some possible 'imperfections' by using compact powder. Dressing, as a form of language, is also an important moment in the process of constructing femininity. It will be through this 'production' when, for the first time, their desire to become *something more* than gays is publicly addressed, even if it is a temporary wish. However, in this phase of transition, it is difficult to know what they want to become until they usually find inspiration in other *travestis* who they meet. Lina remembers that in 1963 or 1964 Coccinelle—the first actress and European transsexual artist with a great worldwide recognition—was hosted at the Hotel Copacabana Palace in Rio de Janeiro. Lina, being a child at that time, saw her bathing in the pool of the hotel and was so impressed that she thought that one day she would become like her. Stories like these, but inspired by anonymous transsexuals or *travestis*, are very common and repeated by the participants.

This period of the first 'productions' is accepted by the group as a necessary stage only when the process of transformation begins. This is a preparatory period to become a *travesti*. Consequently, it is considered that those who 'produce' themselves are not yet *travestis*. However, this statement is problematic. First, it is not my interest to know who is (or not) a *travesti*. Identities are very variable, with porous boundaries which make it difficult to think in a static category that represents *exactly* their experiences (Besnier 2002). Nonetheless, during fieldwork, there were different perceptions on this issue that I could not avoid. On the one hand, and among a minority, there are those *travestis* who—following their own terms—assert that 'one is a *travesti* from the moment one is born,' 'being a *travesti* is at the head of a person,' or 'the feeling of wanting to be like a woman is forever' (Field notes, 11 August 2008). According to this reasoning, it is enough to be dressed 24 hours a day as a woman to affirm that the person is already a *travesti*, independent of the body transformations undertaken. One *is* a *travesti* from the time one is born.

On the other hand, there is a position which assures that it is not enough to dress or be 'produced' as a woman to become a *travesti* since there must be an irreversible process of body transformation to identify someone as such. Some *travestis* say that when consuming hormones they are already a *travesti*, while others—the vast majority—remark that only those who inject up ('pumping') liquid silicone (together with taking hormones) can be considered a *true travesti*. They stress that it is very important to 'have oil'[6] or 'have a plastic'[7] in the body. Being 'all made up' is a very popular and emic expression that refers to having a body all moulded with silicone and prosthesis (Benedetti 2005). This 'made up' body is a symbol of status and admiration among the *travestis*, as long as the body is considered beautiful and has not been deformed by the excessive use of these plastic elements.

In Tiago Duque's (2011) research with adolescent *travestis*, 'being a *travesti*' is developed as a rich network of possibilities and is characterised by the fluidity and contextual use of these identities. He mentions the frequent doubts of adolescents on the fact of whether or not they are *travestis*, when and how it should be, or what is the better occasion to assume the identity of *travestis*. Duque mentions the case of young *travestis* (with a little or no body modification) who, when the situation so requires, undo their 'production' and adopt a considered 'masculine' appearance, while still feeling *travestis*, because it is a way of strategically hiding their *travesti* gender expression.

Hormones That Feminise

Starting to take hormones is an important decision because their body will change, and those transformations begin to be visible and go beyond the use of make-up and clothes to feminise them temporarily. The goal is twofold: to eliminate, as far as possible, their secondary sex characteristics (reducing the effects of androgens) and to induce those corresponding to female sexual characteristics (provide oestrogen). The hormones they ingest decrease the growth of hairs on the body, the skin becomes softer, the breasts are developed, and the body shapes are rounded. In fact, according to the *travestis*, the hormones contribute not only to feminise their bodies but also to incorporate moral qualities considered as belonging to women: sensitivity and delicacy (Benedetti 2005; Pelúcio 2006). They relate their feeling of irritability (being 'nervous,' as they call it), as one of the effects of taking hormones, with a physico-moral situation in which they associate some characteristics as 'feminine.'

Hormones are generally indicated to women as contraceptive methods or for hormonal replacement in cases of menopause. A great number of trademarks and formats (tablets, injections, or patches) are commercialised, and the *travestis* used to be aware of everything since they masterfully have appropriated this knowledge. Accessing these medicines is very easy because they are sold freely in pharmacies in Brazil. In Spain, however, a prescription is required to buy these types of hormones. Nevertheless, this does not mean that they cannot access them. The sooner the treatment begins, the better the results will be. Once an adult, the androgen's previous effects on the body become irreversible. It is not surprising, then, to find *travestis* at the age of 14—who began to take hormones when 11 years old or even earlier—'passing' easily as young women.

Hormones, therefore, as the first procedure to feminise their body shapes, are highly valued by the group because they are cheap, easy to access, and act fairly quickly. They also allow their skins to gain more elasticity for future interventions with silicone (both injectable and prosthesis). However, its use causes a number of side effects, such as fluid retention, weight gain, tiredness, increased irritability, or decreased sexual appetite. The most important obstacle that *travestis* usually mention is related to the difficulty in achieving erections. This disability becomes a real problem if one considers that most of them who are engaged in prostitution are required to keep their erect penises to satisfy a significant number of clients who wish to be penetrated. In order to reverse this situation, they usually space the doses for a longer period or they directly abandon hormonal treatment. In Rio, I interviewed Tony, a current social agent who works with *travestis* in a project of the City Council of Rio and travelled to Paris in the late 1970s to work in the field of sex. Although he/she never identified as a *travesti*, he/she actively integrated and integrates the *travesti* subculture. Tony claims that silicone becomes the main alternative to feminise their bodies against the negative effects of the hormones:

> The *bichas* ['fags,' used as an emic term to refer to the *travestis*] prefer to use silicone. Why? Because with silicone, they do not need to have the intervention of the hormone, the hormone leaves their virility low. It is very interesting this. If you take hormones, hormones remove your sexual desire; you have no erection. (Tony, personal interview, 15 September 2008, Rio de Janeiro)

The clients become great connoisseurs of the *travestis* beautification practices. In particular, they are interested in finding out whether or not they take hormones, due to the (in)ability in achieving erections. In my dislocations through the different *travesti* prostitution venues in Rio, numerous *travestis* recount that, as it has long happened to European clients, Brazilians increasingly want to be penetrated (see Chap. 5). Consequently, many clients reject bodies that are read as very feminine because they have learned to identify such femininity with hormone consumption.

Silicones That Embellish

Among *travestis*, beauty is considered a commodity and a high price is paid to 'acquire' it. In general, since they understand that they are not *naturally* born beautiful, it will only be through great effort and material investment that they will achieve it. Silicone is the main means *travestis* have to beautify themselves.[8] The decision to use it should be well thought out because once the silicone is injected into the body it is very difficult to remove it. However, this practice is widely used by the *travestis*. The 'pumping' process is slow and often very painful. They know they have to bear the so-called pain of beauty because it is a necessary feeling to become *travestis*, as the pain is shared and exposed publicly (Pelúcio 2009). It is, therefore, a form of initiation which marks in the flesh the decision to take the definitive step to becoming a *real travesti*.

In Rio, I was able to participate in at least four sessions of silicone 'pumping.' Two were individual and the other two with multiple interventions; that is, two bodies *were made* at a time. I also interviewed two *bombadeiras* (Alessandra and Roberta), *travestis* who inject the silicone. They told me that had learned this technique by observing and experimenting. The silicone used is liquid, industrial-type, which is easily achieved in specialised stores for products for machinery and cars. Among the group, they talk about the litres of silicone they have in their body: two litres is the measure needed to mould the body 'harmoniously.' But then, the 'retouches' arrive, further doses of silicone that, if not controlled, can deform their bodies. Some needles employed are used in veterinary medicine, thicker than conventional, to better channel the dense texture of the silicone.

On Bodies, Beauty, and *Travesti* Femininity   **89**

Before the *travestis* discovered the use of silicone in the 1970s, those who wanted to transform their bodies used oil or paraffin, dangerous and, in many cases, lethal materials. Those *travestis* who did not have access to these technologies, or did not want to take the risk, employed rubber foam camouflaged under their clothes to obtain the rounded shapes they wanted. They were called 'Pirelli *travestis*,' referring to the material that externally feminised them.

The history of the origin of the use of silicone has never been analysed deeply. Because it is an illegal practice (*bombadeiras* can be charged with a crime of serious bodily injury and illegal medical practice), and everything around this practice is kept under suspicion. During the beginning of the 1970s, the first 'pumped up' (*bombadas*) *travesti* did it in the United States, in New York, with the practitioner Wesser (see Rena 2011).[9] The quality of the work was very good and had nothing to do with rudimentary practices based on oil or paraffin. The few *travestis* who could pay the high prices and injected this silicone in New York were highly praised by the rest. At this time, the Brazilians began to arrive in Europe, specifically, France. One of them, Elisa, who was 'pumped up' in the United States, decided to personally take up this practice in Paris. She bought the silicone in New York and, with great benefits, began to mould many bodies in France. Elisa had the monopoly over the business until Claudia challenged her 'pumping' in Paris, with cheaper prices because she got the silicone right there. In this way, the era of the so-called silicone mafia began. Elisa, who was a very powerful person, exerted much pressure on Claudia to stop her injecting silicone and leave France. The threats were constant and great violence was involved until Claudia finally killed Elisa. The memories of most of the research participants of the 'first generation' allowed me to reconstruct the history of the 'pumping' of silicone. This practice—although not invented—began to be widely diffused by the Brazilian *travestis* in France and from there extended to Brazil and the rest of Latin America. My participants' reconstruction also contributed to the extending idea that the best beauty practices come from 'abroad' (though they were carried out by the Brazilians).

The parts of the body that can be 'pumped up' with silicone are practically all. I handed over enlarged photocopies with the image of a naked woman among the *travestis* of the *casarão* to know what body parts were modified and in what order had been done so or, will be done so.[10] Although there may be variations, they usually began by increasing their buttocks, as it was said to be the main erotic-sexual attraction for both *travestis* and Brazilian women in general. Then, or simultaneously, they thickened the hips. Soon after, they focused on the legs: thighs, knees, and calves. The next step was the breasts. It is a delicate and dangerous area to apply liquid silicone, and the results are not the most satisfactory because they come to form hard breasts, and with no mobility. For these reasons, those who are financially better situated prefer to carry out cosmetic surgeries and use silicone prostheses. The risks are minimal and the result is more favourable. Finally, it was the face. In a similar way as with the breasts, those who were able to pay the higher costs of the procedures preferred to inject authorised substances and undertake a rhinoplasty. For those who could not or did not want to go to a surgeon, the *bombadeiras* were willing to inject liquid silicone into the forehead, cheeks, and mouth.

The first step of the procedure is to determine the points of the body that will be 'pumped up.' The injection is done without an anaesthetic because it is then easier to notice anything going wrong when the silicone is entering the body. The needle should not be introduced into an artery: silicone in an artery can result in death. As soon as blood comes out of a needle, the *bombadeira* must immediately look for another spot to puncture. Once the successive discharges of the syringes have been completed, the holes caused by the needles are closed with contact glue and are then pressed strongly with bits of cotton. Once the process is completed, *travestis* should rest for at least a week, take anti-inflammatories and antibiotics, and wait until the body does not reject the silicone.

The *travestis* appropriate some knowledge coming from mainstream medicine and, at the same time, articulate it with their own expertise (Pelúcio 2009). The 'pumping' of silicone, quintessential *travesti* practice, had its origin from the practice of surgeons who used a silicone of good quality—surgical, non-industrial silicone—to modify the bodies of their patients. *Travestis* appropriated this practice, lowered the costs with industrial silicone, and spread it as never before. On the other hand, they also use antibiotics and anti-inflammatories to mitigate the effects of the silicone injections. They also use sex hormones to create feminine forms

On Bodies, Beauty, and *Travesti* Femininity   **91**

in their bodies. Paradoxically, while these hormones were designed to originally 'adapt' the sex of intersex and transsexual people to intelligible genders that, according to the heteronormative matrix, should reinforce the man/woman dichotomy, *travestis* do not seem to use hormones or any aesthetic technology according to this normalised designation. As Pelúcio notes:

> When *travestis* use this prosthetic and hormonal technology to transform their bodies into 'something else'—they do not become women (and they do not pretend it), and they are not men either—they are denouncing, though unintentionally, that unplanned appropriations of those technologies can be done. It is in this sense that they, the technologies, fail. (2009, 91)

Consequently, *travestis* not only demonstrate that these biopolitical technologies (Foucault 2008) fail, but also make a 'deviant embodiment' of them (Preciado 2007, 384–85).

The dangers of the silicone application are numerous. Infections, skin and muscle necrosis, and blood vessel obstructions (thrombosis) can lead to death. It would also be fatal if the silicone injected into the breasts reaches a lung. During my fieldwork, the main problem I noticed was that the silicone had migrated, descending to parts of the body where it should not be. For example, the silicone of the buttocks usually goes down to the scrotal sac, or in the case of the legs, the silicone descends to the feet and the ankles, leaving them deformed, making it painful and difficult to put on shoes, to walk, or to remain standing for many hours. Despite these dangers, the 'pumping' of silicone does not stop being practised. No matter the risks, immediacy has more value, and the silicone provides an almost 'express' beauty.

This procedure is also largely legitimised by the application prices. Roberta, one of the *bombadeiras*, explained to me that she charged for the litre of silicone—considering the price when fieldwork was done—BRL 200 (about £50), while she bought the litre at BRL 30 (£7.5). To have an idea, a litre of silicone is more than enough to 'pump up' the breasts. Comparing the prices that the plastic surgeons handle, in Brazil, breast implants cost at least BRL 8000 (£2000). In Spain, the practice of 'pumping' is very underdeveloped and a Brazilian *travesti* will hardly inject silicone there. A breast augmentation surgery costs almost £4000 in Spain. The price difference between the two practices is very significant. However, for breast augmentation, *travestis* prefer cosmetic surgeries, even though they have to save money or be indebted for years to get them. The results are better and the prestige they acquire once these surgical implants have been obtained is higher. However, for the buttocks, hips, and legs, the 'pumping' of silicone remains the most required procedure.

For most of my participants, 'pumping' is the way to definitely enter the *travesti* universe. The bodies are 'tailor-made' by the *bombadeiras*, who have 'fairy hands because they make our bodies wonderful' (Samanta, personal interview, 8 September 2008, Rio de Janeiro). They usually ask themselves: 'Who made you?' representing both the power and the prestige of those who have done good 'work.'

Cosmetic Surgeries That Perfect

As Sant'Anna (2016) points out, it was only in the 1960s and 1970s that advertising for plastic surgery gained prominence in the Brazilian press. Brazilian surgeons became well known worldwide, and the images of beautiful women produced surgically started to be accepted as never before. In addition, the growing touristic industry promoted Brazilian women as the icon of sensuality and beauty. In the 1980s, 'Brazil was no longer seen merely as a green paradise but as a paradisiac country for those who, by surgical means, wanted to rejuvenate and beautify themselves' (Sant'Anna 2016, n/a). Due to its low costs[11] and excellence of the techniques of the Brazilian surgeons, it is one of the main destinations for foreigners who contribute to so-called cosmetic surgery tourism (Bell et al. 2011). But cosmetic surgeries do also matter to Brazilians. According to the Brazilian Society of Plastic Surgery (SBCP, in Portuguese), in 2014, 95.6% of the people who performed any plastic surgery were from Brazil, and most of them were between 19 and 35 years. Considering solely cosmetic surgeries, 77.5% were female patients; compared to 2009, this figure decreased while there was an increase in male patients, from 12.0% to 22.5% (SBCP 2016).

The surgeon Ivo Pitanguy has significantly contributed to making Brazil one of the most important centres of plastic surgery in the world. In 1962, he founded the plastic surgery ward at the public hospital Santa Casa in Rio de Janeiro to provide reconstructive procedures for burn victims and working-class people with serious deformations. While very expensive cosmetic procedures are offered in the increasing private clinics, the poor can access low-cost or free services in several public hospitals where the waiting lists are very long and young trainee doctors perform the surgeries.

Brazil became the first country which offers cosmetic surgeries through the national health system (approximately, 15% of the total of procedures). Legally, the public system can only fund reconstructive surgeries, but through misleading redefinitions of what is understood for 'health,' surgeons perform cosmetic surgeries in public hospitals. Indeed, Pitanguy contributed to blurring the limits between reconstructive and cosmetic surgeries because both heal the psyche (Edmonds 2010). Thus, 'the father of plastic surgery' promoted the idea that surgeons were 'psychologists with scalpels' who had to treat ugliness as if it were an illness. He considered that everybody should have the 'right to beauty' (Pitanguy 1984), and poor people could also access cosmetic procedures in order to obtain better chances in life. Physical beauty, thus, defines a great part of the Brazilian national identity and having the right to consume cosmetic surgeries makes people—presumably—part of the modern state. Jarrín (2017, 163) uses the concept of 'cosmetic citizenship' to name working-class people's claim to citizenship through beauty and their contextual perceptions of why beauty matters.

Although cosmetic surgeries seem to be more accessible to (supposedly) anyone who wants to modify and beautify their body, its costs remain very high for the *travestis*, who usually do not want to face (another) discriminatory treatment at public hospitals, and thus make a great effort to pay for these procedures and go to private clinics where they become 'clients' and can feel more respected. Concurrently, as Jarrín (2016, 361) clearly points out, 'not everyone who desires [low-cost] plastic surgery is granted an opportunity.' Considering that the public health system has limited resources for these procedures, plastic surgeons and psychologists have to decide which patients 'deserve' the surgery according to the idea that—formally—only reconstructive surgeries can be performed. The medical team also follows its own prejudices to decide 'which bodies are desirable within the Brazilian body politic—and demonstrate a clear bias toward gender-normative bodies in their choices of what surgeries to approve' (Jarrín 2016, 361). In other words, *travestis* rarely have the chance to be taken seriously to request any body modifications that symbolically would 'threaten' the practice of mainstream surgeons.

Therefore, for *travestis*, these expensive interventions are a 'luxury' they display with pride and ostentation (*dar close*, according to the *travestis'* jargon). It is as important to feel beautiful as it is to show to the rest of their peers and lovers/clients. Following Bourdieu (1984), to *travestis*, this body capital adds to the symbolic capital they obtain through the recognition and admiration of others. As not all of them can access cosmetic surgeries, the aesthetics that are materialised in the bodies will influence the relationships and hierarchies that are established within the group.

As is described in Chap. 7, if the hormones and the 'pumping' of silicone are practices that are initiated almost exclusively in Brazil, cosmetic surgeries are performed both in their country of origin and in Europe. All the surgeons interviewed in Rio and Barcelona agree that *travestis* request interventions on the breasts and face. As the aesthetic surgeon Ernesto points out: 'perhaps what is mostly done on the face is nose and fillings: cheekbones, chin, a little on the forehead—because the collapse of the forehead is very masculine. The most requested surgery, 99%, is Adam's apple [reduction]' (personal interview, 23 December 2010, Barcelona). The implants used are for the breasts and the buttocks (the latter are barely required). For the face, prostheses are no longer employed as they were used on the cheeks or chin; rather injectable products are more common.

Today, silicone prostheses for breasts remain a precious object, as a 'trophy' among the *travestis*, such as 'the dream of all of us, is an accomplishment that is the top' (Priscila, personal interview, 22 May 2008, Rio de Janeiro). In a few years, obtaining large breasts became much more important, among both Brazilian *travestis* and women. However, the 'national preference' continues to be for the buttocks. Surgeons believe that the Brazilian model for female beauty is based on having a thin waist

On Bodies, Beauty, and *Travesti* Femininity   **95**

and wide hips: the 'guitar model' that sexualises (and darkens) the lower body. But it seems that *travestis'* aesthetic demands differ from those of women, as it is revealed by the aesthetic surgeon Lorena:

> The *travesti* comes to construct herself, to sculpt herself as a woman. Then they try to reflect on a woman who exists, for example, Julia Roberts or Elsa Pataky. But they are always very beautiful women, always. They do not look at a normal woman, we are not like that. Because in the end, they recognise that they are not going to be women, they are going to be perfect female sculptures. And that is why they get a little bitter because they will never get it. Then they go looking for a perfect body that they do not get, something that the woman does not seek. The woman does not seek that perfection and that divinity. They tell you 'I am divine,' that word is not sought by a woman. They seek a perfection that is out of reality. (Personal interview, 16 December 2010, Barcelona)

Surgeons believe that the *travestis* 'problem' is not located in their bodies but in the insecurity they have in their 'heads,' and this is the main reason for their constant body dissatisfaction. They are also looking for volumes that surgeons call 'exaggerated,' 'always want more,' and when they establish some limits, they are ensured that other unscrupulous surgeons will end up doing anything for money.

For *travestis*, cosmetic surgery has another meaning. Those who can undergo this procedure are considered 'successful' *travestis*, because it is known that they have overcome some difficulties to be able to afford it. It is almost impossible for someone who has just arrived in Rio de Janeiro to undergo one of these surgeries. It takes time to save the money they would need for it. Within *travestis'* subculture, the body (and the way they get dressed or do their make-up, among other practices) is the main vehicle to situate another *travesti* according to their success/failure scale. Therefore, it is easy to recognise a 'successful' *travesti*: we just have to look at her appearance. There are a lot of corporeal and aesthetics signs that can demonstrate if a *travesti* has taken care of herself or not. For example, whilst it is acceptable to use a razor blade when a *travesti* is beginning her transformation, after a couple of years, undergoing a more permanent laser hair removal treatment is desirable. A smooth cheek and jaw are an aesthetic ideal valued positively among them. But, in order to achieve it, it is necessary to have money, since it is an expensive practice. Thus, *travestis* who could have their beard removed by laser are not only nearer the aesthetic patterns they wish, but also the desired stubble-free skin will act as a display of their socioeconomic status. Another example is if they wear a wig (devalued) versus having natural hair and high-quality hair extensions (desirable).

As we can see, the relationship *travestis* establish between the natural and the artificial requires attention. The natural is valued for some physical characteristics, such as natural hair on the head, but devalued in connection with others, for example, when they let their body hair grow and do not do anything to remove it. On the other hand, artificiality is highly valued because it is a symbol of belonging to the group and, at the same time, demonstrates the investments made in the process of construction of their own subjectivity. It is common to hear the word 'doll' (*boneca*)[12] when they discuss their aspirations regarding cosmetic surgery:

> I wanted a doll's nose. (Priscila, personal interview, 22 May 2008, Rio de Janeiro)[13]

> We have the autonomy to fabricate ourselves; I can conduct plastic surgery ready to look like a doll, as I sometimes look like one. Because I have this autonomy, I am beyond the man-woman aesthetic pattern, then, I can be artificial. Moreover, I like being artificial. Everything money can provide me, the resources, I use them on myself. (Reyna, personal interview, 6 May 2008, Rio de Janeiro)

While the contemporary techniques of cosmetic surgeons tend to achieve more 'natural' results (Edmonds 2010), a *travesti* would be pleased if her new nose were so small it looked artificial. The artificial nose is the expression of the idea: 'This is my beautiful nose because I have paid for it.' It is another step towards beauty and the *travestis'* claim for social recognition, starting with their peers and lovers/clients. For them, being 'natural' is being ugly and having a plastic and 'artificial' body is something that confers *travestis* with prestige. In addition, as beauty is considered a commodity, there are no limits in obtaining the body shapes and features desired (as looking like a 'doll') once they have the money to 'acquire' them. According to the *travestis*, women's 'naturalness' makes them (women) careless about their aesthetic appearance. When a woman provokes a *travesti*, saying 'I do not have any cosmetic surgery,' a *travesti* responds, as Reyna explained teasingly during her interview, 'I can see you don't have any, you ugly woman!'

Travestis beautification practices have been employed diversely by different generations of *travestis*. There is a broad consensus that the first generations 'exaggerated' much with the amount of silicone they injected into their bodies. Today, there is a tendency to create what they believe to be more 'natural' and 'feminine' bodies, with a greater intervention of the hormones, a decreased prominence of injected silicones, and an increasingly widespread use of cosmetic surgeries. During fieldwork, I have been able to observe that this tendency to the 'naturalness' of the youngest *travestis* is evident. There is a greater inclination to value the 'scalpel' over liquid silicone. However, I also met many young *travesti* sex workers just arriving in Rio who expressed their desire to be 'pumped up,' despite the excellent effects hormones have had on them. Although the silicone is injected with more restraint than in the past, the practice of 'pumping' continues to have an important role in their body transformations.

Beauty and Health

As Pelúcio points out (2009), for the *travestis*, feeling beautiful also means taking care of themselves, that is, beauty is related to health. Bodies should be healthy and the *travestis* are aware—although they may not always meet it—that they need to 'have head,' as they express it, to not make an abusive use of drugs and alcohol, or maintain relations with clients without using condoms. We have seen that they modify their bodies without any medical follow-up, with the exception of the cosmetic surgeries. They self-medicate and engage in practices like the 'pumping' of silicone that can have very tragic consequences. *Travestis* are unprotected in their bodily and identity transits as they remain unintelligible subjects for the health care system. In Brazil, the few public hospitals which provide free sex reassignment surgeries follow a very straight psychiatric definition to identify those transsexuals who would *really* need the surgery once they 'fit' under the gender identity disorder diagnosis. *Travestis*, as they generally want to keep their genitalia and are thus outside the medical category of 'transsexual,' remain invisible and ignored (Jarrín 2016). Colombian trans anthropologist Andrea García Becerra (2009, 140) warns that:

> when it comes to categorise, define and pathologise the experiences of the body, the medical and health institutions perform an excellent job; but the health system fails to cover the rights of a group of people who are on the margins of citizenship.

Similarly, in Brazil the health system focuses exclusively on the genital surgery, denying any other surgery requested as being 'too cosmetic.' Within this context, *travestis* are 'regarded as the invisible underside of the biomedical treatment of transsexuality, and as an abject other to the system in place' (Jarrín 2016, 360–1). Health institutions struggle to deal with *travestis'* particularities because, although they are very visible within Brazilian popular culture, they generate disconcert and the lack of knowledge is great, as any non-normative gender identity is generally subsumed under the medicalised category 'transsexual.' I find it useful to introduce Briggs and Mantini-Briggs' (2003, cited in Ochoa 2014) analysis of the 1991 cholera epidemic in Venezuela among the Warao people. They coined the term 'sanitary citizenship' to explain the disproportionate number of deaths within the indigenous community and how they were excluded from modernity and ultimately considered responsible for the transmission of the disease. For Briggs and Mantini-Briggs,

> *Sanitary citizenship* is one of the key mechanisms for deciding who is accorded substantive access to the civil and social rights of citizenship. Public health officials, physicians, politicians, and the press depict some individuals and communities as possessing modern medical understandings of the body, health, and illness, practicing hygiene, and depending on doctors and nurses when they are sick. These people become *sanitary citizens*. People who are judged to be incapable of adopting this modern medical relationship to the body, hygiene, illness and healing – or who refuse to do so – become *unsanitary subjects*. (10, emphasis in original)

Travestis seem to be relegated to the status of unsanitary subjects as they are outside the medicalised epistemologies described above. They are not *incapable* of becoming sanitary citizens, but their unintelligible bodies—together with people's prejudices and ignorance—exclude them from the care and healing medical circuits. *Travestis* face many prejudices and discrimination when they need to access health services, which are generally not prepared to attend to them with respect.

Graciele was a family doctor in a pioneering project, a collaboration between the City Hall of Rio de Janeiro and a private university where she was teaching. This project aimed to provide basic medical assistance to people in the Lapa area with limited opportunities to go to health care centres (whether they were too old or too unmedicalised subjects as with the *travestis*). Therefore, practitioner Graciele visited *travestis* at the *casarão*, where she delivered condoms, listened to their demands, and advised them if needed. She considered that 'health services have always discriminated against them. They called them with their masculine names and if they had to be admitted, they were hospitalised in a male infirmary, provoking embarrassed situations all the time' (personal interview, 19 August 2008, Rio de Janeiro). These experiences do not encourage *travestis* to consider health services as valid references to their health problems. It is also true to recognise, as practitioner Graciele and Helena from the NGO Stop SIDA in Barcelona indicate, that health is not one of their priorities. Body aesthetics, work, and money have a greater preponderance in their daily experiences.

There is an increasing awareness of *travestis'* special needs. With the pressure of political movements, the Brazilian Health Ministry published in 2013 an official report considering LGBTI health priorities in which is recognised 'travestis as a unique subjectivity whose needs should be considered separately from other LGBT minorities' (Jarrín 2016, 370). There was a project to create an Integral Health Care Centre for *Travestis* and Transsexuals in Rio, but it did not prosper. Nevertheless, in São Paulo, there are two projects which provide respectful and depathologising health care to the demands of trans people. Similarly, in Spain, there is an alternative model to the traditional biomedical one which has introduced positive changes among the trans community. Since 2012, there is a Catalan pioneer outpatient care service which does not pathologise trans people, respects their gender diversity, and is attentive to trans needs. This public service provides information on health care and psychological support only if it is requested, because the gender identity disorder diagnosis is not required or important for providing attention.

According to practitioner Graciele, *travestis'* main health difficulties are skin problems (scabies)[14]; sexually transmitted diseases, especially HIV/AIDS; drug and alcohol use; and depression. Considering the HIV/AIDS, there is a lot of discretion around this syndrome, and few are encouraged to have the tests (the 'truth test,' as they call it), because they prefer to ignore the results than to face the situation. Graciele recounts that

> There are girls [*travestis*] there [at the *casarão*] that I see they are not well, I see that are sick, I see they need an exam. I ask them to do it and they say no because they are not prepared and 'you cannot force us to do it.' So many tell me 'I'm not ready because if I have the positive result I will not know what to do, I'll throw myself out the window, I'll kill myself.' (Personal interview, 19 August 2008, Rio de Janeiro)

In addition, it is very common that those who know the positive test results do not ask for treatment because they prefer to avoid the prejudices and stigma of people living with HIV/AIDS. The treatment is free both in Brazil and Spain. Graciele considers that those who do accept treatment are usually older *travestis*, with a more clear vision of their future and goals to achieve, and with higher self-esteem than the rest. On the other hand, younger *travestis* become more resistant to treatment because they feel more insecure, think only about the present, and have no family ties or personal mentors to help them to situate more powerfully in the world. Generally, most of these young *travestis* already arrive in Rio infected with the virus, although without developing AIDS. They do not consider themselves 'ill' because they feel well. However, after three or five years, they do develop AIDS if there is no treatment.

Helena, from Stop SIDA in Barcelona, reveals that HIV-positive *travestis* who come to Europe have the belief that the drug which is given in Spain is better than in their countries of origin. They also consider that the attention is better, as there is a greater sensitivity to sexual and gender diversity. Helena says that 'for these reasons they are more receptive to go and ask for attention in the centres here in Spain than in their countries' (Helena, personal interview, 5 January 2011, Barcelona). Nevertheless, she also admits that most of the HIV-positive *travestis* she knows, very few are in treatment. In Barcelona, out of a sample of 111 trans interviewed for the TranSex2010 study done by the NGO Stop SIDA (Fernández-Dávila and Morales 2011), approximately 17% self-reported having tested positive for the last HIV test, of which 56% received no treatment. The degree of vulnerability of *travestis* regarding HIV/AIDS is disturbing. In Spain, it was found that trans sex workers together with male sex workers have a much higher prevalence of HIV infection (22% and 12%, respectively) than that analysed in women who engage in prostitution (1%) (Rojas et al. 2009). Trans people have much more risk of HIV infection than any other population worldwide, although—epidemiologically—they are usually invisibilised and included within the statistics as 'men who have sex with men' (Infante et al. 2009; Padilla et al. 2016, 261).

Although it is not one of their priorities, (good) health is an element that is also related to beauty. It is much harder to feel beautiful if somebody is involved with drugs and alcohol, if AIDS is developed and is not being treated, or if others sexually transmitted diseases (syphilis, hepatitis C) have been acquired. These diseases, together with depression, the stigma of those who are HIV positive, and the limited rights and great discrimination towards trans people, delimit a scenario where a beautiful *travesti* can hardly emerge or even survive.

Empowered Beauty

For the strongest—the *travestis* who manage to survive—feeling like beautiful *travestis* provides them with a different perspective from which to position themselves. Although beauty is an ephemeral and precarious good, we have advanced that they establish certain internal, symbolic, and corporeal hierarchies that organise them as 'successful' or not, according to the degree of beauty achieved. *Travestis'* bodies are, thus, constructed as a metaphor of morality (Douglas 1966); that is, they become evidence of the morality of the person. For example, a person who, after years of living as a *travesti* (meaning one who is not newly initiated), still wears a wig, has hardly taken hormones, and does not have silicone injected is, according to Samanta, a '*travesti* apprentice.' They are usually seen as people who have problems with drugs or health, are heavily indebted, and have other concerns before thinking about spending money on their appearance, since money is always required to feel beautiful. Once in Rio de Janeiro, those who want to become *travestis* tend to start their processes of bodily transformation almost immediately (at least by taking hormones and having liquid silicone injected into their bodies). If changes are not initiated after a certain time, they are criticised and judged by the rest as 'careless.' The same happens if they do not know how to dress or perform 'correctly,' according to a particular understanding of femininity. In starting a serious career as a *travesti*, the goal is to look *like* a woman. Anyone who fails in this endeavour by not being careful enough will be met with reproaches and mockery from the rest.[15]

As discussed throughout this chapter, I understand *travesti* beauty not as a mere superficiality or a faithful reproduction of a certain understanding of femininity that reinforces gender-related inequalities. Rather, the pursuit of beauty allows *travestis* to construct themselves as social subjects who feel powerful and desired. As Samanta explains:

> After I became a *travesti*, I believe discrimination was greater. Society is very hypocritical with *travestis*: the doors are often closed to us when we are transformed.
> (Julieta: As gay you were more accepted?)

> Society believed that was better, but it wasn't for me. Fuck society, then, I owe nothing to society, I turn my back on society. As a *travesti* I feel much better, although society wanted me to be gay, as a man. I am brave enough to assume my identity as a *travesti*, to rebel and face society in a skirt.
> (Samanta, personal interview, 8 September 2008, Rio de Janeiro)

On Bodies, Beauty, and *Travesti* Femininity   **103**

Travestis associate their past with ugliness. As young, effeminate gays, they were simply considered *bichas*, 'regular men' criticised and rejected for their effeminacy. Although less accepted and more marginalised in society, as *travestis*, they feel powerful. They are aware of how brave and strong they need to be to face a society that discriminates against them. Therefore, their current lives, while characterised by suffering, are also associated with beauty and self-esteem. Again, Samanta considers that

> I feel better, I feel good like this through the eyes of men. Because when I was gay they did not look at me. Today as a *travesti*, I walk out onto the street and I feel them looking at me, desiring me when I step close.

As can be seen, the *travestis'* ways of making sense of what they *are* is constructed precisely in relation to the gaze of others. For Samanta and other *travestis*, the male gaze is not a synonym for oppression, but a symptom of becoming legible, beautiful, and desired subjects. Therefore, feeling beautiful is as important as displaying it to men and also to one's peers. Through this act of display, they are claiming legibility, the only way they can show they are more than *bichas*, and disclosing a 'spectacular' way of presenting their femininity (Ochoa 2014, 208). Instead of considering beauty practices as normalising *travestis'* bodies while following (hetero)normative beauty standards, they appropriate certain aesthetic ideals to give sense to their own existence. Once they feel beautiful, they discover that the capacity they have to attract attention, especially from men, gives them power, as it reinforces their self-esteem. As we have examined at the beginning of the chapter, beauty is not simply a form of self-affirmation or oppression, but something more complex in which beauty exists in its continuous *doing* and through a relational interaction. According to Reyna:

> Frankly, between being a simple woman and a *travesti* – everyone sees that I am a *travesti*, a doll – I prefer to be like a doll, a *travesti*. I don't want to pass as a woman, to go unnoticed, no, absolutely not. I really want to succeed; I want to be a tasty *travesti*, powerful. (Personal interview, 6 May 2008, Rio de Janeiro)

To conclude, I have proposed an understanding of beauty as a way of becoming *travesti*. It is through beauty that *travestis* 'produce' themselves as subjects and can be situated, however precariously, in the world. Not least, the techniques for feeling beautiful have both affective and material consequences. Beauty is also about pain and suffering, and is typically achieved in a long, expensive, and risky process. Beauty, then, cannot be interpreted as the merely superficial practice of people eager to embody a 'spectacular' way of displaying femininity. Indeed, for *travestis*, beauty has effects over their lives—I was more interested in what beauty *does*, rather than what beauty *is*—and gives sense to their everyday reality and existence in a country where (beautiful) bodies and the skin tone matter. For *travestis* ready to face society in a skirt and high heels, their willingness to achieve beauty makes them feel desired and, at least temporarily, loved.

Notes

1. This expression is originally employed by Garfinkel (1967). In any case, Bordo (1993) recognises that when talking about cultural normalisation, it does not imply that women are considered as 'cultural dopes'—as unreflective and submissive to the oppressive regime of beauty.
2. *Truque* is an emic category that refers to the techniques employed by the group to deceive something in order to improve their appearance.
3. Younger *travestis* do not aspire to become 'artists' like the older ones who were inspired by the Hollywood stars.
4. However, Williams (2014, 460, emphasis in original) suggests that within sex tourism in Salvador, Brazil, 'the standard of *sensuality* privileges women of African descent.' Although whiteness is privileged as the standard of beauty, for foreign tourists black and *mulata* women sex workers are more sexually desired than the white ones. Therefore, sex tourism is 'one of the few social spaces where black women are "preferred" over white' (460). See also Carrier-Moisan (2015).
5. Plastic surgery is a medical speciality that is divided into two fields: *reconstructive surgery* that deals with rebuilding congenital or caused by a catastrophe/accident deformations, and *aesthetic* or *cosmetic surgery* that modifies those parts of the body that are unsatisfactory to the patient. Cosmetic surgeries denote elective procedure and are undertaken to enhance the appearance, although they are not medically needed. Thus,

On Bodies, Beauty, and *Travesti* Femininity **105**

while the reconstructive surgeries refer to health and physical functionality, cosmetic ones accentuate the improvement of self-esteem and social status of those who request it (Balsamo 1999).

6. *Travestis* use this expression to talk about the vegetable oil that was used in the past to shape their bodies. Although the same technique was used as the current 'pumping' of silicone, the product was very harmful and caused a lot of damage to their bodies. Today, the word 'oil' is only used as a synonym of industrial-type liquid silicone.

7. An emic expression that refers to both undertaking a cosmetic surgery and also the body's ostentation of silicone prostheses obtained in such surgeries.

8. Working-class women do also use liquid silicone to shape their bodies (Edmonds 2007b).

9. There is another version that refers to a nurse as the one who, clandestinely, began 'pumping' in New York. However, I keep the information about Dr Wesser because it is the only one I have been able to corroborate. I also publish his full name since he died in 2008 and his medical performances are publicly known.

10. I am grateful to Don Kulick for suggesting to me the use of this method of inquiry.

11. For example, in the United Kingdom, a breast augmentation surgery costs around £3500–£7000; in Brazil, it can be paid £2000–£5000 in a private clinic.

12. When analysing a Brazilian trans beauty pageant (*Miss T Brasil*) held in Rio de Janeiro (2012–2015), Silva Junior (2017) describes how the *Miss Boneca Pop* pageant (1974–1976) was used as an inspiration to the current *Miss T Brasil* in order to obtain more legitimacy and visibility while reinforcing a politicised discourse around 'trans culture.' According to one of his participants, in the 1970s, the word '*boneca*' was very popular to refer to effeminate gays and *travestis*. As the category '*travesti*' started to be used in a pejorative way, *boneca* was the chosen option to refer to the various shows or beauty pageants in those times.

13. This was her way of explaining the rhinoplasty surgery she had had.

14. Graciele explained that the sheets and towels used by the inhabitants of the *casarão* were washed with very little regularity, and the lack of cleanliness was what commonly generated these infections.

15. In Rio, I noticed that friendship ties were very weak amongst the group and solidarity was not strong enough to criticise those who made fun of the rest. Indeed, mockery was a legitimised practice within the group.

References

ABIHPEC, Brazilian Association of the Personal Hygiene, Perfumery and Cosmetics Industry. 2016. https://abihpec.org.br/publicacao/panorama-do-setor-2016-2/. Accessed 1 Apr 2017.

Adelman, Miriam, and Lennita Ruggi. 2008. The Beautiful and the Abject: Gender, Identity and Constructions of the Body in Contemporary Brazilian Culture. *Current Sociology* 56 (4): 555–586.

Aizura, Aren. 2009. Where Health and Beauty Meet: Femininity and Racialisation in Thai Cosmetic Surgery Clinics. *Asian Studies Review* 33 (3): 303–317.

Balsamo, Anne. 1999. *Technologies of the Gendered Body. Reading Cyborg Women.* Durham: Duke University Press.

Bast, Elaine. 2016. Número de salões de beleza quase quadruplicou nos últimos quatro anos. *Jornal Hoje GLOBO*, June 8. http://g1.globo.com/jornal-hoje/noticia/2016/06/numero-de-saloes-de-beleza-quadruplicou-nos-ultimos-quatro-anos.html. Accessed 6 Apr 2017.

Becerra, Andrea García. 2009. Tacones, siliconas, hormonas y otras críticas al sistema sexo-género. Feminismos y experiencias de transexuales y travestis. *Revista Colombiana de Antropología* 45 (1): 119–146.

Bell, David, Ruth Holliday, Meredith Jones, Elspeth Probyn, and Jacqueline Sanchez Taylor. 2011. Bikinis and Bandages: An Itinerary for Cosmetic Surgery Tourism. *Tourist Studies* 11 (2): 139–155.

Benedetti, Marcos. 2005. *Toda feita: o corpo e o gênero das travestis.* Rio de Janeiro: Garamond.

Bertão, Naiara. 2016. Brasil já é um dos maiores mercados 'fitness' do mundo. *Revista Exame*, May 26. http://exame.abril.com.br/revista-exame/brasil-ja-e-um-dos-maiores-mercados-fitness-do-mundo/. Accessed 6 Apr 2017.

Besnier, Niko. 2002. Transgenderism, Locality, and the Miss Galaxy Beauty Pageant in Tonga. *American Ethnologist* 29 (3): 534–566.

Bordo, Susan. 1990. Reading the Slender Body. In *Body Politics. Women and the Discourses of Science*, ed. Mary Jacobus, Evelyn Fox Keller, and Sally Shuttleworth, 83–112. London/New York: Routledge.

———. 1993. *Unbearable Weight. Feminism, Western Culture and the Body.* Berkeley: University of California Press.

Bourdieu, Pierre. 1984. *Distinction. A Social Critique of the Judgement of Taste.* Cambridge, MA: Harvard University Press.

On Bodies, Beauty, and *Travesti* Femininity 107

Briggs, Charles, and Clara Mantini-Briggs. 2003. *Stories in the Time of Cholera: Racial Profiling During a Medical Nightmare*. Berkeley: University of California Press.

Caldwell, Kia L. 2004. 'Look at Her Hair': The Body Politics of Black Womanhood in Brazil. *Transforming Anthropology* 11 (2): 18–29.

———. 2007. *Negras in Brazil. Re-envisioning Black Women, Citizenship, and the Politics of Identity*. New Brunswick/London: Rutgers University Press.

Cameron, Liz. 2006. *Sexual Health and Rights: Sex Workers, Transgender People and Men Who Have Sex with Men: Thailand*. New York: Open Society Institute.

Carrier-Moisan, Marie-Eve. 2015. 'Putting Femininity to Work': Negotiating Hypersexuality and Respectability in Sex Tourism, Brazil. *Sexualities* 18 (4): 499–518.

Chapkis, Wendy. 1986. *Beauty Secrets*. Boston: South End Press.

Charles, Christopher. 2003. Skin Bleaching, Self-Hate, and Black Identity in Jamaica. *Journal of Black Studies* 33 (6): 711–728.

Colebrook, Claire. 2006. Introduction. *Feminist Theory* 7 (2): 131–142.

Coleman, Rebecca. 2010. Dieting Temporalities: Interaction, Agency and the Measure of Online Weight Watching. *Time and Society* 19 (2): 265–285.

Craig, Maxine. 2006. Race, Beauty, and the Tangled Knot of a Guilty Pleasure. *Feminist Theory* 7 (2): 159–177.

Davis, Kathy. 1991. Remaking the She-Devil: A Critical Look at Feminist Approaches to Beauty. *Hypatia* 6 (2): 21–43.

———. 2003. *Dubious Equalities and Embodied Differences. Cultural Studies on Cosmetic Surgery*. Lanham: Rowman and Littlefield Publishers.

Douglas, Mary. 1966. *Purity and Danger: An Analysis of Concepts of Pollution and Taboo*. London: Routledge and Kegan Paul.

Duque, Tiago. 2011. *Montagens e Desmontagens: desejo, estigma e vergonha entre travestis adolescentes*. São Paulo: Annablume.

Edmonds, Alexander. 2007a. 'Triumphant Miscegenation': Reflections on Race and Beauty in Brazil. *Journal of Intercultural Communication* 28 (1): 83–97.

———. 2007b. 'The Poor Have the Right to Be Beautiful': Cosmetic Surgery in Neoliberal Brazil. *Journal of the Royal Anthropological Institute* 13 (2): 363–381.

———. 2010. *Pretty Modern: Beauty, Sex, and Plastic Surgery in Brazil*. Durham: Duke University Press.

Elias, Ana, Rosalind Gill, and Christina Scharff. 2017. Introduction. In *Aesthetic Labour: Rethinking Beauty Politics in Neoliberalism*, ed. Ana Elias, Rosalind Gill, and Christina Scharff, 3–49. Basingstoke: Palgrave Macmillan.

Felski, Rita. 2006. Because It Is Beautiful. New Feminist Perspectives on Beauty. *Feminist Theory* 7 (2): 273–282.

Fernández-Dávila, Percy, and Adriana Morales. 2011. Estudio TranSex 2010. *Conductas de riesgo y detección de necesidades para la prevención del VIH/ITS en mujeres transexuales trabajadoras sexuales.* Stop SIDA: Barcelona (Unpublished technical report).

Figueroa, Mónica Moreno. 2013. Displaced Looks: The Lived Experience of Beauty and Racism. *Feminist Theory* 14 (2): 137–151.

Foucault, Michel. 2008. *The Birth of Biopolitics. Lectures at the College de France, 1978–1979.* New York: Palgrave Macmillan.

Freyre, Gilberto. 1987. *Modos de homem, modas de mulher.* Rio de Janeiro: Record.

———. 1992. *Casa-Grande & Senzala: formação da família brasileira sob o regime da economia patriarcal.* Rio de Janeiro: Record.

Fry, Peter. 2005. *A Persistência da Raça. Ensaios Antropológicos sobre o Brasil e a África Austral.* Rio de Janeiro: Civilização Brasileira.

Garfinkel, Harold. 1967. *Studies in Ethnomethodology.* Englewood Cliffs: Prentice-Hall.

Gill, Rosalind, and Ana S. Elias. 2014. 'Awaken Your Incredible': Love Your Body Discourses and Postfeminist Contradictions. *International Journal of Media and Cultural Politics* 10 (2): 179–188.

Gimlin, Debra. 2007. Accounting for Cosmetic Surgery in the USA and Great Britain: A Cross-Cultural Analysis of Women's Narratives. *Body and Society* 13 (1): 41–60.

Goldenberg, Mirian. 2010. The Body as Capital: Understanding Brazilian Culture. *Vibrant – Virtual Brazilian Anthropology* 7 (1) 220–238. http://www.vibrant.org.br/issues/v7n1/mirian-goldenberg-the-body-as-capital/. Accessed 20 Mar 2017.

Goldstein, Donna. 2003. Color-Blind Erotic Democracies, Black Consciousness Politics, and the Black Cinderellas of Felicidade Eterna. In *Laughter Out of Place: Race, Class, Violence, and Sexuality in a Rio Shantytown*, 102–135. Berkeley/London: University of California Press.

Gomes, Nilma. 2006. *Sem Perder a Raiz: Corpo e Cabelo como Símbolos da Identidade Negra.* Belo Horizonte: Autentica.

Gordon, Doreen. 2013. A beleza abre portas: Beauty and the Racialised Body Among Black Middle-Class Women in Salvador, Brazil. *Feminist Theory* 14 (2): 203–218.

Gulbas, Lauren. 2013. Embodying Racism: Race, Rhinoplasty, and Self-Esteem in Venezuela. *Qualitative Health Research* 23 (3): 326–335.

Heyes, Cressida. 2009. All Cosmetic Surgery Is 'Ethnic': Asian Eyelids, Feminist Indignation, and the Politics of Whiteness. In *Cosmetic Surgery: A Feminist Primer*, ed. Cressida Heyes and Meredith Jones, 191–208. Burlington: Ashgate Publishing.

Holliday, Ruth, and Joanna Elfving-Hwang. 2012. Gender, Globalization and Aesthetic Surgery in South Korea. *Body and Society* 18 (2): 58–81.

Holliday, Ruth, and Jacqueline Sanchez-Taylor. 2006. Aesthetic Surgery as False Beauty. *Feminist Theory* 7 (2): 179–195.

Infante, Cesar, Sandra Sosa-Rubi, and Silvia Cuadra. 2009. Sex Work in Mexico: Vulnerability of Male, Travesti, Transgender and Transsexual Sex Workers. *Culture, Health and Sexuality* 11 (2): 125–137.

ISAPS, International Society of Aesthetic Plastic Surgery. 2016. *International Survey on Aesthetic/Cosmetic.* https://www.isaps.org/Media/Default/global-statistics/2016%20ISAPS%20Results.pdf. Accessed 24 Mar 2017.

Jarrín, Alvaro. 2015. Towards a Biopolitics of Beauty: Eugenics, Aesthetic Hierarchies and Plastic Surgery in Brazil. *Journal of Latin American Cultural Studies* 24 (4): 535–552.

———. 2016. Untranslatable Subjects. Travesti Access to Public Health Care in Brazil. *Transgender Studies Quarterly* 3 (3–4): 357–375.

———. 2017. *The Biopolitics of Beauty: Cosmetic Citizenship and Affective Capital in Brazil.* Oakland: University of California Press.

Kando, Thomas. 1973. *Sex Change: The Achievement of Gender Identity Among Feminized Transsexuals.* Springfield: Charles Thomas Publishers.

MacKenzie, Gordene. 1994. *Transgender Nation.* Bowling Green: Bowling Green State University Popular Press.

Malysse, Stephane. 1998. Em busca do corpo ideal. *Sexualidade, Gênero e Sociedade* 7 (8): 12–17.

Menon, Alka. 2017. Reconstructing Race and Gender in American Cosmetic Surgery. *Ethnic and Racial Studies* 40 (4): 597–616.

Monro, Surya. 2005. *Gender Politics: Activism, Citizenship and Sexual Diversity.* London: Pluto Press.

Novaes, Joana. 2010. *Com que corpo eu vou? Sociabilidade e usos do corpo nas mulheres das camadas altas e populares.* Rio de Janeiro: Ed. PUC/Pallas.

Ochoa, Marcia. 2014. *Queen for a Day: Transformistas, Beauty Queens, and the Performance of Femininity in Venezuela.* Durham/London: Duke University Press.

Ouellette, Alicia. 2009. Eyes Wide Open: Surgery to Westernize the Eyes of an Asian Child. *The Hastings Center Report* 39 (1): 15–18.

Padilla, Mark, Sheilla Rodríguez-Madera, Nelson Varas-Díaz, and Alixida Ramos-Pibernus. 2016. Trans-Migrations: Border-Crossing and the Politics of Body Modification Among Puerto Rican Transgender Women. *International Journal of Sexual Health* 28 (4): 261–277.

Pelúcio, Larissa. 2006. O Gênero na Carne: sexualidade, corporalidade e pessoa – uma etnografia entre travestis paulistas. In *Política e Cotidiano: estudos antropológicos sobre gênero, família e sexualidade*, ed. Miriam Grossi and Elisete Schwade, 189–216. Florianópolis: Nova Letra.

———. 2009. *Abjeção e Desejo: uma etnografia travesti sobre o modelo preventivo de aids*. São Paulo: Annablume, Fapesp.

———. 2011. 'Amores perros' – sexo, paixão e dinheiro na relação entre espanhóis e travestis brasileiras no mercado transnacional do sexo. In *Gênero, sexo, amor e dinheiro: mobilidades transnacionais envolvendo o Brasil*, ed. Adriana Piscitelli, Glaucia de Oliveira Assis, and José M. Nieto Olivar, 185–224. Campinas: Unicamp/PAGU.

Pereira, Cláudia da S. 2008. *Gisele da Favela: Uma análise antropológica sobre a carreira de modelo*. PhD dissertation, Federal University of Rio de Janeiro, Brazil.

Pinho, Osmundo. 2004. O efeito do sexo: políticas de raça, gênero e miscigenação. *Cadernos Pagu* (23): 89–119.

Pitanguy, Ivo. 1984. *Direito à Beleza: Memórias do Grande Mestre da Cirurgia Plástica*. Rio de Janeiro: Record.

Pravaz, Natasha. 2003. Brazilian *Mulatice*: Performing Race, Gender, and the Nation. *The Journal of Latin American and Caribbean Anthropology* 8 (1): 116–146.

Preciado, Beatriz. 2007. Entrevista com Beatriz Preciado (por Jesús Carrillo). *Cadernos Pagu* 28: 375–405.

Reischer, Erica, and Kathryn Koo. 2004. The Body Beautiful: Symbolism and Agency in the Social World. *Annual Review of Anthropology* 33: 297–317.

Rena, Laura M. 2011. The High Price of Looking Like a Woman. *New York Times*, August 19. http://www.nytimes.com/2011/08/21/nyregion/some-transgender-women-pay-a-high-price-to-look-more-feminine.html. Accessed 29 Jan 2012.

Rial, Carmen. 2008. *Rodar*: The Circulation of Brazilian Football Players Abroad. *Horizontes Antropologicos* 4, Selected Ed. http://socialsciences.scielo.org/scielo.php?script=sci_arttext&pid=S0104-71832008000100007&lng=en&nrm=iso. Accessed 3 Apr 2017.

Rojas, Daniela, Iván Zaro, and Teresa Navazo. 2009. *Trabajadoras transexuales del sexo: el doble estigma*. Madrid: Fundación Triángulo.

Sansone, Lívio. 2003. *Blackness Without Ethnicity: Constructing Race in Brazil*. New York: Palgrave Macmillan.

Sant'Anna, Denise. 2016. O imperativo da beleza no Brasil. *Confins* (Online) 26. http://confins.revues.org/10741. Accessed 1 Apr 2017.

SBCP, Brazilian Society of Plastic Surgery. 2016. Análise Comparativa das Pesquisa 2009 e 2015. Situação da Cirurgia Plástica no Brasil. *Sociedade Brasileira de Cirurgia Plástica* (not published report).

Silva, Hélio. 2007. *Travestis: entre o espelho e a rua*. Rio de Janeiro: Rocco.

Silva Junior, Aureliano L. 2017. Para uma história dos concursos de beleza trans: a criação de memórias e tradição para um certame voltado para travestis e mulheres transexuais. *Cadernos Pagu* (online) 50. https://doi.org/10.1590/18 094449201700500015. Accessed 14 Oct 2017.

Stryker, Susan. 1994. My Words to Victor Frankenstein Above the Village of Chamounix. *GLQ: A Journal of Gay and Lesbian Studies* 1: 237–254.

Sullivan, Nikki. 2003. *A Critical Introduction to Queer Theory*. Edinburgh: Edinburgh University Press.

Tate, Shirley. 2016. *Skin Bleaching in Black Atlantic Zones: Shade Shifters*. Basingstoke: Palgrave Macmillan.

Telles, Edward. 2004. *Race in Another America: The Significance of Skin Color in Brazil*. Princeton: Princeton University Press.

Twine, France. 1998. *Racism in a Racial Democracy: The Maintenance of White Supremacy in Brazil*. New Brunswick: Rutgers University Press.

Ünaldi, Serhat. 2011. Back in the Spotlight: The Cinematic Regime of Representation of *Kathoeys* and Gay Men in Thailand. In *Queer Bangkok: Twenty-First-Century Markets, Media, and Rights*, ed. Peter Jackson, 59–78. Hong Kong: Hong Kong University Press.

Vartabedian, Julieta. 2016. Beauty That Matters: Brazilian *Travesti* Sex Workers Feeling Beautiful. *Sociologus: Journal for Social Anthropology* 66 (1): 73–96.

Wade, Peter. 2009. *Race and Sex in Latin America*. London: Pluto Press.

Williams, Erica. 2014. Sex Work and Exclusion in the Tourist Districts of Salvador, Brazil. *Gender, Place and Culture* 21 (4): 453–470.

Wolf, Naomi. 1990. *The Beauty Myth*. London: Chatto and Windus.

Wong, Yin Wuen. 2005. The Making of a Local Queen in an International Transsexual Beauty Contest. Paper presented at the *Sexualities, Genders, and Rights in Asia*, 1st International Conference of Asian Queer Studies, Bangkok, July 7–9.

5

On Clients, *Maridos*, and *Travestis'* Sexualities

In this chapter, I focus on the particular ways in which *travestis* interact sexually and socially with their clients and *maridos* (husbands). Before describing these categories and how the construction of *travesti* gender identities is also closely related to the emotional and erotic relationships they establish—mostly—with men, I examine how sexuality and gender have been discussed theoretically to situate the following discussion.

Gender and Sexuality

From the middle of the nineteenth century to the second half of the twentieth century, medical discourses assumed that gender and sexuality were 'natural' phenomena, based on biology and thought of in fixed terms. Heterosexuality was considered a universal principle from which to explore homosexuality. Many cases of non-normative sexualities were analysed 'in ways that have reproduced sexual and gender "coherence"' (Richardson 2007, 460). Homosexuality was studied as a symptom of a

---

An earlier version of this chapter can be found in Vartabedian (2014).

© The Author(s) 2018
J. Vartabedian, *Brazilian* Travesti *Migrations*, Genders and Sexualities in the Social Sciences, https://doi.org/10.1007/978-3-319-77101-4_5

'sexual inversion,' as Havelock Ellis called it. That is, homosexual men and women were perceived to have 'unusual proportions' of female and male elements, respectively. Thus, 'effeminate' men and 'manly' women were seen as people whose bodies 'cross gendered' (Richardson 2008) and rejected any sexual and gender coherence.

Feminists challenged these predetermined essentialist frameworks for understanding gender and sexuality. However, social constructionist accounts did not disengage both concepts from each other (Alsop et al. 2002). For example, French materialist feminists such as Delphy (1993) and Wittig (1992) considered gender as a consequence of the social and economic oppression experienced by women. Marriage and family institutions allowed men to access both women's labour and bodies. Women were, therefore, constituted as a class dominated by another class (men). As Diane Richardson (2007, 461) states, '[g]ender categories would not exist if social divisions did not exist. In this conceptual framework, the binary divide between heterosexuality and homosexuality is seen to derive from gender.' In this way, Richardson considers that, within this approach, gender is prioritised over sexuality.

During the second-wave of feminism, some scholars like Rich or MacKinnon produced writings on gender and sexuality in which, according to Richardson (2007, 2008), sexuality was prioritised over gender. Rich's essay, 'Compulsory Heterosexuality' (1980), was a response to the assumption of heterosexuality as the 'normal' choice of most women. She proposed the idea of a 'lesbian continuum' as a safe space for women. MacKinnon (1982) introduced a Marxist analysis of capitalism to a feminist analysis of gender and sexuality. She stressed that gender is determined by sexuality, which is defined as a 'social process which creates, organizes, expresses, and directs desire, creating the social beings we know as women and men' (516). In this hierarchical organisation, male's sexuality dominated and subjugated the female one. These approaches provided a negative view of sexuality in which heterosexuality

> is by definition oppressive, as this sexual practice is constructed for male pleasure, subordinates women and oppresses other sexual practices such as lesbianism and homosexuality. … The emphasis on male power … negates sexual pleasure and stresses the dangers of sexual desire and curiosity for women. (Alsop et al. 2002, 121)

The feminist postulates that examined gender and sexuality together remained almost unchallenged until the emergence of poststructuralist and queer approaches during the 1990s (Richardson 2007, 2008). Rubin's 'Thinking Sex' (1984) is a first reference. She developed both a radical perspective on sexuality to displace sexuality's fears and negativities constructed through history, and a methodological distinction between gender and sexuality. She believed that, 'although sex and gender are related, they are not the same thing, and they form the basis of two distinct arenas of social practice' (308), and used the example of the oppression of lesbians. From a feminist perspective, this oppression is analysed in terms of women's oppression. Nonetheless, 'lesbians are also oppressed as queers and perverts, by the operation of sexual, not gender, stratification' (288). Eve Sedgwick (1990) agreed with this point of view. Although related, 'gender and sexuality represent two analytic axes that may productively be imagined as being as distinct from one another as, say, gender and class, or class and race. Distinct, that is to say, no more than minimally, but nonetheless usefully' (Sedgwick 1990, 30). Sexuality is therefore not limited to gender because there are multiple dimensions related to the choice of the desired object (not just same/opposite sex, homosexuality/heterosexuality). Sedgwick's position allows for the thinking that 'sexual desires, practices and identities do not depend on a person's gender for their meaning' (Richardson 2008, 16).

The distinction between gender and sexuality proposed by Rubin and Sedgwick has been questioned by Butler (1994). In an article entitled 'Against Proper Objects,' she problematises the way in which analytical fields have been institutionalised around gender and sexuality. A methodological distinction is usually made to affirm that gender *belongs to* feminist studies, whereas sexuality *corresponds to* gay and lesbian studies. Such separation, which denies the history of feminism in its struggle to achieve the sexual liberation of women, limits and desexualises the feminist project by reducing its interest exclusively to gender. For Butler, 'the institution of the "proper object" takes place, as usual, through the mundane sort of violence' (6). The author argues that it is politically unfeasible to establish an extreme separation between, on the one hand, feminism, and on the other, radical sexual theory (queer studies). Butler proposes that feminist and queer studies should engage in dialogue and go beyond and

116   J. Vartabedian

against this institutional separatism that only leads to maintaining narrow and sectarian analyses. Many other scholars have also considered that both categories cannot be fully separable (Howe et al. 2008; McLaughlin et al. 2006; Valentine 2007). We have seen that, as Richardson (2008, 16) clearly summarises:

> modernist understandings of sexuality and gender as fixed, coherent and stable have been challenged by recent trends in social theory that conceptualize these categories as plural, provisional and situated. And if there are multiple genders and multiple sexualities, then it is also likely that there will be multiple relationships between these categories.

Yet, analysing the points of encounter and disagreement between both categories allows us to problematise and further complicate the limits of this relationship. Throughout this chapter, I discuss the intersections, disputes, and negotiations that are established between gender and sexuality while analysing the organisation and construction of the *travesti* sexualities according to the clients and *maridos* categories. I also problematise a spreading idea—even among some *travestis*—of considering them 'homosexuals.'

Regarding the 'Active'/'Passive' Model of Sexuality

In Brazil, the construction of femininity and masculinity are based not only on the sexed bodies but also on the practices associated with sexuality. It is the organisation and distinction of the 'passive' and 'active' roles that structure the notions of masculinity and femininity, that is, a man who has sex with another man does not 'sacrifice' his masculinity as long as he assumes the 'active' role (penetrator). On the other hand, those who assume a 'passive' attitude, one that is traditionally assigned to women, whether in a sexual or social interaction, 'devalue' their own masculinity (Parker 1999). This system of classification is also called the 'Mediterranean homosexuality' model because it is found 'in the Latin countries of Europe and the Americas, in the Islamic countries of the Mediterranean, as well as in the Balkans' (Dall'Orto 2016 [1990], 796), among other regions. Therefore, this model is not limited to Brazil (Benedetti 2005; Fry 1982; Klein 1999; Kulick 1998; Parker 1991, 1999), but is extended to other Latin American realities such as Nicaragua (Lancaster 1992), Mexico (Cantú 2002; Howe et al. 2008; Prieur 1998), Costa Rica (Sikora 1998), Cuba (Lumsden 1996), Dominican Republic (Padilla 2007), Spain (Guasch 2011), Spanish ex-colonies like the Philippines (Johnson 1997), and even Tonga (Besnier 2002).

It is important to recognise that while the active/passive model is useful for examining the erotic practices and social interactions of *travestis*, these distinctions cannot always be (re)presented in such a linear and dichotomous way. As Hines (2009, 94) stresses, 'sexual identities are subject to temporal and contextual shifts.' Some research on homosexual relationships between women (Facchini 2008) and men (França 2010) also suggests that those who are involved in these types of relationships perceive their sexual practices in a more flexible way, considering the performance of *fully* 'active' or 'passive' roles as limited. Therefore, they do not perceive that, because they are gay men or women, they have to behave socially and sexually in a 'feminine' or a 'masculine' way, respectively. The concerns about a person's 'masculinity' or 'femininity' correspond more to prescriptions regarding sexual behaviours that *must be* fulfilled in specific contexts, for example, when certain men need to become intelligible subjects to relate emotionally and sexually with other men (França 2010, 218). However, in other contexts, these same people may blur such sexual and gender prescriptions to move continuously along the masculine/feminine polarity. In short, although I find limitations when analysing sexuality in binary terms, it is also worth noting that the active/passive model gave sense to *travestis'* own performances of their sexualities and social interactions with their clients and *maridos*. In addition, although *travestis* employ a rigid and binary conception of what is perceived as masculine and feminine, they also move fluidly between the two margins of sexuality and gender, blurring constantly the transgression/conformity duality.

In the active/passive classification, the 'masculine' pole is valued, while the 'feminine' one is devalued and stigmatised, since those assigned as men at birth who occupy this position destabilise—more strongly—the heteronormative dynamics of gender. Peter Fry (1982) considered that this masculine, hierarchical, and popular relationship model is presented as the main (but not the only) classificatory system of homosexuality in Brazil and is closely related to the working classes of the country (see also Garcia 2009).[1] The active/passive opposition—from which other oppositions such as macho/fag, strong/weak, or virile/effeminate are derived—does not correspond to physical characteristics per se but gives meaning to the different forms in which the body is used in homoerotic encounters. At the same time, this model reinforces the construction of two categories: *homens* (men) and *bichas* (fairy, fag). 'Active' men are not perceived as gay. On the contrary, only the 'passive' *bichas* are considered gay (Cornwall 1994), as they represent the supposed submission of femininity. In Brazil, it is very popular to use the verbs *comer* (to eat) and *dar* (to give) to refer to the act of penetrating and being penetrated, respectively. Whoever 'eats' the other, at the same time, is possessing and dominating him/her symbolically. *Dar* (the anus or vagina) represents an act of submission.

Prieur (1998) offers us the example of the Mexican *jotas* (young effeminate gays) and *vestidas* (local expression for *travestis*) whose femininity enables their partners and clients to accept these relationships and not consider them homosexual encounters. They, who are recognised as 'men,' continue to feel like 'machos' and the *jotas* and *vestidas*, as long as they assume their 'passive' role, are the *maricas* (fairy) or, in the best case, their 'wives.' According to this scheme, the masculinity of these 'men' is not being compromised. Similarly, in Brazil, the feminine appearance and the supposed 'passive' role of the *travestis* contribute to not questioning their *maridos'* and—in some cases—clients' masculinity. Next, we see how this system is organised among the *travestis*.

Travestis' Sexualities

For this popular and hierarchical model of classification, the boundaries between the masculine and feminine are not based on the sexed bodies, as the sexual practices and the values associated with masculinity and femininity establish who behaves as a 'man' or a 'woman.' However, as we see

On Clients, *Maridos*, and *Travestis'* Sexualities **119**

later, *travestis* make a rigid and binary use of what is perceived as masculine and feminine through their sexual and erotic interactions: 'real' men should only penetrate; *travestis* should only *dar* and be possessed. Moreover, the rigidity of values and meanings attributed to the sexual practices categorise *travestis* as if they were homosexual or *viados* (Benedetti 2005). Indeed, most of the *travestis* consider themselves as homosexuals or *bichas* (Klein 1999; Kulick 1998) to describe who they *are*.[2] It is useful to take into account that the construction of *travesti* identities is crossed by an 'erotic engineering' (Denizart 1997) that not only guides the construction of a highly sexualised body but also organises the desire. From the moment they decide to modify their bodies, feminising and beautifying themselves, *travestis* are, simultaneously, heterosexualising the desire (Butler 1990) as they construct intelligible bodies that will supposedly maintain some coherence through the active/passive sexual practices. It is no longer a 'male' body that will relate to another 'male' body; rather, it is a *travesti* with a considered feminine appearance that interacts sexually with men. Within this model of sexuality, the homosexual (self-)definition depends more on the roles assumed in their sexual interactions than on the sexual-object choice (that is, being two 'men' together).

Those who have a greater political awareness and participate in social movements have reflected more on *travesti* identities and distinguish that it is not the same *being travestis* as *being* homosexuals. Mara, who was the president of ASTRA Rio (Association of Transsexuals and Transsexuals of the State of Rio de Janeiro), discussed with other activists that homosexuality is a sexual orientation, while *travesti* expressions remain at the level of (gender) identities. Therefore, according to her, *travestis* could *be* homosexual, heterosexual, or bisexual. She stated that a *travesti* should not be identified directly as a homosexual. In this way, she moved away from an analysis of sexuality following the active/passive model and approached a more egalitarian one based on the heterosexual/homosexual axis. She described that based on the recognition that a *travesti* is not a man or a woman, 'A *travesti* who has sex with a man has a heterosexual relationship. A *travesti* who has sex with a woman has a heterosexual relationship. And a *travesti* who has sex with another *travesti* maintains a homosexual relationship' (Field notes, 18 April 2008). It is observed that she did not define a person as homosexual according to their 'passive' role in the sexual encounter; on the contrary, she focused on the orientation of the desire (among men, women, or *travestis*). Thus, as soon as *travestis* do not recognise themselves as men, and feel desire for men, they are heterosexualising the desire. However, this way of understanding *travesti* sexuality does not represent the majority of *travestis* who remain immersed in the active/passive model of sexual intercourses and self-identify as *bichas*.

Next, I describe the ways in which *travestis* relate sexually with their clients, lovers, and *maridos*. The construction of *travestis'* femininity is also closely related to their relationship with men (Benedetti 2005). When they feel desired *as* women, *travestis* are reinforcing their femininity. According to Kulick (1998, 228),

> The idiom (and the practice) of penetration is the axis around which every aspect of travesti life turns. An individual's self-discovery as a travesti is signalled by attraction to males—an attraction that inexorably, sooner or later, leads to her being anally penetrated.

Kulick's beautiful ethnography has been criticised for simplifying *travestis'* reality while not acknowledging that their 'sexual practices have been plural, far beyond the barrier of penetrating/being penetrated binarism' (Silva 2013, 149). Although there are *travestis* who are engaged sexually and emotionally with other *travestis,* or women, the vast majority of *travestis* who I met during my fieldwork were attracted to men. Thus, it is not my aim to minimise the complexity of *travestis'* reality, but the participants' own accounts and experiences are the ones that led me to this analysis.

Clients

Most of the *travestis* have a structured discourse that is based on hegemonic and binary notions of the meaning and way femininity and masculinity are articulated in society to make sense of their own identity constructions. Therefore, they assume that it is when they adopt the 'female' role in their sexual interactions that they are satisfied and can construct and express their femininity. For example, Reyna says:

On Clients, *Maridos*, and *Travestis'* Sexualities   **121**

Look, my nature is passive, who taught me to be active were men, but my nature is passive, and I being female is when I complete myself, being possessed. (Personal interview, 6 May 2008, Rio de Janeiro)

However, many of them do not have any qualms about recognising that they love penetrating. They all know that, in the sex market, those who are more sexually vigorous will work more because, as everyone says, most of their clients want to assume the 'passive' role. In this way, when they penetrate the clients, or receive oral sex, there is a kind of 'pollution' of their femininity as their sexual practices distort the gender roles that they are expected to perform. Yet, it is in the street, within prostitution— where the sexual practices are not regulated and can be potentially transgressive because there is a commercial transaction—that the 'disorder' is accepted and even enjoyed among some *travestis* (Pelúcio 2009).

No one is forced to penetrate their clients; there are *travestis* or those who self-identify as transsexuals who do not want to 'violate their female essence,' as they say, or cannot do it because of the hormones that compromise their virility (Field notes, 23 June 2008). However, it is clear that, for those working in the sex marketplace, the possibility of penetrating provides the main economic benefits. According to some participants:

I would rather prefer to be passive, more woman. [Being] active only at work, just because of the money itself. I get twice as much of a *programa*[3] when I am active. (Keila, personal interview, 23 May 2008, Rio de Janeiro)

I did not like being active and what did I do? To earn my money, I did what he [the client] wanted; I did it and enjoyed it for him. (Roberta, personal interview, 7 August 2008, Rio de Janeiro)

Many *travestis* find it difficult to understand why most of their clients prefer to *dar* when, in front of them, there are 'beautiful and feminine' *travestis* who have invested much effort and money into looking *like* women and, furthermore, most of their clients wish to be possessed. For example, Francisca explained that:

The *travesti* is not sought after as a woman, but for something different. And this is, for us, difficult because we have suffered a lot. But we can get around it, the psychological hurts, it is very embarrassing, you know? Because if you spend years and years taking hormones, you go through the pain of surgery, you go through emotional pain because the family sometimes has greater discrimination, or they reproach you. Unfortunately, we have to be the husband of the story, the man in the story. (Francisca, personal interview, 30 July 2009, Barcelona)

They also recognise—as professional sex workers—that in the realm of desires and fantasies, men can be very sexually 'vicious.' In fact, *travestis* believe that the clients are attracted to the conjunction of a person with a feminine image that—at the same time—has a penis (and the bigger the better). As Samanta says in Rio: 'Clients pay for our silence with money. They like to fantasise that a woman is penetrating them' (Field notes, 7 July 2008). On the one hand, in the erotic-sexual imagery of many men, *travestis* represent 'women with something else' that attracts them considerably (Pelúcio 2009). On the other hand, as clients believe, desiring *travestis* does not imply being recognised as gay because they desire 'beautiful women.' This is stated by Cristina, a *travesti* of the so-called 'first generation':

They want a different woman, they want a woman with a cock, let's say like this [laughs]. Really, *travestis'* clients do not like being in the bed with another man; if you were dressed as a man, he would not go to the bed with you. He has to see something feminine because they want to believe that they are not homosexuals. (Personal interview, 12 September 2008, Rio de Janeiro)

I did not contact *travestis'* clients during my fieldwork. That would have required designing another, new research. Yet, Pelúcio (2009) entered the network of the so-called T-lovers (*Travesti* lovers), that is, men who like to have sex with *travestis* and are organised in major cities of Brazil through off-line meetings and Internet discussion forums. They consider their sexual and erotic practices with *travestis* as 'natural' and 'desirable' for 'real' men. They not only identify themselves as 'normal' men but inscribe their behaviour within the matrix of a masculinity understood as hegemonic. The majority—white, married, and middle-class men—reinforce their masculinity and identity as heterosexual in interactions with other T-lovers to avoid any type of association with homosexual practices and, ultimately, with a gay identity—characteristics highly devalued within the group. Thus, beyond their practices and desires, it is important to describe, among their peers, a *travesti's* femininity in order to reaffirm precisely how 'masculine' they are. However, even if they are penetrated by *travestis*, they continue to publicly assume their virile position, as they are the ones who control the situation: they choose the *travestis*, pay for their services, and determine the practices that will be carried out.

Many clients do care about the degree of femininity achieved by *travestis*, as hormones compromise their virility and mean they cannot penetrate. Therefore, these clients would accept less feminine and only dressed up *travestis* who can guarantee the service required. However, as Cristina declared, a minimum degree of femininity is necessary so that the clients do not believe that they are with 'men.' We have seen in Chap. 4 that the use of liquid silicone allows *travestis* to become feminine without compromising their ability to penetrate.

According to the *travestis*, most of their clients are men. Although some participants mentioned a few cases of married couples that ask for their services to penetrate the women, this is less frequent and also a more expensive practice. *Travestis* categorise their clients in two big groups: those considered 'men' (*homens*) and 'fagots' (*mariconas*). The first group of *homens* include young clients who usually belong to the same social strata of *travestis*, that is, they share generational codes that make them very attractive. Generally, they have low economic resources and mobilise on foot to contact them.[4] They are those who exclusively penetrate in sexual intercourse, which means that they are mostly interested in their female shapes, disdaining any contact with their penises. As 'real,' young, and handsome men, according to *travestis'* aesthetic patterns, they become an important object of desire. So much so that potential clients become sporadic lovers who are not charged. It is also very frequent that they become their future *maridos*. *Mães* and *madrinhas* used to warn the youngest and inexperienced *travestis* to avoid these practices as harmful to the incomes of those who try to live from sex work.

In the second group, that of the *mariconas*, there is a high percentage[5] of clients of *travestis* who prefer to *dar*. Frequently, they are white and older men, living a heterosexual life, and belonging to the middle and higher social classes. According to the *travestis*, they usually negotiate the services from their luxurious cars.[6] These clients, even if they supply their main source of income, are despised by the *travestis*, as they are directly linked to the feminine side, an aspect that devalues them socially and sexually. Moreover, they believe that their clients 'disguise their true nature and pretend to be something that they are not' (Kulick 1998, 225). The pejorative appellation of 'fag' that *travestis* use refers to the contempt which generates from not recognising publicly—as *travestis* do—their sexual desires, turning them into people with a double life, without honour or the courage to be themselves in front of society.

These descriptions should not be thought of as two fixed ways of describing *travestis*' clients. On the contrary, these presentations could be more flexible. For example, there are young and handsome clients who, although they seem to be 'real' men, want to be penetrated. There are also *mariconas* who are far from being solvent, have very low economic resources, and openly express their femininity. Therefore, the heterogeneity of clients can be as rich and complex as their experiences and desires.

Teixeira (2011) analyses the relationships that a group of Brazilian *travestis* maintain with their Italian clients in Milan. Her research participants classify them as (a) *street client*, very frequent, little 'faithful,' and very little valued by *travestis*; (b) *drugged client*, who introduces drugs during the sexual encounter. Some *travestis* 'with head,' as they say, develop some strategies—without displaying them—to not to consume drugs and avoid becoming drug addicts. With this type of clients, they earn enough money because the time they spend for the service is always greater; and (c) *refined client*, who is the favourite of the *travestis*, and the only one who, potentially, can become a *marido* because he shows kindness and refinement in the way he treats them. *Refined clients*, particularly Italian or Swiss men, are educated, with money, give them presents, and invite them to dinner or to go for walks. Beyond the sexual practices assumed in this relationship, conquering a *refined client* is highly valued among the *travestis* because, once he becomes a *marido*, it assures them of protection and 'help' in their migratory projects in Italy—where *travestis*

On Clients, *Maridos*, and *Travestis'* Sexualities   **125**

are frequently undocumented and face situations of vulnerability. As we discuss in Chap. 7, the term 'help' (*ajuda*) is an emic category that refers to the networks involved for the *travestis* to travel to cities in Europe or within Brazil. In the case of the Italian *refined clients/maridos*, affective relationships are engaged to justify the 'help'; that is, they are not always translated in economic terms (for example, when the *refined clients/maridos* offer themselves as guarantors so that they can rent apartments or teach them the Italian language).

In a European context, the work of Teixeira (2011) reveals that the clients, before being classified as 'men' or 'fags,' are mostly valued according to the capacity they have to 'help' *travestis* and introduce them in Italy. *Travestis* and their *refined clients/maridos* therefore build relationships based on friendship, eroticism, desire, or affection. In these economic, sexual, social, and symbolic exchanges, they find advantages that make sense only in their migratory context. In Brazil, even if there are educated and kind clients, they would hardly assume the role of protector of Italian *refined clients*, not only because *travestis* at home are—apparently—less vulnerable, but the prejudices are greater to 'help' them even as a lover or good friend.

In the case of Spain, the relationships they establish with their clients seem to be different from in Italy (Milan). In Barcelona, only one of the participants (Márcia) was married to a Catalan man, a former client, with whom she lived before the wedding.[7] However, I did not meet any *travesti* with a more established relationship during my fieldwork in Barcelona. To begin with, all of the participants considered Spanish clients to be more 'vicious.' Francisca was categorical when expressing that they 'have the vice in the blood' and before greeting her, they would ask what is her penis size as 'they only think about sex.' Pelúcio accessed two important Spanish websites where Latin American *travesti* sex workers offer their services, and there are online forums organised among the clients. The author describes how Spanish clients are more demanding about the sexual practices because *travestis* have to frequently offer more practices that are not generally requested in Brazil (Pelúcio 2011). At the same time, *travestis* complain about the clients' 'lack of hygiene' (referring to Europeans in general) and their constant haggling for prices (the Spanish, in particular). Rosanne, who lived more than seven years in Barcelona,

126   J. Vartabedian

complained that the Catalans are 'badly accustomed': they want a lot and pay little. Nevertheless, there are some 'good' clients who are faithful and give them 'pieces of gold,' as Francisca, a *travesti* who works with a high-class clientele, told me in her private apartment in Barcelona. Nonetheless, in general, the Spanish clients do not get the same respect as the Milanese *refined clients* and are rather included within the *maricona* category.

The binary model *travestis* use to classify their clients follows similar lines to the one analysed by the anthropologist Néstor Perlongher (2008 [1987]), who created an ethnography with male sex workers (called popularly *michês*) during the 1980s in São Paulo. Perlongher points out that these young *michês*, from the working-class, offer their virility in exchange for money to older and socioeconomically more powerful *mariconas* who seek—in this model of *michê*-macho—a way to satisfy their sexual desires. The exaggerated masculinity of the *michês* and the supposed premise that they only penetrate become valuable symbols to affirm that they do not consider themselves 'homosexuals.' Perlongher classifies clients through a series of indicators such as the (1) socioeconomic status, poor clients are considered the *lied mariconas*, while the rich ones are the *rotten mariconas*, clients who show that with their money can 'buy' whoever they want; (2) gender, according to the degree of femininity/masculinity of the client; in general, they are all seen as *bichas*. In addition, there is, to a lesser extent, the 'macho' client, who self-identifies as a heterosexual and 'active' man. This client has difficulty in agreeing—at least publicly—on a service with a *michê* that also allows him to appear socially as a 'man,' and (3) age: *maricona*, old *bicha*, or 'aunt' are the terms which refer to gays over 35 years. These categories, which are not exhausted here and are much more numerous in Perlongher's work, overlap with each other and are articulated with other indicators such as race, because being black is a factor of inferiority in the gay ghetto of São Paulo.

In sum, we can distinguish that the *homen/maricona* model that *travestis* use to classify their clients reproduces the more general active/passive model in which they are also inserted. In the same way that *travestis* repudiate the *mariconas* because they are 'not assumed fags,' *travestis* are themselves repudiated by society because they occupy an even more marginalised position. In fact, the 'offence' *travestis* provoke is twofold:

not only are they considered 'fags' because they perform the 'passive' role with clients, lovers, or *maridos*, but mainly because *travestis* have declined to *naturally* become men. By choosing to live their lives *like* women, *travestis* radically dismantle—if unintentionally—the foundations of a heteronormative society that positively values the exaltation of masculinity. Consequently, as their sexuality and gender 'affront' a binary society that privileges men, they are sanctioned as 'fags' or *viados*, excluded from citizenship, stigmatised, and even murdered.

Maridos

I kept the word *maridos* in italics throughout the book because it is an emic category that names *travestis'* partners, regardless of the duration of the relationship or the existence of any formal link (Teixeira 2011). If *travestis* can perform both sexual roles with their clients, the situation is different with the *maridos*: according to them, the man of the house cannot be a 'fag.' As described by Kulick (1998), these men are generally very young, handsome, muscular, and well endowed, and share the same social origins as *travestis*. These boyfriends, who can immediately become symbolic *maridos*, are very possessive and, in some cases, can even physically mistreat *travestis*. Many *travestis* who want to follow the most stereotyped gender roles, accept and even somehow 'appreciate' this situation of relative powerlessness as 'submissive women' in front of their violent and virile *maridos* (Garcia 2009). Pleasure and violence intersect to shape these relationships (Klein 1999). Thus, the masculine characteristics of their *maridos* are enhanced to counteract their own fantasies linked to femininity.[8] But if, on the one hand, in the private sphere, many *travestis* understand femininity in a very normative way, that is, as 'housewives' who suffer the despotism of their *maridos*, on the other hand, we have seen that they also experience their own femininity as a means of empowerment: when they become ('all made up') *travestis*, they feel desired and are self-confident sex workers who earn the money to maintain their home. However, the combination of these two models of femininity cannot always be sustained. Luciana, interviewed by Denizart (1997, 76), recounts:

> I lost three years with my *marido*, deceiving myself, believing that one day I would be the housewife, that we would have a puppy, a poodle, and that we would have a family: me, him and the dog... cooking, washing, ironing... and the thing did not work well... That's not our reality. Our reality is to 'wear our T-shirt' [of *travesti* sex workers], go out there, struggling and showing off a beautiful body, a healthy head, money in the wallet to save, a travel to Europe...

It would be very simplistic, therefore, to think of *travestis* solely as 'victims' of oppressive *maridos* if they choose this more 'traditional' model of femininity (Kulick 1998). I believe that *travestis* make a strategic use of certain characteristics attributed to femininity because, in fact, having a *marido* implies an act of empowerment. The *travestis* are the ones who accept them (and not the other way around) and maintain them economically. The vast majority of their *maridos* do not work, so they live exclusively on the earnings of the *travestis*. In Italy, although they may engage in another type of relationship with their Italian *maridos*, *travestis* reproduce the same model as in Brazil with their Brazilian *maridos* who travel with them to Milan: they are usually maintained by the *travestis* (Teixeira 2011). Yet, we cannot say that they are *travestis'* pimps, because they generally do not intervene in the field of sex work. It happens that this economic dependence causes the relationship to become paradoxical because, even though they are the 'machos' who control the *travestis* (at least sexually), *travestis* dominate them since they are the ones who provide all the money for the home and their expenses. This is also a way to buy their loyalty.

In Rio, only the *marido* of Samanta lived in the *casarão*. I barely exchanged a few words with him. He was in his 20s, very introverted, and spent all day outside the *casarão*. His routine was to spend—on gambling and beer—the money that, each day, Samanta provided for his personal expenses. I can imagine that the absence of Samanta's *marido* from the *casarão* came from an instruction of hers, to avoid jealousy, conflicts, and seductions by the other *travestis* who lived near and who passed by. A man in the house is someone to look after and control. It is very common for a *marido,* after ending a relationship with a *travesti*, to get involved with another friend or acquaintance. The business of 'love' ends up being very profitable for these men who, in general, seem to have little desire to work. Although Samanta's *marido* had lived with her for more than three years, respected her, and was very reserved, conflicts also appeared in the *casarão*. I witnessed the day when Paula decided to leave the *casarão* because she had argued with Samanta, who accused her of being a 'viper' for having lied and betrayed her friendship. Samanta got the information that Paula warned the other *travestis* not to walk in the *casarão* with tiny shorts because Samanta's *marido* would be on top of them all. Paula, who did not deny the accusation, left the *casarão* after the repudiation of the rest.

The money and gifts that the *maridos* receive from the *travestis* are part of the construction and maintenance of this relationship. As Kulick (1998) mentions, a poor *travesti* has no *marido*. The intervention of money is part of a common practice that delineates the erotic encounters of men and *travestis* outside the sex work market. Leandro de Oliveira (2009) analyses the dynamics involved in a night club in the suburbs of Rio. This is a place where *travestis*, gays with a masculine appearance, gays who cross-dress, and 'real' men meet. The latter, like those who present a performance understood as 'masculine,' enter the club without paying. Those who pay (*travestis* and cross-dressers) do so with the motivation to interact erotically with 'real' men. In the club, there are spaces to have intimate meetings between two or more people. Here, in this space of pleasure, the *travestis* stop working since they do not charge the partner/ sporadic lover they choose to engage with sexually. At the same time, those considered 'men' or 'real men,' who claim that they only like women and *travestis*, agree to maintain relationships with gay men only when there is some material benefit (invitation for a beer, or some money) and could not 'conquer' a *travesti* or cross-dresser during the night. Among these 'men,' their sexual activity has great prestige and strengthens their masculinity. However, these 'men' have to justify—through a certain economic gain that they *must* accept and demand—that they are not gay. If they did not do it, they would be degraded and it could highlight the incongruity between their sexual behaviours and the gender they perform. In short, 'men' reinforce their masculinity by being attracted to people with a feminine appearance and this mutual erotic desire between 'men' and *travestis* means that there is no financial intervention in the

130   J. Vartabedian

context of these fleeting sexual encounters. On the contrary, in the case of gays who do not have a feminine appearance, being supposedly less desirable, the material retribution must exist to support this encounter. As Oliveira sums up:

> Money, far from representing a universal equivalent for relations of exchange, operates as a sign marked by gender, from the interaction context in which it is actuated, expressing the recognition of the masculine *status* that a *man* holds. (2009, 135, emphasis in original)

Money, then, structures the organisation of a *marital* relationship where *maridos*, far from being perceived as 'maintained,' find that their masculinity is being recognised and cared for. On the other hand, while the *travestis* are materially reinforcing the masculinity of their *maridos*, at the same time, they are strengthening their own femininity. Money is only a vehicle to understand this game of practices and interests that are sustained according to the dynamics that tighten the poles of femininity and masculinity. Yet not everyone wants to, and can, support a *marido*. Many *travestis* prefer to avoid 'parasites' who only want to 'eat, sleep and watch television' (Denizart 1997, 73).

But it is important to emphasise that, whatever the reasons and interests of this union, in the bed, the *maridos* are those who have the power. Or, at least, they *should* have it because they are symbolically constructed as very masculine and virile men. From the moment they want to be penetrated or even caress *travestis'* penises, they are immediately displaced to the female pole of the relationship. Equated to the *travestis*, they are disqualified as 'good' *maridos* and excluded from the *travesti* circle: no one will want them in marriage (Benedetti 2005; Kulick 1998). That is why one of the biggest insults among *travestis* is the sentence, '*Seu marido é viado*' ('Your husband is a fag'). They want a 'man' in the house. Some of the participants say:

> I would never do anal penetration with him. For me, I see the image of him, for me, he is a man. Because if I had to find anal sex, I would look for it on the street. For me, at home, I want a man. (Samanta, personal interview, 8 September 2008, Rio de Janeiro)

> There are men with whom I like to bring out my feminine side, [like] woman, being passive; with others, I have fantasies and I end up being active ... with my fixed partner, I prefer to do only woman. (Priscila, personal interview, 22 May 2008, Rio de Janeiro)

Finally, it is very rare that *travestis* and *maridos* socialise together or interact with their respective friends or relatives, if these exist. Kulick (1998) described two reasons for this kind of *marital* isolation: jealousy (on both sides) and shame. The latter is what their *maridos* usually feel when they are presented publicly as their partners. Recognising that they *only* penetrate *travestis* and, thus, are supposed to not be 'gay,' does not completely prevent them from feeling ashamed. *Travestis*, socially repudiated as *bichas*, are severely stigmatised for their double 'infringement' of gender and sexuality. Indeed, those who are publicly recognised as their *maridos* are on the edge of respectability. In the case of Spain, Pelúcio (2011, 207) admits that very few clients fall in love with *travestis* and are able to take on the challenges that this relationship implies in their lives. These men prefer to attribute these 'love failures' to the 'closed mind' of society or to the *travestis* who only think of money and work, instead of recognising that they themselves are not ready to openly accept this type of emotional relationship with all its consequences.

In this chapter, we have seen that the relationship between gender and sexuality has largely been problematised—mainly—within feminism. Although they are distinct categories, they should be examined together to enrich the analysis. Throughout *Brazilian Travesti Migrations*, we have seen that *travesti* gender identities are expressed through the materialisation in their bodies of the desire to feel *like* women. In the field of sexuality, it matters less who they *are* and more what they *do* (Cornwall 1994); that is, the practices rather than the identities give meaning to how they construct their own ways of understanding femininity and masculinity. *Travestis*' gender constructions are then also closely linked to the relationship they establish—mostly—with men (*maridos* and clients). Based on one of the ways in which sexuality is organised in Brazil, there is a hierarchical relationship between, on the one hand, those who are considered 'real' men, that is, 'virile' and 'active' ones, and on the other hand, those who are feminised, devalued, and stigmatised for being 'passive' and sexually submissive to those who want to *comer* them. The men who occupy this position are considered *bichas* or *viados* in Brazil.

In the case of *travestis*, there is a paradoxical situation that avoids recognising them *simply* as gays. Their ability to simultaneously penetrate and be penetrated allows them to position themselves on both sides of the masculine/feminine polarity. Indeed, considered as 'women with something else,' they become very attractive to a large number of clients (called *mariconas* among the *travestis*) who seek to be penetrated by them. The feminine appearance that many *travestis* embody allows them to heterosexualise their erotic and affective practices with men. In addition, in the field of intimacy and private life, *travestis* praise their *maridos'* masculinity and rage. The fact of maintaining a *marido* economically becomes an act that empowers *travestis* as it allows them to reinforce their own femininity. Indeed, *travestis* employ a rigid and binary conception of what is perceived as masculine and feminine, and they use it to organise their sexual and erotic interactions through a more 'traditional' framework.

In short, it has been analysed that, in these forms of social and sexual interaction between *travestis*, clients, and *maridos*, it is important to distinguish the way in which the gender roles are acted and interpreted in order to understand the sexual practices that will end up defining people as masculine and/or feminine. However, the boundaries between these identities are always diffuse and can cross areas where some 'infractions' can easily be made, turning clients and *maridos* into the devalued (the feminine) pole. Finally, *travestis*—even if they move fluidly between the two margins of sexuality and gender—are at the same time considered *bichas* by a heteronormative society that still discriminates and stigmatises *travestis'* decision to publicly assume their gender identity.

Notes

1. The other model of sexuality—mainly among middle-upper classes—defines gay identities according to the sexual-object choice, instead of the sexual roles that emulate the heterosexual norms. This is a more egalitarian system, based on the heterosexual/homosexual axis, in which all men who have sexual and affective relationships with other men are considered gay.

On Clients, *Maridos*, and *Travestis'* Sexualities 133

2. Pelúcio (2009, 93) partially agrees with this gender classification system based on the sexual roles adopted in *travesti* erotic encounters. In her research, she also refers to a more rigid model of interpretation in which *travesti* gender identity appears *naturally* linked to sex. In this way, *travestis* ultimately recognise themselves as 'men' who deride the 'norms of nature.' I could not go deeper into Pelúcio's statement because the data of my research do not allow me to go further. However, there is one exception. Daniela, an inhabitant of the *casarão* in Rio, told me one day that they [the *travestis*] 'will be punished by God for being men who try by all means to have a woman's body' (Field notes, 9 July 2008). This idea arose when she emphasised that she would never have vaginal surgery because people who want to change their penises are punished (by God). This issue deserves more attention in future research.

3. A *programa* is the sexual service offered to a client in exchange for money.

4. While this observation is only anecdotal, we can say that not all the clients identified as 'men' are low-income, but the vast majority of them are. I was in Rio de Janeiro during the scandal of the Brazilian football player Ronaldo who asked for the service of three *travestis* at the end of April 2008. One of the *travestis* accused him of not paying what was agreed upon (it is said that she had extorted him and asked for more money) and went to the police with Ronaldo's stolen driving licence. It was a media scandal (see, for example, Simpson 2008). To defend himself, the internationally recognised Ronaldo argued that he believed he was with 'female prostitutes.' For Ronaldo, it was unthinkable to accept the embarrassment of publicly acknowledging that he sought the sexual services of *travestis*. According to the participants, no one accepted Ronaldo's 'confusion' because he came precisely from the popular strata of Rio and was prepared to perfectly recognise a *travesti*. Ronaldo also met them in the west area of Rio, in Barra da Tijuca, where an important focus of *travesti* prostitution is concentrated in the city. In addition, Garcia (2009, 619) states that scandal is one of the strategies *travestis* use to keep clients in a 'submissive position.' Kulick and Klein (2003) believe that scandal acts as a political weapon *travestis* employ to threaten and discredit the clients in order to obtain more economic profits.

5. Although it is not possible to present reliable data, *travestis'* own perceptions of the percentage of clients who want to be penetrated by them oscillate between 70% and 80%.

6. Perlongher (2008 [1987]), when analysing young male prostitutes in São Paulo, describes that the brand of the cars of their possible clients is highly valued among the sex workers. Some even set aside their economic interests in order to exhibit themselves in a luxury car.
7. In Spain, a law came into effect in July 2005 to legalise same-sex marriage.
8. Urrea and La Furcia (2014) reveal the use of the same stereotyped roles among Colombian trans women from popular social strata.

References

Alsop, Rachel, Annette Fitzsimons, and Kathleen Lennon. 2002. *Theorizing Gender*. Cambridge: Polity Press.

Benedetti, Marcos. 2005. *Toda feita: o corpo e o gênero das travestis*. Rio de Janeiro: Garamond.

Besnier, Niko. 2002. Transgenderism, Locality, and the Miss Galaxy Beauty Pageant in Tonga. *American Ethnologist* 29 (3): 534–566.

Butler, Judith. 1990. *Gender Trouble: Feminism and the Subversion of Identity*. New York: Routledge.

———. 1994. Against Proper Objects. *Differences: A Journal of Feminist Cultural Studies* 6: 1–26.

Cantú, Lionel. 2002. De Ambiente. Queer Tourism and the Shifting Boundaries of Mexican Male Sexualities. *GLQ: A Journal of Lesbian and Gay Studies* 8 (1–2): 139–166.

Cornwall, Andrea. 1994. Gendered Identities and Gender Ambiguity Among *Travestis* in Salvador, Brazil. In *Dislocating Masculinity*, ed. Andrea Cornwall and Nancy Lindisfarne, 111–132. London: Routledge.

Dall'Orto, Giovanni. 2016 [1990]. Mediterranean Homosexuality. In *The Encyclopedia of Homosexuality*, ed. Wayne Dynes, vol. II, 796–798. London: Routledge.

Delphy, Christine. 1993. Rethinking Sex and Gender. *Women's Studies International Forum* 16 (1): 1–9.

Denizart, Hugo. 1997. *Engenharia erótica: travestis no Rio de Janeiro*. Rio de Janeiro: Zahar.

Facchini, Regina. 2008. *Entre umas e outras. Mulheres, (homo)sexualidades e diferentas na cidade de São Paulo*. PhD dissertation, State University of Campinas, Brazil.

França, Isadora L. 2010. *Consumindo lugares, consumindo nos lugares. Homossexualidade, consumo e subjetividades na cidade de São Paulo.* PhD dissertation, State University of Campinas, Brazil.

Fry, Peter. 1982. *Para inglês ver: identidade e política na cultura brasileira.* Rio de Janeiro: Zahar.

Garcia, Marcos R.V. 2009. Identity as a 'Patchwork': Aspects of Identity Among Low-Income Brazilian *Travestis. Culture, Health & Sexuality* 11 (6): 611–623.

Guasch, Oscar. 2011. Social Stereotypes and Masculine Homosexualities: The Spanish Case. *Sexualities* 14 (5): 526–543.

Hines, Sally. 2009. A Pathway to Diversity?: Human Rights, Citizenship and the Politics of Transgender. *Contemporary Politics* 15 (1): 87–102.

Howe, Cymene, Susanna Zaraysky, and Lois Lorentzen. 2008. Transgender Sex Workers and Sexual Transmigration Between Guadalajara and San Francisco. *Latin American Perspectives* 158 (35/1): 31–50.

Johnson, Mark. 1997. *Beauty and Power. Transgendering and Cultural Transformation in the Southern Philippines.* Oxford/New York: Berg.

Klein, Charles. 1999. 'The Ghetto Is Over, Darling': Emerging Gay Communities and Gender and Sexual Politics in Contemporary Brazil. *Culture, Health and Sexuality* 1 (3): 239–260.

Kulick, Don. 1998. *Travesti: Sex, Gender and Culture Among Brazilian Transgendered Prostitutes.* Chicago: University of Chicago Press.

Kulick, Don, and Charles Klein. 2003. Scandalous Acts: The Politics of Shame Among Brazilian *Travesti* Prostitutes. In *Recognition Struggles and Social Movements. Contested Identities, Agency and Power*, ed. Barbara Hobson, 215–238. Cambridge: Cambridge University Press.

Lancaster, Roger. 1992. *Life Is Hard. Machismo, Danger, and the Intimacy of Power.* Berkeley: University of California Press.

Lumsden, Ian. 1996. *Machos, Maricones, and Gays: Cuba and Homosexuality.* Philadelphia: Temple University Press.

MacKinnon, Catharine. 1982. Feminism, Marxism, Method, and the State: An Agenda for Theory. *Signs* 7 (3): 515–544.

McLaughlin, Janice, Mark Casey, and Diane Richardson. 2006. At the Intersections of Feminist and Queer Debates. In *Intersections Between Feminist and Queer Theory*, ed. Diane Richardson, Janice McLaughlin, and Mark Casey, 1–18. Basingstoke: Palgrave.

Oliveira, Leandro. 2009. Diversidade sexual e trocas no mercado erótico: gênero, interação e subjetividade em uma boate na periferia do Rio de Janeiro. In *Prazeres dissidentes*, ed. Elvira Díaz Benítez and Carlos Fígari, 119–145. Rio de Janeiro: Garamond.

136   J. Vartabedian

Padilla, Mark. 2007. *Caribbean Pleasure Industry: Tourism, Sexuality, and AIDS in the Dominican Republic*. Chicago: University of Chicago Press.

Parker, Richard. 1991. *Bodies, Pleasures and Passions: Sexual Culture in Contemporary Brazil*. Boston: Beacon Press.

———. 1999. *Beneath the Equator: Cultures of Desire, Male Homosexuality, and Emerging Gay Communities in Brazil*. New York: Routledge.

Pelúcio, Larissa. 2009. *Abjeção e Desejo: uma etnografia travesti sobre o modelo preventivo de aids*. São Paulo: Annablume, Fapesp.

———. 2011. 'Amores perros' – sexo, paixão e dinheiro na relação entre espanhóis e travestis brasileiras no mercado transnacional do sexo. In *Gênero, sexo, amor e dinheiro: mobilidades transnacionais envolvendo o Brasil*, ed. Adriana Piscitelli, Glaucia de Oliveira Assis, and José M. Nieto Olivar, 185–224. Campinas: Unicamp/PAGU.

Perlongher, Néstor. 2008 [1987]. *O negócio do michê: Prostituição viril em São Paulo*. São Paulo: Editora Fundação Perseu Abramo.

Prieur, Annick. 1998. *Mema's House, Mexico City: On Transvestites, Queens, and Machos*. Chicago: University of Chicago Press.

Rich, Adrienne. 1980. Compulsory Heterosexuality and Lesbian Existence. *Signs: Journal of Women in Culture and Society* 5: 631–660.

Richardson, Diane. 2007. Patterned Fluidities: (Re)Imagining the Relationship Between Gender and Sexuality. *Sociology* 41 (3): 457–474.

———. 2008. Conceptualizing Gender. In *Introducing Gender and Women's Studies*, ed. Diane Richardson and Victoria Robinson, 3rd ed., 3–19. Basingstoke: Palgrave.

Rubin, Gayle. 1984. Thinking Sex: Notes for a Radical Theory of the Politics of Sexuality. In *Pleasure and Danger: Exploring Female Sexuality*, ed. Carole Vance, 267–319. London: Routledge.

Sedgwick, Eve. 1990. *Epistemology of the Closet*. Berkeley: University Of California Press.

Sikora, Jacobo S. 1998. *De ranas a princesas: sufridas, atrevidas y travestidas*. San José de Costa Rica: Ilpes.

Silva, Joseli Maria. 2013. Espaço interdito e a experiência urbana travesti. In *Geografias malditas: corpos, sexualidades e espaços*, ed. Joseli Silva, Marcio Ornat, and Alides Chimin Jr., 143–182. Ponta Grossa: Todapalavra.

Simpson, Richard. 2008. Brazilian World Cup star Ronaldo Takes Three Prostitutes to His Hotel Room… Only to Discover They Are MEN. *Daily Mail Online*, April 29. http://www.dailymail.co.uk/news/article-562742/Brazilian-World-Cup-star-Ronaldo-takes-prostitutes-hotel-room--discover-MEN.html. Accessed 24 Mar 2017.

Teixeira, Flávia do B. 2011. *Juízo e Sorte*: enredando *maridos* e *clientes* nas narrativas sobre o projeto migratório das travestis brasileiras para a Itália. In *Gênero, sexo, amor e dinheiro: mobilidades transnacionais envolvendo o Brasil*, ed. Adriana Piscitelli, Glaucia de Oliveira Assis, and José M. Nieto Olivar, 225–262. Campinas: Unicamp/PAGU.

Urrea, Fernando, and Angie La Furcia. 2014. Pigmentocracia del deseo en el mercado sexual Trans de Cali, Colombia. *Sexualidad, Salud y Sociedad – Revista Latinoamericana* 16: 121–152. https://doi.org/10.1590/S1984-64872014000100007. Accessed 23 Mar 2017.

Valentine, David. 2007. *Imagining Transgender. An Ethnography of a Category*. Durham/London: Duke University Press.

Vartabedian, Julieta. 2014. Sobre travestis, clientes y *maridos*: género y sexualidad en la construcción de las identidades de travestis brasileñas trabajadoras del sexo. *Revista de Antropología Social* 23: 237–261.

Wittig, Monique. 1992. *The Straight Mind and Other Essays*. Boston: Beacon Press.

6

Travesti Sex Workers' Bodily Experiences and the Politics of Life and Death

Bodies, as capital, information, and markets, move rapidly across the world. In recent decades, there has been a significant growth in cross-border circuits for making a living. One of the most important of these global circuits—which Sassen (2002) calls 'counter-geographies of globalization'—is sex work. Although it is part of the global economy, commercial sex is also situated at the margins of the formal economy, that is, it constitutes the so-called shadow globalisation (Penttinen 2004). In most countries worldwide, the exchange of sex for money occurs in a quasi-legal context, where sex work is not illegal, but the criminalisation of activities such as pimping or sex advertising restricts prostitution and—paradoxically—leads sex workers to situations of more vulnerability and exploitation (Hubbard et al. 2008; Hubbard 2012).[1] However, the sex industry[2] continues to grow and create great benefits in the context of neoliberal state policies (Brents and Sanders 2010). Unemployment, poverty, and shrinking state resources are some of the reasons which motivate people to migrate to more lucrative scenarios to live and work within the sex industry. Sex workers can earn significantly more money in fewer hours than in any other job (Willman 2010). However, as we see

© The Author(s) 2018

J. Vartabedian, *Brazilian* Travesti *Migrations*, Genders and Sexualities in the Social Sciences, https://doi.org/10.1007/978-3-319-77101-4_6

139

in this and the next chapters, when discussing *travestis'* motivations for migrating and engaging in sex work, people's sexualities, desires, and genders also shape their decisions to move. My aim is to challenge understandings of (migrant) sex workers as 'passive' subjects isolated from the social circumstances in which they are situated. In this way, as other scholars have analysed (Agustín 2007; Smith 2016, 375, my emphasis), I consider that sex work is 'deeply implicated *in*, but not determined *by*, social relations of power in complex ways that may, at times, serve to subvert and destabilise existing power relations as well as to reinforce them.' Thus, structure and agency are co-constituted in a flexible, ambiguous, and contested way (Smith 2012).

In *Brazilian Travesti Migrations*, I also analyse sex work through the lens of non-heteronormative genders and sexualities to decentre the tight association between (non-trans) 'women' and 'sex work.' The lack of inclusion of male and trans sex workers within research agendas and public policies is quite evident (Dennis 2008; Pitcher and Wijers 2014; Smith and Laing 2012). As Smith (2012, 590) describes, it is considered, empirically, that 'the focus on women tends to be justified (if it is justified at all) on the grounds that the "vast majority" of sex workers are female'; based on empirical evidence which has never been really interrogated. Yet, the diversity among sex workers is underestimated and read through a 'heterosexual matrix' (Butler 1990) in which sex workers are assumed to be heterosexual women and clients heterosexual men. Although some relevant contributions focus on male sex workers (Aggleton 1999; Aggleton and Parker 2015; Castañeda 2013; Minichiello and Scott 2014; Padilla 2007; Whowell 2010), trans sex workers remain almost ignored (with some exceptions such as Howe et al. 2008; Kulick 1998; Ochoa 2014; Pelúcio 2009; Silva and Ornat 2014).

In this chapter, I describe the different meanings that sex work has for the *travestis* and how this activity shapes their social interactions, bodies, and lives. I situate this discussion in Mbembe's concept of *necropolitics* to understand 'the structural exclusions that dehumanize and diminish gender non-conforming bodies' (Aizura 2014, 129; Haritaworn et al. 2014). That is, as Butler described (2004), some (queer) bodies are ungrievable or left to die. *Travestis* are the target of violence and death, while they are also excluded from 'neoliberal productivity' (Edelman 2014, 183) with almost no chance of finding a job outside sex work. However, although they are the 'bad' citizens who embody institutional abandonment, *travestis* also occupy a position as racialised or colonised 'others' within the circuits of capital: they have an economic value as hypersexualised sex workers (Aizura 2014). It is through sex work that most of the *travestis* display their own strategies to move—within and outside Brazil—and obtain economic, social, and symbolic benefits from their work, thus, constructing themselves as intelligible and desired subjects who negotiate the dynamics of the contemporary globalised world. I follow 'a fleshy, embodied understanding of sex work' (Loopmans 2016, 310) because it is through their bodies that *travesti* sex workers give sense to their varied experiences. Sex work not only allows them to earn money to survive and invest in their bodily transformations and processes of beautification but also enables them to feel desired, more confident, and have a place— although precarious—in the world.

The Meanings of Sex Work

There is no unique way of understanding sex work, as *travesti's* experiences are different and determined by variations in age, education, race, social class, or family support. To begin with, mainly among the 'first generations' of *travestis*[3] with more economic and social resources, sex work is perceived in negative terms, associated with criminality and marginality. Older *travestis* generally differentiate themselves from the 'others,' those younger and poorer ones who, according to them, are engaged in prostitution to steal clients and take the benefits. For example, Lina, in her 60s, the owner of a recognised hair salon and who also worked as an artist in the remaining theatre shows in Rio, recounted:

> I was born to be a hairdresser, an artist. I was not born to be a prostitute, to do this kind of work. I was raised in a good family … I am against marginality, right? Those who use prostitution to steal, to blackmail, I am against this, they are marginal people … I do not like working with artists who are doing prostitution, I do not like to mix myself. (Personal interview, 6 August 2008, Rio de Janeiro)

After this interview, other *travestis* of the same generation as Lina who knew her very well, let me know that Lina was also a 'prostitute' when she moved to France in the late 1970s and never worked as an 'artist' in the prestigious nightclub *Le Carrousel* of Paris, as Lina assured me. If we assume that all the stories are, indeed, fictions, I was less interested in finding 'the truth' rather than understanding why Lina chose certain facts (and possibly omitted others) to reconstruct her life trajectory. It is more relevant then to comprehend that she rejected any association with prostitution because she considered it 'marginal' and that the 'prostitute stigma' (Pheterson 1996) would interfere with her construction as an artist and famous hairdresser. The distinctions that Lina and other 'artists' established with the 'other' *travestis* who were perceived as 'marginal' and 'with no future' allowed them to construct an 'us' with the memories of the best years of the theatre shows, their trips to Europe, the admiration men and women professed towards them, and the halo of 'glamour' that surrounded their lives.

Other *travestis* of the 'first generation,' such as Cristina and Bibi, although currently working in the field of entertainment as artists who lip-synch to famous singers, claimed that they had to engage in prostitution out of 'necessity,' even though they did not like it. When she recounted her experience in Spain, Bibi proudly stated, 'but my prostitution was an honest and dignified one. I did not get lost, did not keep bad company, I never got mixed up in the world of drugs, junk, mafia or anything like that' (personal interview, 12 September 2008, Rio de Janeiro). Analysis of *travesti* sex workers' migration to Europe reveals that during the second half of the 1970s, *travestis* took great economic advantage of a very profitable scenario within the sex work marketplace, as discussed in Chap. 7. Money empowered them in front of other *travestis* and their families upon their return to Brazil, where they settled down more comfortably if they bought at least a house or an apartment. Those 'survivors,' like Bibi or Cristina, needed to 'have head' to strategically take some distance from drugs, conflicts with other colleagues, clients and avoid risky behaviours that would have killed them as *travesti* sex workers. Evidently, they also needed some 'luck' to survive, as it is not an election to 'escape' from transphobia and other structural constraints. We know that *travesti* sex workers are more vulnerable to HIV infection, violence, and death; discrimination is greater and they usually suffer from a lack of social, health, and legal support (Edelman 2014; Infante et al. 2009; Padilla et al. 2016).

Samanta and Keila from the *casarão* told me that they did not like some *travestis* of the 'first generation' such as Lina and Regina (presented below) because they thought that Lina and Regina felt 'better' than the sex workers and put a lot of distance between them. According to Keila, 'every *travesti* goes through prostitution, even if she is a doctor. She will always be treated as a whore' (Field notes, 2 September 2008). We can see that through the way the 'first generation' of *travestis* reject sex work, they are reproducing a discourse of respectability in which some trans people are constructed as 'proper' subjects (Irving 2008) 'deemed to be the deserving recipients of transgender rights' (Aizura 2014, 135). In this way, they keep a distance from the 'others,' those sex workers who, according to Shah (2010), are simultaneously 'produced as vectors of HIV contamination and seen as the repository of risk' (in Aizura 2014, 139), which leads them to be highly criminalised, as a threat to homonormativity (Duggan 2003). Some scholars use the concept-metaphor 'queer necropolitics' to make sense 'of the symbiotic co-presence of life and death' (Haritaworn et al. 2014, 2) in which some (queer) bodies are 'fostered for living' (Puar 2007, 36), while others are let die. For example, Edelman (2014) employs the term *necronationalism* to distinguish the hetero and homonationalistic discourses of viable life. He describes that necronationalism 'focuses on the ways in which the erasure and death of the bad (queer) citizen—worker body carves out the ideological and physical space for the good (queer) citizen—worker body to emerge' (174). These institutionalised processes valorised whiteness, domesticity, and a depoliticised LGBTI culture based on consumption and productivity. The 'non-domesticised' others, the trans women sex workers who are 'framed as risky or deviant individuals whose disappearance from the streets makes life safe for others' (Aizura 2014, 140), in their survival, take the ultimate revenge against a heteronormative system that emphasises the responsibility of the individual for their 'irrational and risky' choice of life. In other words, the politics of life and death construct a fragile line between legitimate subjects and illegitimate non-subjects who, ultimately, *must* die (Quinan 2016).

Despite this moral and very carnal division between the 'good' and the 'bad' *travesti*, it is a fact that sex work is one of the most profitable activities that most of the participants can carry out, as other ethnographic research has shown (Benedetti 2005; Kulick 1998; Ochoa 2014; Padilla et al. 2016; Pelúcio 2009; Prieur 1998). In heteronormative contexts where gender non-conforming people are stigmatised and discriminated against, *travestis* are also—as Keila mentioned—immediately associated with prostitution (Aizura 2014), even though there are a few exceptions who manage to face social rejection and dismantle this close connection.

During fieldwork, almost all the participants were outdoor sex workers. Posso and La Furcia (2016) describe that in Colombia many *travestis* are also hairdressers in very low-income salons; however, in Rio, I just met Lina and Martine working as hairdressers (though in middle-class hair salons). Posso and La Furcia (2016) recount that prostitution and hairdressing are the only two professions in which trans women are accepted, and even *naturalised*, because they can express their gender identities without concealment. Another activity available for the *travestis* is housekeeping, which is a very devalued work and only those who cannot afford (and do not want) to work within sex work are informally employed in other *travestis'* houses to earn very little money, or at least have a place to sleep or something to eat. I could witness the great informal economy developed in the *casarão* among trans and non-trans people, as this old house functioned as a 'social centre' for the *travestis* in Lapa. For example, Samanta used to sell latex panties and Silvia served lunch in her bedroom, which had the only stove available in the house. Thus, *travestis* become 'good' consumers, if we consider not only their material constraints (for not having a kitchen to cook) but also the 'outside' discrimination that makes *travestis* pay higher prices for renting a room to a *mãe/madrinha* or having a hairdresser in the *casarão* to avoid rejection from one of the hair salons of the neighbourhood. Finally, more experienced *travestis* become *mães*, *madrinhas* or *bombadeiras* to take advantage—with great benefits—of their networks and influence to *produce* and materially sustain the dynamics of *travestis* within prostitution. Coming back to Lina, she clearly states:

Nobody gives a job to a *travesti*, you know it very well, a *travesti* has no job. You're going to be a hairdresser and even then you're going to have it difficult to work in certain places. People do not accept us yet, thus, you're going to be a prostitute. I do not see a *travesti* working either in a bank or in another wonderful job, I do not see it. I only see *travestis* who are prostituting themselves and living very poorly. Very few *travestis* live well, those who are my age live well because they started as men, and they made their living, bought their apartments, lived in a period with more facilities for shows in Europe. (Lina, personal interview, 6 August 2008, Rio de Janeiro)

Unemployment and underemployment are issues that deeply impact on trans people's lives worldwide (Edelman 2014; Padilla et al. 2016). In Brazil, younger *travestis*, with less education and family support than Lina and other middle-class *travestis*, find a 'refuge' in prostitution—paradoxically, dangerous and uncertain—from where to start to construct their identities and make a living. Prejudices and transphobia do not allow them to access the formal job market, even within the lower-paid occupations. As Lina expressed, those *travestis* in their 60s who are now in a better economic position had the opportunity to study with a male appearance and later took great advantage of the 'golden era' of *travesti* prostitution in Europe. According to Pedro, a former business owner of nightclubs for *travestis* and cross-dressers' shows during the 1970s in Rio, those *travestis* working in prostitution were 'marvellous.' But today, he continues, the new generations 'have lowered the standard because there is no longer a *travesti* with a certain status, culture, no, no, it does not exist anymore' (personal interview, 13 September 2008, Rio de Janeiro). In Chap. 3, I remarked that there are some *travestis* who managed to go to the university and get jobs outside sex work in current times. However, they are still a small minority who do not represent the majority of the participants of this research.

When analysing the experiences of non-normative migrant sex workers within the UK sex industry, Nick Mai (2012, 582) explains that this activity is potentially empowering because it allows them to 'escape the insecurities engendered in them by the degree of homophobia and discrimination they find in the "straight" world and in "straight" jobs' (if that would be possible in the case of *travestis*). However, whilst marginality,

146   J. Vartabedian

social stigma, and poverty determine the day-to-day of many *travestis*, it would be limited to understand prostitution *only* through its economic advantages to 'improve' *travestis'* lives. As other scholars have also discussed (Benedetti 2005; Garcia and Lehman 2011; Kulick 1998), sex work, thus, does not only represent their main professional option, it is also the space of construction and learning of femininity, and of reaffirmation of their bodily transformations. This means that sex work has a strong influence on the construction of *travestis'* identities. It is in the space of prostitution where they socialise with other *travestis*, learn how to make-up and dress up 'properly,' discover the techniques to transform and feminise their bodies, and feel admired and desired by their clients, lovers, and possible future *maridos*. In other words, the gender of *travestis* is mainly learned and examined through sex work. As Samanta relates: 'it was from there [sex work] that I became what I am today, if it were not for prostitution, I would not be the Samanta I am today' (personal interview, 8 September 2008, Rio de Janeiro).

Even for the new generations of *travestis* who can study, who are supported by their parents, and who do not 'need' to prostitute themselves, sex work remains an important reference for their identitarian experiences, since it is the space par excellence where the transgression of gender norms is accepted (Duque 2011). Unlike spaces such as the family and the school, where heteronormativity is imposed and any other variant of gender or sexual orientation continues to be sanctioned, within prostitution, these sexual and gender variants are accepted, valued, and monetised. Spanish self-identified transsexual activist Beatriz Espejo says that 'many transsexuals find legitimacy and personal fulfilment through the economic and real valuation that men demonstrate towards them, reinforcement that they do not find in other social areas in which they have previously been despised' (2008, 133). Therefore, for the young *travestis* who have access to other resources to live, sex work becomes equally attractive as a space to build their processes of feminisation. Similarly, Infante et al. (2009, 133), in their research with trans women sex workers in Mexico, recount that although those who can work in beauty salons are safer and more protected than if they were working on the streets, the hairstylists still 'missed the glamour and competitiveness to get greater number of clients' when they were sex workers.

As explained earlier, almost all of the participants, both in Rio and Barcelona, have experienced or are living from sex work. Either in a professional, systematic way, or through some 'friends' who provide them with 'gifts,' the vast majority find in these economic, sexual, and symbolic exchanges to be one of the main means not only to survive but to live and reaffirm their own identities. Those who never experienced sex work were Martine and Regina (and apparently Lina) of the so-called 'first generation' of *travestis*. Martine identified herself as a white transsexual and, as mentioned, was a hairdresser, although she was also recognised as a writer and actress. Regina, one of the first *travesti* actresses to arrive in Europe to work in *Le Carrousel* of Paris and one of the most famous *travestis* in the Brazilian media, was an artist and had always lived exclusively from acting. In fact, when she came back from Paris in the 1980s, she called herself a *transformista* to dissociate from the 'street *travestis*' (Hutta and Balzer 2013, 76).[4]

Feminist scholars have stressed upon the autonomy and agency of the people who choose sex work as the best labour option compared with low-paid and precarious jobs (Agustín 2005, 2007; Kempadoo and Doezema 1998; O'Connell Davidson 1998; Osborne 1991; Pheterson 1989, 1996). In the case of trans people, the options available are much narrower than for female and male sex workers as they are more affected by stigma and discrimination (Aggleton 1999; Blanchette and Silva 2011; Infante et al. 2009). However, most of the *travestis* do not consider prostitution a 'fatality' (nor for many other female and male sex workers). I am concerned with highlighting the productive effects that this activity has over *travestis*, avoiding any victimising approach. In this sense, prostitution is a key element in their becoming *travestis* as it allows them, in many cases, to leave an oppressive home and become self-sufficient to face their 'new' lives. According to Roberta: 'To leave the house I had to prostitute myself. Then I started to make money, rented a room and started buying my things, you know? From there to here I've been growing' (personal interview, 7 August 2008, Rio de Janeiro). Once engaged in sex work, those who want to go a step further and live *as travestis* make an important decision to 'cut' with a severe familiar context in which they were punished as *viados*.[5] In this way, *travestis* are actively interfering—as empowered sex workers—in the social relations in which they are submerged; in some cases subverting power relations but also reinforcing them.

We have to consider that sex work is also associated with pleasure among many *travestis*. In the *casarão*, while the *travestis* were getting ready before going to the streets, it was quite common to hear 'I love being a whore!' In Chap. 5, we have analysed that those young and handsome men—according to *travestis'* aesthetic ideals—who perform masculinity socially and sexually are much desired by the *travestis* and, some of them, become their lovers or *maridos*. Although there are *travestis* who desire other *travestis* or women, most of my participants were attracted to men and enjoyed being penetrated by them. Thus, *travestis'* self-esteem may be reinforced when they feel desired by men. As sex workers, they have the opportunity—sometimes a unique opportunity—to expose themselves to clients, future lovers, and *maridos* as beautiful and desired *travestis*. Viviana, an inhabitant of the *casarão*, told me that she loved her work because 'clients tell me that I am beautiful and, in addition, they pay me' (Field notes, 11 August 2008). Pleasure, alongside the ability to feel desired, allows them to live prostitution as an ideal place from which to perform and display their ways of understanding femininity, making this activity an important experience throughout their lives.

To conclude this section, sex work is—paradoxically—also the territory which *travestis* associate most with violence and death. In a study with *travestis* living in the Brazilian city of Ponta Grossa, Cabral et al. (2013) observe that almost half of the interviewees see sex work in terms of violence (physical, sexual, or psychological). They do also relate it to vulnerability, fear, and death. *Travestis* have more chances of being attacked while they work as sex workers. The streets are the territory that represents them most, and it is also where they are more dangerously visible (Lewis 2012). It is not by chance that sex workers in Brazil referred colloquially to their work as 'battling' (Williams 2014) to express the violence and harassment they have to face daily. Hence, I do not pretend to soften an activity in which many *travestis* suffer violence and die.[6] Nevertheless, it would not be fair to invisibilise other meanings of prostitution that—simultaneously—define *travestis'* experiences and were evident during all the research. As described in Chap. 3, society has a love/hate relationship with *travestis*, and this is reflected within sex work, where the fine line between life and death shapes *travestis'* daily lives. In the next section, we explore how their bodies—and the importance of beauty—play a role as professional sex workers.

Embodying Beauty Within Sex Work

We start with some reflections of the participant sex workers to understand what they think about their bodies:

> Like any profession, you have to engage in this, if you earn with your body, your appearance … you have to invest in your profession and you will work, you will also have a return, do you understand? (Priscila, personal interview, 22 May 2008, Rio de Janeiro)

> We have a more beautiful body because we work on the streets. We seek to improve it, get more body [with silicone], have a beautiful body, and look after it. I believe that we have to give that good image for men, you have to be good for them. So I think we take more care, it's better. (Samanta, personal interview, 8 September 2008, Rio de Janeiro)

> When we are on the streets, you are making more money, investing in yourself, becoming more beautiful so clients come to appreciate you more. Because an ugly *bicha*, an ugly *travesti* does not make money on the street. (Roberta, personal interview, 7 August 2008, Rio de Janeiro)

> At work, if you do not have a beautiful body, you will not work … everything you invest in yourself is rewarded. The appearance, the well-made face, the nails, the well-treated skin: everything attracts attention. (Keila, personal interview, 23 May 2008, Rio de Janeiro)

In this profession, irrespective of the gender of the sex workers, appearance is important, and *travestis* are aware that they have to 'invest' and 'improve' their bodies to succeed, that is, become more feminine and desired to be chosen by the clients. As street-based sex workers, they are publicly exposed and have to compete continuously to sell sex. The most feminine and beautiful ones will be chosen. However, as stated in Chap. 5, most of the clients became experts in declining the services of those *travestis* who look *too* feminine because it is supposed that they are taking hormones, which would compromise their erections and virility. *Travestis*, thus, have to regulate the doses of hormones or not use them at all, employing industrial silicone instead as a means to feminise their bodies. But beyond these 'adjustments,' beauty allows *travesti* sex workers to feel confident and desired, given that they believe they will attract more clients if they are constantly 'retouched' aesthetically.

Alessandra, *māe* and *bombadeira*, complains about those who only think of pleasing clients through their bodies: 'But that's where they end up ruined because clients only want them for an hour, they do not want them to go with them during the day. So they are pleasing the client but they will not recognise them [the *travestis*] on the street' (personal interview, 21 May 2008, Rio de Janeiro). Alessandra's comment that the *travestis* 'ruin' their bodies refers to the fact that those who are more dissatisfied with the results of sex work are those who most want to undergo repeated sessions of silicone injections and/or, for the *travestis* who can afford it, cosmetic surgeries. Alessandra also recounts that 'prostitution creates insecurity due to the street itself. Because if one has slightly larger buttocks, the other one wants to get more because she believes that the client has chosen the other one because she has larger buttocks' (personal interview, 21 May 2008, Rio de Janeiro). These physical changes give them a security that, in fact, is finite. As Alessandra mentioned, after three days or a week without working, they want to get even more silicone because they believe that they will make money again. For many, it is difficult to recognise that these periods without working are bad gaps or phases that people go through when they work in the sex industry.[7]

In the next chapter, when the spatial variable intersects with our analysis of beauty, *travestis'* identities, and sex work, we explore the importance that injecting silicone had for the first Brazilian *travestis* who travelled to Europe and created 'exuberant' bodies to display their femininities. However, few participants of this 'first generation' use their silicone-free bodies as a way to differentiate them from those sex workers who have 'ruined' their bodies. For example, Regina told me that she never introduced silicone into her body, as she believed, contemptuously, that it was a practice associated with those who engaged in prostitution and who had not thought through the possible terrible consequences of the injections. She considered that the use of silicone was an issue of class and of a lack of objectives in life. Today, younger *travestis* who have more family and social networks, better education, and more chances to not engage in prostitution, presumably, do not need to modify their bodies with silicone injections. Nevertheless, all of the younger *travestis* I met during the

Travesti Sex Workers' Bodily Experiences and the Politics... 151

research were sex workers, and all of them, sooner or later, had started to mould their bodies with silicone but—generally—following more 'natural' and less 'exuberant' shapes.

I contend that it is too limited to think of *travesti* sex workers' beautification as solely strategy to obtain clients on the basis of an exclusively economic rationality. As I expressed earlier, their seeking of beauty cannot be detached from their subject formation, more generally, and prostitution contributes to this becoming *travestis*. Although sex work requires a minimum feminine aesthetic to attract the clients, throughout *Brazilian Travesti Migrations*, beauty and their bodily transformations allow them to situate themselves—though precariously—in the world. Roberta puts it in these words:

> It changes, the life of all of us changes when we start to transform our bodies. It changes because of the family, the people, the friends, everybody starts to treat you differently. The friends start to look at you in another way, the men start to admire you, and they want to stay with you. Your female friends admire you and call you 'beautiful,' they want to look like you. The family in the beginning does not accept you but later it does. (Personal interview, 7 August 2008, Rio de Janeiro)

Beauty, however, is finite, and immediate 'success' as sex workers can drastically change over the years. The other side of their stories of beautification and empowerment is ageing. Blanchette and Silva (2011) describe that age creates great pressure over people whose main occupational field values youth. The authors focus particularly on female (non-trans) sex workers in Rio de Janeiro where an older woman who has to compete with younger sex workers must work harder or move to less-exclusive venues (where the services offered are cheaper) to maintain her income. In the case of *travestis*, they are also seen as less attractive when they are getting old (Garcia and Lehman 2011). Siqueira (2004) and Antunes and Mercadante (2011) examine the experiences of Brazilian *travestis* in old age. They reveal that those who can 'survive' become even more invisible in society and among the *travestis* who do not value ageing. *Travestis* are almost 'denied' this possibility because once a few of them grow old, they dress like 'men' in an attempt to obtain, ultimately, better chances in life.

They have embodied too many prejudices along with their lives, and those who did not manage to make some savings will have a less dignified old age. While working, *travestis* feel useful, productive, and, therefore, young and beautiful (Antunes and Mercadante 2011). For old *travestis*, it is also very difficult to try to switch their activity. Garcia and Lehman (2011, 1217) recount that, unlike female (non-trans) sex workers who can 'hide' their previous or current profession, 'the *travesti* cannot because of the easily identified body transformations that have stigmatized her.' Considering the stigma, loneliness, and great difficulties that some *travestis* experience when they grow old, it is easier to understand how my older participants clung to the memories of their best years as artists or sex workers in Europe in order to give greater meaning to their present. Finally, *travestis* know that they have to take advantage of sex work when they are still young, and the idea of going to Europe is based on the projection of the future that some of them who 'have head' make. We move on to understand the bodily impact that Brazilian *travesti* sex workers have once in Europe, so as to know why they are sought after in transnational contexts.

Embodying 'Brazilianness' in Transnational Contexts

When accessing the transnational sex market, *travestis* have the opportunity to reflect on and compare the corporeal aesthetics that the clients desire according to the different places through which they travel. In this way, they consider, roughly speaking, that European clients prefer thin *travestis* with prominent breasts, while Brazilians are inclined to bodies with curves and prominent buttocks. Although women's beauty ideals are increasingly being homogenised (in the case of Brazilian *travestis* and women, the desire to increase their breasts is an indicator of globalised aesthetics' embodiments), *travestis* are aware of the kind of body considered more attractive to their clients in Brazil and Europe. This does not mean that they unfailingly 'sculpture' their bodies according to the clients, but they will strategically enhance some characteristics to present themselves as more desirable.

In the context of their migrations to Europe, they frequently highlight their 'Brazilianness' as an identity that gives them 'value' in commercial sex. As Adriana Piscitelli (2011) describes when analysing Brazilian female (non-trans) sex workers in the Spanish sex industry, the national construction of the highly sexualised *mulata* can explain the notoriety that the Brazilians have in the transnational sex industry as 'exotic' and 'erotic' consumer goods. In migratory contexts, being Brazilian is strongly associated with prostitution (Mayorga 2011; Pontes 2004). Only women with more schooling, who are not considered black, and who have a better social position in the receiving countries, may be 'less affected by these notions of Brazilianness' (Piscitelli 2011, 15). Similarly, Carrier-Moisan (2015, 501) asserts that Brazilian women (*mulatas* and non-*mulatas*) are eroticised in the global sexual marketplace, 'as Brazil is typically imagined by foreigners as a "tropical paradise" full of black or mixed-raced women who are readily available and sexually adventurous.' This is what Pope (2005) calls the consumption of a 'tropicalized fantasy,' when describing how Cuban women in sex tourism are constructed—as a consequence of the paradoxes of colonialism—as 'hypersexual yet romantic, liberated yet loving, educated yet submissive, mulatta wom[e]n' (103) (for a deeper analysis, see the intersection of beauty and race in Chap. 4, and also Williams 2014).

Coming back to Brazilian female (non-trans) sex workers in Spain, Silva and Ornat (2016) use Aparicio and Chávez-Silverman's concept of 'tropicalization' (1997, 8), which means 'to trope, to imbue a particular space, geography group, or nation with a set of traits, images' to understand how the Brazilians are 'tropicalised' in Spanish society (both by men and women), as they are highly hypersexualised. However, going beyond the hegemonic/subversive tropicalisation, the Brazilian sex workers use the stereotypes ('sensual,' 'submissive,' 'hot,' 'poor') to take advantage of the competitive sexual marketplace, 'concealing and exaggerating their "Brazilianness" according to the interactions and spatialities that they consider to be advantageous or disadvantageous for the conquest of power' (Silva and Ornat 2016, 339; see also Piscitelli 2007, 2011).

Like female (non-trans) sex workers, when the *travestis* present themselves as 'hot Brazilian *mulatas*' in transnational contexts, they are racialising their bodies while employing their 'Brazilianness' strategically (Pelúcio 2011; Piscitelli 2011). This is a way of capitalising on their place of origin whilst they simultaneously challenge and reproduce sexual and racial stereotypes (Mai 2012). Some of the participants assure that:

> People say that the Brazilian is already privileged to have such a beautiful body, to be so striking, to have sensuality, sex appeal … [laughing] most of them have too much sex appeal! (Rosanne, personal interview, 27 August 2009, Barcelona)

> [Brazilian] *travestis* are very beautiful, very beautiful and very feminine. And for the sexual game the Brazilians are great because everyone, like the monkey, loves being naughty. That's why the Brazilians won and win a lot of money out there. And they are well-endowed, they are well-endowed and like making love. (Tony, personal interview, 15 September 2008, Rio de Janeiro)

Silva and Ornat (2014) also analysed the importance of being Brazilian in the Spanish trans/*travesti* commercial sex industry, where the construction of a racialised nationality positions Brazilians favourably compared to other nationalities. As the previous and other participants repeatedly said to me, they were 'different,' but they privilege their bodies as the main identity markers of their 'Brazilianness': they feel like beautiful and good lovers. For example, they explained to me that:

> It is rare that there is a *travesti*, a transsexual, with a beautiful body in Spain. Did you already see a really nice Spanish *travesti*? And Brazilian you have already seen several! … Perfect body, tan lines from the bikini [proudly exposed], Brazil, always! (Roberta, personal interview, 7 August 2008, Rio de Janeiro)

> The Brazilian *travesti* is the one that works the most in the sex market. Why? Because of the fame of the Brazilians of being well-endowed, more vicious, and hotter. (Francisca, personal interview, 30 July 2009, Barcelona)

There is a belief among the *travestis*—increasingly questioned by the beauty achieved by the new generations of Venezuelan or Colombian *travestis*—that they are 'unique,' that the particularity of their bodies distinguishes them from the rest. This conviction has its origins in the great importance that the arrival of the Brazilian *travestis* had at the end of the 1970s, in the European sex work marketplace, and in the influence that they had in the diffusion of some techniques of beautification. As Reyna clearly relates: 'the whole world seeks the Brazilian prototype so much so that in silicone applications we are the best, even in plastic surgery, we have the best plastic surgeons in that field. We are then copied all over the world, we are sought after' (personal interview, 6 May 2008, Rio de Janeiro). Brazilian *travestis*, thus, once they cross the borders of their country, recognise themselves/are recognised as 'the most beautiful.' Their 'perfect' bodies become the main hallmark that distinguishes them from other *travestis* in Europe. These notes, which will be expanded upon in the next chapter when discussing their national and transnational mobilisations, contribute to our understanding that *travestis* are bound to corporeality and, once in Europe, they negotiate, rebuild, and take advantage of their 'Brazilianness' to stand out in the sex marketplace.

To sum up this chapter, while sex work is the main space where *travestis* can work and empower themselves by reaffirming their gender identities and sexualities, feeling desired as 'beautiful' and 'feminine' *travestis*, it is also the place of violence and death, where intense competition and lack of work can make them more vulnerable and dependent on continuous corporal modifications which can 'ruin' their bodies (and lives). Throughout *Brazilian Travesti Migrations*, we explore how *travestis'* identities are constructed not only through their sexual practices and desires, but through the processes of bodily transformations which are—in most cases—achieved through sex work. Their bodies, therefore, are a fundamental axis to organise their identitarian and life experiences as *travestis* in and outside Brazil, where they can perform their 'Brazilianness' and benefit from their eroticised bodies and 'uniqueness' in transnational settings where they are highly valued. This chapter viewed the meanings of sex work through the lens of the participants to analyse the non-heteronormative and embodied experiences of prostitution. Concurrently, prostitution allowed us to think about the politics of life and death and how there is a sharp division between those trans subjects who 'deserve' to live and those who do not. Most of my participant *travesti* sex workers are situated as abject-others without value as citizens in a neoliberal scenario which, paradoxically, renders them economic value as racialised and hypersexualised Brazilian sex workers. Once again, we can see how *travestis* embody the biopolitical and economic contradictions that intertwine desire, beauty, and money, but also violence, criminalisation, and death. Aizura clearly synthesises these contradictions to 'understand transphobia as imbricated in transnational circuits of reproductive labour and biopolitical control: the same gender variant bodies on which violence is visited also circulate as valuable within global capital' (2014, 130–1). Life and death are inextricably part of the *travesti* sex workers' experiences, and we cannot comprehend trans necropolitics without considering the mobility of *travesti's* bodies and the circuits of capital.

Notes

1. I employ both 'sex work' and 'prostitution' to name the activity in which sexual services are offered in exchange for money (see endnote 1 in Chap. 1 for a further explanation).
2. Sex work is included within a wider sex industry which involves, according to Agustín (2005, 622) 'bars, restaurants, cabarets, clubs, brothels, discotheques, saunas, massage parlours, sex shops with private booths, hotels, flats, dungeons for bondage and domination, Internet sites, cinemas and anywhere that sex is offered for sale on an occasional basis, such as stag and hen events, shipboard festivities or "modelling" parties.' Moreover, the sex industry is not limited to those who sell sex directly and their customers, other social actors such as waiters, business owners, drivers, doctors, travel agents, among others, are also included.
3. Many of them identify with the less-stigmatised term 'transsexual.'
4. I have kept here, though, her pseudonym name.
5. During my fieldwork in Brazil, I met some people who self-identified as *bichas* (effeminate gay male) and only cross-dressed for working on the streets to earn more money as sex workers. Contrary to *travestis*, they made a strategic use of their transitory female appearance.
6. This manuscript does not adhere to an abolitionist position regarding prostitution and does not consider the *travesti* sex workers as 'victims who need to be saved.' Although this activity can expose the *travestis* to situations of more vulnerability, I support sex workers' emancipatory use of this profession (see also endnote 1 in Chap. 1).
7. Paradoxically, *mães* and *madrinhas*, like Alessandra and Reyna, press hard for the *travestis* to pay their 'debts' towards them (the renting of the room/bed they have to pay daily, the injections of silicone, the financing to arrive in Rio or Europe, and so on).

References

Aggleton, Peter, ed. 1999. *Men Who Sell Sex: International Perspectives on Male Prostitution and HIV/AIDS*. Philadelphia: Temple University Press.

Aggleton, Peter, and Richard Parker, eds. 2015. *Men Who Sell Sex: Global Perspectives*. Abingdon/New York: Routledge.

Agustín, Laura. 2005. The Cultural Study of Commercial Sex. *Sexualities* 8 (5): 618–631.

———. 2007. *Sex at the Margins*. London: Zed Books.

Aizura, Aren. 2014. Trans Feminine Value, Racialized Others and the Limits of Necropolitics. In *Queer Necropolitics*, ed. Jin Haritaworn, Adi Kuntsman, and Silvia Posocco, 129–147. Abingdon/New York: Routledge.

Antunes, Pedro S., and Elisabeth F. Mercadante. 2011. Travestis, envelhecimento e velhice. *Revista Kairós Gerontologia Temática* 14 (5): 109–132.

Aparicio, Frances, and Suzanne Chávez-Silverman, eds. 1997. *Tropicalizations: Transcultural Representations of Latinidad*. Hanover: University Press of New England.

Benedetti, Marcos. 2005. *Toda feita: o corpo e o gênero das travestis*. Rio de Janeiro: Garamond.

Blanchette, Thaddeus, and Ana P. Silva. 2011. Prostitution in Contemporary Rio de Janeiro. In *Policing Pleasure: Sex Work, Policy, and the State in Global Perspective*, ed. Susan Dewey and Patty Kelly, 130–145. New York: New York University Press.

Brents, Barbara, and Teela Sanders. 2010. Mainstreaming the Sex Industry: Economic Inclusion and Social Ambivalence. *Journal of Law and Society* 37 (1): 40–60.

Butler, Judith. 1990. *Gender Trouble: Feminism and the Subversion of Identity*. New York: Routledge.

———. 2004. *Precarious Life: The Power of Mourning and Violence*. New York: Verso.

Cabral, Vinicius, Joseli M. Silva, and Marcio J. Ornat. 2013. Espaço e morte nas representações sociais de travestis. In *Geografias malditas: corpos, sexualidades e espaços*, ed. Joseli Silva, Marcio Ornat, and Alides Chimin Jr., 273–307. Ponta Grossa: Todapalavra.

Carrier-Moisan, Marie-Eve. 2015. 'Putting Femininity to Work': Negotiating Hypersexuality and Respectability in Sex Tourism, Brazil. *Sexualities* 18 (4): 499–518.

Castañeda, Heide. 2013. Structural Vulnerability and Access to Medical Care Among Migrant Street-Based Male Sex Workers in Germany. *Social Science and Medicine* 84: 94–101.

Dennis, Jeffrey. 2008. Women Are Victims, Men Make Choices: The Invisibility of Men and Boys in the Global Sex Trade. *Gender Issues* 25: 11–25.

Duggan, Lisa. 2003. *The Twilight of Equality: Neoliberalism, Cultural Politics and the Attack on Democracy*. Boston: Beacon Press.

Duque, Tiago. 2011. *Montagens e Desmontagens: desejo, estigma e vergonha entre travestis adolescentes*. São Paulo: Annablume.

Edelman, Elijah A. 2014. 'Walking While Transgender.' Necropolitical Regulations of Trans Feminine Bodies of Colour in the Nation's Capital. In *Queer Necropolitics*, ed. Jin Haritaworn, Adi Kuntsman, and Silvia Posocco, 172–190. Abingdon/New York: Routledge.

Espejo, Beatriz. 2008. La prostitución desde una visión transexual. In *Prostituciones*, ed. I. Holgado Fernández, 123–138. Barcelona: Icaria.

Garcia, Marcos R.V., and Yvette P. Lehman. 2011. Issues Concerning the Informality and Outdoor Sex Work Performed by *Travestis* in São Paulo, Brazil. *Archives of Sexual Behavior* 40: 1211–1221.

Haritaworn, Jin, Adi Kuntsman, and Silvia Posocco. 2014. Introduction. In *Queer Necropolitics*, ed. Jin Haritaworn, Adi Kuntsman, and Silvia Posocco, 1–27. Abingdon/New York: Routledge.

Howe, Cymene, Susanna Zaraysky, and Lois Lorentzen. 2008. Transgender Sex Workers and Sexual Transmigration Between Guadalajara and San Francisco. *Latin American Perspectives* 158 (35/1): 31–50.

Hubbard, Phil. 2012. *Cities and Sexualities*. Abingdon/New York: Routledge.

Hubbard, Phil, Roger Matthews, and Jane Scoular. 2008. Regulating Sex Work in the EU: Prostitute Women and the New Spaces of Exclusion. *Gender, Place and Culture* 15 (2): 137–152.

Hutta, Jan, and Carsten Balzer. 2013. Identities and Citizenship Under Construction: Historicising the 'T' in LGBT Anti-violence Politics in Brazil. In *Queer Presences and Absences*, ed. Yvette Taylor and Michelle Addison, 69–90. Basingstoke: Palgrave Macmillan.

Infante, Cesar, Sandra Sosa-Rubi, and Silvia Cuadra. 2009. Sex Work in Mexico: Vulnerability of Male, Travesti, Transgender and Transsexual Sex Workers. *Culture, Health and Sexuality* 11 (2): 125–137.

Irving, Dan. 2008. Normalized Transgressions: Legitimizing the Transsexual Body as Productive. *Radical History Review* (100): 38–59.

Kempadoo, Kamala, and Jo Doezema, eds. 1998. *Global Sex Workers: Rights, Resistance, and Redefinition*. London: Psychology Press.

Kulick, Don. 1998. *Travesti: Sex, Gender and Culture Among Brazilian Transgendered Prostitutes*. Chicago: University of Chicago Press.

Lewis, Vek. 2012. Volviendo visible lo invisible: hacia un marco conceptual de las migraciones internas trans en México. *Cuicuilco* 54: 219–240.

Loopmans, Maarten. 2016. Commercial Sexualities: Section Introduction. In *The Routledge Research Companion to Geographies of Sex and Sexualities*, ed. Gavin Brown and Kath Browne, 307–312. Abingdon/New York: Routledge.

Mai, Nick. 2012. The Fractal Queerness of Non-heteronormative Migrants Working in the UK Sex Industry. *Sexualities* 15 (5/6): 570–585.

Mayorga, Claudia. 2011. Cruzando fronteiras. Prostituição e imigração. *Cadernos Pagu* 37: 323–355.

Minichiello, Victor, and John Scott, eds. 2014. *Male Sex Work and Society*. New York: Harrington Park Press/Columbia University Press.

O'Connell Davidson, Julia. 1998. *Prostitution, Power and Freedom*. Ann Arbor: The University of Michigan Press.

Ochoa, Marcia. 2014. *Queen for a Day: Transformistas, Beauty Queens, and the Performance of Femininity in Venezuela*. Durham/London: Duke University Press.

Osborne, Raquel. 1991. *Las prostitutas: una voz propia (Crónica de un encuentro)*. Barcelona: Icaria.

Padilla, Mark. 2007. *Caribbean Pleasure Industry: Tourism, Sexuality, and AIDS in the Dominican Republic*. Chicago: University of Chicago Press.

Padilla, Mark, Sheilla Rodríguez-Madera, Nelson Varas-Díaz, and Alixida Ramos-Pibernus. 2016. Trans-Migrations: Border-Crossing and the Politics of Body Modification Among Puerto Rican Transgender Women. *International Journal of Sexual Health* 28 (4): 261–277.

Pelúcio, Larissa. 2009. *Abjeção e Desejo: uma etnografia travesti sobre o modelo preventivo de aids*. São Paulo: Annablume, Fapesp.

———. 2011. 'Amores perros' – sexo, paixão e dinheiro na relação entre espanhóis e travestis brasileiras no mercado transnacional do sexo. In *Gênero, sexo, amor e dinheiro: mobilidades transnacionais envolvendo o Brasil*, ed. Adriana Piscitelli, Glaucia de Oliveira Assis, and José M. Nieto Olivar, 185–224. Campinas: Unicamp/PAGU.

Penttinen, Elina. 2004. *Corporeal Globalization. Narratives of Subjectivity and Otherness in the Sexscapes of Globalization*. Tampere: Tapri.

Pheterson, Gail, ed. 1989. *A Vindication of the Rights of Whores*. Seattle: Seal Press.

———. 1996. *The Prostitution Prism*. Amsterdam: Amsterdam University Press.

Piscitelli, Adriana. 2007. Corporalidade em confronto. Brasileiras na indústria do sexo na Espanha. *Revista Brasileira de Ciências Sociais* 22 (64): 17–32.

———. 2011. ¿Actuar la brasileñidad? Tránsitos a partir del mercado del sexo. *Etnográfica* 15 (1): 5–29.

Pitcher, Jane, and Marjan Wijers. 2014. The Impact of Different Regulatory Models on the Labour Conditions, Safety and Welfare of Indoor-Based Sex Workers. *Criminology and Criminal Justice* 14 (5): 549–564.

Pontes, Luciana. 2004. Mulheres brasileiras na mídia portuguesa. *Cadernos Pagu* (23): 229–256.

Pope, Cynthia. 2005. The Political Economy of Desire: Geographies of Female Sex Work in Havana, Cuba. *Journal of International Women's Studies* 6 (2): 99–118.

Posso, Jeanny, and Angie La Furcia. 2016. El fantasma de la puta-peluquera: Género, trabajo y estilistas trans en Cali y San Andrés Isla, Colombia. *Sexualidad, Salud y Sociedad – Revista Latinoamericana* 24: 172–214. https://doi.org/10.1590/1984-6487.sess.2016.24.08.a. Accessed 14 June 2017.

Prieur, Annick. 1998. *Mema's House, Mexico City: On Transvestites, Queens, and Machos*. Chicago: University of Chicago Press.

Puar, Jasbir. 2007. *Terrorist Assemblages: Homonationalism in Queer Times*. Durham: Duke University Press.

Quinan, Christine. 2016. Queering the Politics of Life and Death. *Reviews in Cultural Theory* 6 (1): 31–36.

Sassen, Saskia. 2002. Women's Burden: Counter-Geographies of Globalization and the Feminization of Survival. *Nordic Journal of International Law* 71: 255–274.

Shah, Svati. 2010. Fear, Sexuality and the Future: Thinking Sex (Panic), Monstrosity and Prostitution. *Sarai Reader* 8: 142–148. http://archive.sarai.net/files/original/ac6a8e1f46fd506a118286b5905d889e.pdf. Accessed 12 July 2017.

Silva, Joseli M., and Marcio J. Ornat. 2014. Intersectionality and Transnational Mobility Between Brazil and Spain in *Travesti* Prostitution Networks. *Gender, Place and Culture* 22 (8): 1073–1088.

———. 2016. Sexualities, Tropicalizations and the Transnational Sex Trade: Brazilian Women in Spain. In *The Routledge Research Companion to Geographies of Sex and Sexualities*, ed. Gavin Brown and Kath Browne, 331–340. Abingdon/New York: Routledge.

Siqueira, Mônica. 2004. Sou senhora: um estudo antropológico sobre travestis na velhice. MA dissertation, Federal University of Santa Catarina (Brazil).

Smith, Nicola. 2012. Body Issues: The Political Economy of Male Sex Work. *Sexualities* 15 (5/6): 586–603.

———. 2016. The Global Political Economy of Sex Work. In *The Handbook on Gender in World Politics*, ed. Jill Steans and Dani Tepe, 370–377. Cheltenham/Northampton: Edward Elgar.

Smith, Nicola, and Mary Laing. 2012. Introduction: Working Outside the (Hetero)norm? Lesbian, Gay, Bisexual, Transgender and Queer (LGBTQ) Sex Work. *Sexualities* 15 (5/6): 517–520.

Whowell, Mary. 2010. Male Sex Work: Exploring Regulation in England and Wales. *Journal of Law and Society* 37 (1): 125–144.

Williams, Erica. 2014. Sex Work and Exclusion in the Tourist Districts of Salvador, Brazil. *Gender, Place and Culture* 21 (4): 453–470.

Willman, Alys. 2010. Let's Talk About Money. In *Sex Work Matters: Exploring Money, Power, and Intimacy in the Sex Industry*, ed. Melissa H. Ditmore, Antonia Levy, and Alys Willman, 143–146. London/New York: Zed Books.

7

Trans Migrations: Brazilian *Travestis'* Spatial and Embodied Journeys

This chapter focuses on the *travestis'* spatial trajectories to interweave the analyses described so far with their identity constructions regarding beauty, sexualities, and experiences as sex workers. I examine how their bodily and spatial mobilisations shape their processes of gender transformation. I depart from Lefebvre's (1991) understanding of space: it is through the body that space is perceived, lived, and produced. Within this phenomenological perspective, people are situated in the world through their bodies, and the lived experience of the body in the space has a central role in people's identity positions (Rose 1995). When exploring Brazilian *travesti* bodily modifications in relation to their national and transnational displacements, we can see that the *travestis* are simultaneously constructing themselves as legible subjects while reaffirming their own identities. That is to say, bodies are permanently moving and transitioning not only through gender but also through (other) borders and spaces (Cotten 2012).

However, spaces are not neutral or unified and must be thought of relationally and according to an ongoing production process in which the relationship between the subject and her/his material environment is crossed by social and power relations. People's spatial interactions are

© The Author(s) 2018
J. Vartabedian, *Brazilian* Travesti *Migrations*, Genders and Sexualities
in the Social Sciences, https://doi.org/10.1007/978-3-319-77101-4_7

163

inscribed by various elements such as sexuality, gender, class, ethnicity, age, or race, which intersect and define their personal experiences of space (Baydar 2012; Brown 2012). Feminist geographers have contributed to the study of the ways in which gender relations both impact upon and are produced over/by space (Massey 1994; McDowell 1999; Rose 1993). Although geographers have been troubling gender for many years (Johnston 2016), it is only very recently that more fluid and non-binary gender categories are used in social and cultural geography research (Browne 2004; Doan 2010). The so-called queer geographies (Nash 2010) or LGBTIQ gender geographies (Johnston 2016) theorise 'more unstable and oscillating intersections between identity/subjectivity, sexual desire, embodiment and spatial organization' (Nash 2010, 581).

Concurrently, from the early beginning of the 2000s onwards, feminist and queer studies have challenged heteronormative assumptions that have traditionally characterised all immigrants as heterosexuals. A growing body of research on queer diaspora and sexual/queer/trans migrations have contributed to deepen new critical frameworks on the intersections of sexuality, gender, race, class, space, diaspora, migration, citizenship, colonialism, and globalisation (Ahmed et al. 2003; Cantú 2002; Cantú et al. 2009; Carrillo 2004; Cotten 2012; Fortier 2003; Gopinath 2005; Luibhéid and Cantú 2005; Manalansan 2006; Parker 1999; Patton and Sánchez-Eppler 2000; Puar 2002a, 2007). This body of work aims to examine 'the interlocking structures of oppression and agency that characterize the experiences of both queer and LGBTQI migrants' (Lewis and Naples 2014, 912).

In what follows, I describe some scholars' analysis on how spaces are normative spaces and the difficulties non-heteronormative sexualities and genders have in finding safe places in contemporary cities. Next, I problematise the metaphor of 'home' as a tool to examine trans people's gender and spatial mobilisations. I also introduce the so-called sexual migration and queer migration to then describe the specificity of trans migrations to examine Brazilian *travesti* national and transnational displacements. I focus particularly on the different prostitution venues they transit in Rio de Janeiro and Barcelona to understand their embodiments in the ongoing process of the *travestis'* identity formations.

The Privilege of a Safe Space

Several studies problematise the relationship of spaces with a 'proper' form, which is heterosexual, to make use of them. In this way, spaces are regulated according to a sexual order that establishes who is included in, or excluded from, them. For example, Michael Brown (2000) considers that, for heterosexual people, all spaces are straight; that is, it is assumed that they are 'normally' heteronormative. As a result, gay people often are 'out of place' in most spaces that are heteronormativised. Brown also discusses the everyday experiences of gay men in relation to the metaphorical and material use of the 'closet' as a place of exclusion. The 'closet' is both the place of secrecy, to keep their sexuality hidden, and the place of autonomy and security, as if it were a kind of 'prison' where it is safe to be gay. Similarly, for Cresswell (2004), the creation of a place necessarily implies the definition of what remains outside. He says that 'a place does not have meanings that are natural and obvious but ones that are created by some people with more power than others to define what is and is not appropriate' (27). When analysing the relations of sexual citizenship to the city, Bell and Binnie (2000) describe how, although big cities seem to be friendly to queer citizenship, there are 'clean-up' movements which reveal homophobic politics in urban social space. Likewise, Manalansan (2005) recounts the construction of exclusive gay bars and expensive apartments in two historically gay areas in New York as clear politics of eradication and invisibilisation of queer people of colour.

Doan (2010) describes her experiences as a transsexual woman to affirm that spaces are also gendered. The rigid and binary gender categorisations prevent intersexual and transsexual people from accessing spaces in the same way as the rest. Consequently, those who transgress gender norms, or those who are constrained by them, experience a 'gender tyranny' in their daily social interactions. Following an auto-ethnographic account, Doan develops her own experience of this 'tyranny' through the use of different public and private spaces such as public restrooms, parking lots, the workplace, and home. She concludes her article (649):

166   J. Vartabedian

Gender strongly influences the ways that spaces are perceived and the kinds of activities that are possible, acceptable, or even safe within them. The tyranny of the gender dichotomy is an artifact of the patriarchal structuring of gendered space and it is time to lay it aside, not just for trans people, but for us all.

Namaste (2006) considers how the definition of public space is intimately linked to the social sanctions that are carried out in relation to dissident gender identities. Trans people are at risk in both 'ordinary' public spaces and in gay and lesbian areas. In the streets of Montreal, Canada, the main victims of violence are not as a result of their sexual orientation, but because of the way in which the presentation of gender is seen as a threat to the male and heterosexual domain of public space. Namaste employs the term 'genderbashing' to name precisely the violence experienced on a daily basis by people living outside heteronormativity. Doan (2009) also examines how trans people are the most vulnerable and marginalised population in the cities of the United States. They are the target of the highest rates of violence and, contrary to trans men, many trans women's *failing* in 'passing' make them more visible and, therefore, to feel more insecure and unsafe in public spaces. Although trans people seem to feel more comfortable in 'queer' community spaces that 'should' be inclusive to non-normative gendered embodiments, many of these spaces 'may be unwelcoming' and exclude those 'unwanted' trans people (Johnston 2016, 671).

Finally, Bailey (2011) analyses the ballroom culture in Detroit, USA, and explains the strategic performances used by black queer people 'to unmark themselves as gender and sexual nonconforming subjects' (366) in the outside world. His participants know they can be more easily beaten, attacked, or even murdered with impunity as queer, black, and working-class subjects. Being safe and visible in the public space are privileges that many trans people cannot afford. 'Passing' or adjusting themselves to 'realness' are strategies used to minimise and avoid race, class, gender, and sexual violence and discrimination.

For *travesti* sex workers, going out in public spaces during the day is presented as a challenge for most of my participants due to possible aggressions that they may suffer. As other ethnographies with Brazilian *travestis* have shown (Benedetti 2005; Kulick 1998; Pelúcio 2009), the 'day' and the 'night' are two space-time categories that structure *travestis'* experiences. During the day, they know they are more openly exposed to inquisitive looks that repudiate their gender non-conforming bodies. Thus, they constantly feel unsafe and uncomfortable in public spaces as sudden transphobic reactions can interpellate them at any time. Their rejection from certain places 'can occur subtly, through constraints, such as accusatory looks, smiles of debauchery and humiliation' (Silva 2013, 158). In Brazil, *travestis* employ some strategies to evade these subtle, or even violent, transphobic situations: for example, they try to go out in groups of at least two *travestis* together or avoid attracting attention in the way they dress or wear their make-up during the day. All the *travestis* I met in the *casarão* remained resting in the house almost all day, and if they had to go out, they went only to the supermarket or bakery at the corner of their street. If they did not eat at home, they had lunch at the restaurants or bars nearby. In other words, they hardly moved from the two or three blocks of their neighbourhood in Lapa in which they felt relatively secure.[1] Going to the beach or to popular markets to buy some clothes were perceived as 'great' events which required a certain organisation to combine these 'excursions' with somebody else's movements. As we see throughout this chapter, Europe is represented as safer than Brazil. This is why one of my interviewees from Barcelona told me that 'they only go out at night in Brazil, not during the day, they remain more at home' (Márcia, personal interview, 31 July 2009, Barcelona).

On the other hand, and paradoxically, during the night is where they feel 'more protected' because as sex workers, it is in the corners where the *travestis* can 'have the sensation of belonging somewhere' (Pelúcio 2009, 70). Generally, the family home is seen as a threat, a space where they first experienced rejection. As we have described in Chap. 6, sex work becomes a 'refuge' to construct themselves as *travestis* and the streets 'host' them and introduce them to the rough—but also pleasurable—experiences of the nights. *Mães* and *madrinhas* have contributed to creating a self-protection network in which some police officers, drug dealers, taxi drivers, or owners of bars in the prostitution venues may act, to various extents, to guarantee certain fluidity in *travestis'* professional work. Although violence is also lethally present in the streets during the night (and alongside *travestis'* lives), the night/street has its own rules and—at least precariously—provides *travestis* with a way to survive as sex workers.

The Limits of the 'Home' Metaphor

In the next section, we move on to examine the metaphor of 'home' as a way to analyse some trans narratives as a 'journey,' in their attempt to reach a 'safe' and 'coherent' place. As Aizura (2006, 289) points out, 'to speak about gender-variant bodies is often to engage in a metaphorical slippage between geography and gender.' We question how the home/border distinction has been used to give sense to the transsexual experiences on gender transitions but in a quite linear and finalist way, thus excluding other transsexual narratives with different (trans)gender trajectories.

The Limits of the 'Home' Metaphor

In his critiques to the performative theory of gender, Jay Prosser (1998) makes a distinction between trans narratives that claim the 'authenticity' of their gender and search their gendered 'homes,' and those based on queer theory that aim to destabilise gender and inhabit the 'borderlands' of 'no gender'—an 'interstitial space between sexes' (Prosser 1998, 201). He wants, therefore, to avoid any universalisation of trans identities and distinguishes transsexuals' claim for belonging and gendered 'realness' from transgenders' celebration of gender ambiguity. Prosser's recounting of transsexuals' narratives based on 'being trapped in the wrong body' or childhood feelings as 'wanting to play with dolls' (transsexual women) or 'being a tomboy' (transsexual men) follow the sense of a journey to reach 'a stable destination,' a way to produce 'a coherent sense of self' (Alsop et al. 2002, 208). In this way, finding a 'home' is an attempt to arrive at one's proper place, a very corporeal experience that follows a clear trajectory with a beginning, transition, and end.

Although important, the distinction between transsexual/transgender is also problematic because, as Hines states (2006, 51), in 'viewing transsexuality as representative of an "authentic" experience, the transgenderist is positioned as an almost frivolous postmodern player.' Moreover, the gender-variant community is very heterogeneous and diverse, and not all transsexual experiences are alike, and so Prosser runs the risk of essentialising transsexuality. Prosser's analysis of transsexuality is based on a rigid gender boundary which relies on a linear crossing in which the masculine and feminine bodies are seen as two endpoints of a continuum, which are presented as static and with a finalist aim to rest at 'home.' According to Aizura (2006, 296):

> The call to find a proper home once one has crossed the border of sex reassignment forecloses the possibility that some people never wholly cross that particular border; or that for some, gender transition might be a lifelong project. It also precludes the possibility that transpeople may not, for many reasons, blend into normality once sex reassignment is 'over.' Moreover, it assumes that there is a homogeneous sphere of normality in which to blend.

Drawing upon post-colonial studies, Halberstam (1998) discusses Prosser's articulation of identities as 'homes,' a stable place from where 'coherent' narratives of transsexuals' lives can be inhabited (Alsop et al. 2002). Rather, for Halberstam, 'some bodies are never at home, some bodies cannot simply cross from A to B, some bodies recognize and live with the inherent instability of identity' (1998, 164). Post-colonial work has influenced the discussions on gender by shifting the debate away from 'real' and 'pure' subjectivities to focus on the 'politics of transgender mobility' (Hines 2006, 51). Identities are constructed on the borderlands of gender. In fact, the opposition to home/border can be dismantled by assuming that 'for many people home is a borderland' (Alsop et al. 2002, 213; see Anzaldúa 1987). In other words, there are people (and bodies) that are permanently dislocated from 'home' and never arrive at a stable place nor pretend to aim for it.

Becoming a *travesti* requires a process of continuous work and dedication. This journey, in fact, never has an end. Consequently, more than the 'home' to which one returns, or the destiny at which one aspires to arrive, *travesti* identities are experienced in these permanent transits. In this way, *travesti* narratives do not follow gender hegemonic constructions that claim a linear and finalist transition from one gender to another one. Rather, their *journeys* are shaped by untidy and multidimensional borders that are constantly reconstructed in their becoming *travestis*. Before describing in detail *travestis'* bodily and geographic displacements, we analyse recent research interested in trans/transgender migrations as a line of inquiry with its own specificities, which it is better not to analytically subsume under the broader umbrella category of sexual or queer migrations.

Trans Migrations

In the early 1980s, the status of women as dependents of migrant men and reproducers par excellence of tradition—in hegemonic migration studies of the past decades—was questioned (Sharpe 2001). Feminist scholars described how women also migrated following their own initiatives while becoming active subjects in the labour market (Morokvasic 1984; Phizacklea 1983). However, this body of work continued to focus mainly on the economic motivations of female migration, and sexuality was understood only as reproductive heterosexuality that perpetuated family life. In the last few years, an increasing number of researchers have shown that migration decisions cannot 'be adequately explained in terms of rational responses to economic and political forces' (Gorman-Murray 2009, 444) and that the heterosexual model is limited to understand current mobility flows. Scholars have incorporated the articulation of categories such as gender, affection, emotion, desires, and sexuality to comprehend the motivations to migrate. In the junction of transnational, globalisation, and migration studies with sexuality/queer studies, the so-called sexual migration (Cantú 2002; Cantú et al. 2009; Carrillo 2004; Parker 1999) and queer migration (Ahmed et al. 2003; Gorman-Murray 2007, 2009; Luibhéid and Cantú 2005) go beyond to the exclusively 'push' and 'pull' economic framework to suggest that sexuality, as widely conceived, is one of the main motivations for transnational relocation and movement (Manalansan 2006). These studies emphasise people's agency and how their sexual desires, non-normative identities, and practices are involved in their decision to displace and choose another place to live. Thus, as Manalansan (2006, 243) distinguishes, there is a move from the 'laboring gendered agent' to the 'desiring and pleasure-seeking migrant subject.' In the contemporary globalised world, Puar (2002b, 125)—inspired by the work of Kaplan (1996)—argues that 'the experiences of location, displacement, mobility, and travel are crucial to the constitution of the modern subject.' In this way, identity formation processes are constantly shaped by interaction with the environment (Lewis 2014), and the construction of the self emerges in dialogue with the new location in which 'intricate realignments of identity, politics, and desire take place' (Patton and Sánchez-Eppler 2000, 3). Bodies are moving, but so are the discourses on these bodies, as 'bodies carry with them ideologies, practices, desires, longings, and imaginings about ways of enacting sexuality differently in faraway locations' (Carrillo 2004, 68).

Sexual and queer migrations, although very useful as a theoretical framework within which to situate my research on Brazilian *travestis*, focus almost exclusively on gay and lesbian displacements and do not make visible trans people's particularity in crossing many borders, not only across gender but also through spatial territories in which they can embody both pleasure and social rejection. As advanced, the idea of a gender journey is usually displayed in transsexual autobiographies, which use a metaphorical language to describe their own transitions as bodily gender crossings. Doan (2016, 240) notes that some of these trans life journeys are framed in terms of 'the diaspora in a gender crossing,' reflecting the ambivalence of joy and loss in some queer diaspora recounts (Gopinath 2005; Patton and Sánchez-Eppler 2000). For example, referring to gay and lesbian narratives, Fortier (2003) equates the idea of 'coming out' with 'diaspora' because both concepts suggest the unlikely return to the place of origin, the loss of a heterosexual 'origin,' and the childhood family home.

Moving beyond the sexual/queer migrations and the queer diaspora frameworks, and considering an 'untidy' trans gender journey which, in many cases, does not aim to arrive at a stable place or 'home,' I argue that the so-called trans or transgender migrations problematise more adequately trans people's experiences of the institutionalisation of exclusion, stigma, and criminalisation (this is what Lewis [2012, 226] calls 'structural violence') that simultaneously intersects with other categories such as identity, sexuality, gender, class, or race, to better understand trans people's mobilities in space. Trans mobilities are, therefore, acts of survival, ones that also 'enables and empowers both the spatial journey and the embodied journey of transformation' (Doan 2016, 245).

García and Oñate (2010) describe how the journey of Ecuadorian 'transsexual' women to Murcia, Spain, is not only motivated to earn money, and to gain more respect and freedom in Europe, but also to transform their bodies: the journey leaves its marks on their bodies. Padilla et al. (2016) analyse Puerto Rican trans women's migrations and travels abroad as being integrated within a transnational network of body modification practices and technologies. Whether they do not trust in the national practitioners, or do not have access to the interventions in Puerto Rico, trans women have to deal daily with stigma and discrimination in social, legal, and healthcare services, together with a precarious work situation resulting in poverty that contributes to their searching for new ways to transform their bodies.

Lewis (2012) examines trans women's internal migrations in Mexico as a response to social and structural constraints, but also as an opportunity to live more safely, with a better quality of life. Vogel (2009) argues that, in the case of the Venezuelan *transformistas*[2] decisions to move to Europe, various factors intervene: the desire to earn money and escape from a context of marginality and stigma, and a willingness to display their 'beauty' and return to their country with a 'new' identity, that is, more feminine, beautiful, and successful. Vogel employs the concept of 'liminality' as a rite of passage 'inherent both in *transformistas*' migration from Venezuela to Europe and in their bodily transformation from male to female' (2009, 368). Finally, the work of Howe et al. (2008) describes the transmigratory experience of Mexican sex workers leaving Guadalajara to find the possibility of modifying and feminising their bodies through hormonal and surgical/aesthetic practices in San Francisco. Trans sex workers also decide to migrate to earn money in order to help their families when they return to Mexico, that is, the participants all agree that their stay in the United States is temporary. San Francisco is internationally recognised for its 'tolerance' as a 'gay mecca.' However, despite the best structural, economic, and service conditions found in the city, the vast majority decide to return to their native country. This is because they find great limitations caused by the lack of family and local networks' support, their marginalisation as 'undocumented,' language barriers, and, above all, working in a considered illegal activity such as prostitution.

These ethnographic examples show us that trans people move to find greater freedom and respect to better express and live their gender identities and sexualities, but also to seek an advantageous economic scenario in which to develop a work activity (sex work) and modify their bodies. In this way, trans migrations cannot be isolated from the social, political, and economic constraints that mobilise such migrations, together with the gender transformations. Trans migrations display both the capacity of agency as sexualised and gendered subjects, as well as the economic processes in which migrants are inserted. In other words, the particularity of trans migrations lies in that they are not only crossing spatial borders (national or transnational) to have better economic chances, but rather, they have the ability to become legible subjects, as their mobilities allow them, in many cases, to modify and feminise their bodies while they look for a safer place in which to live.

My aim in this chapter is to explore the embodied dimension of *travestis'* migrations. As Gorman-Murray (2009, 444) argues, migrants 'are not "disembodied actors"; sensual corporeality, intimate relationality and other facets of emotional embodiment also suffuse relocation processes.' *Travestis'* negotiations of gender and sexualities through their (trans) national displacements are grounded in their bodies. Next, I describe *travestis'* spatial and gender trajectories in Brazil and Spain. I also examine the different territories of *travesti* prostitution, both in Rio de Janeiro and Barcelona, and the impact that travel to Europe had/has in their lives. In summary, this chapter interweaves the precedent chapters by establishing a close relationship between body and space, while accounting for the structural violence *travestis* have to face in their search for survival.

First Displacements: From Somewhere to Rio

The mobilisations of Brazilian *travestis* are defined by both their transnational and national migrations. In fact, before arriving in Europe, the vast majority have already experienced various displacements within Brazil, seeking big cities like Rio de Janeiro or São Paulo as one of their main destinations. It is very complicated (but not impossible) to become a *travesti* in their place of birth and, consequently, these first national displacements are necessary in order to begin to transit their identity processes and 'escape' from oppressive milieus.

Halberstam (2005) questions dominant narratives of queer lives in which the coming out is usually enabled by leaving home and moving to big cities to live freely with their own sexualities. In these narratives, the characterisation of the urban as a place of freedom and tolerance is opposed to the representation of the rural as oppressive, intolerant, and hostile to non-normative bodies and sexualities. Halberstam uses the term 'metronormativity' as a way to naturalise these narratives, which devalue the rural and exalt the urban as the main reference for queer visibility (Wang 2014) or as a 'gay mecca.' In this way, 'it is easy to equate the physical journey from small town to big city with the psychological journey from closet case to out and proud' (Halberstam 2005, 37). Herring (2010), a queer anti-urbanism theorist, recounts that rural or small cities are becoming more open and tolerant to sexual diversity and currently attract gay people coming from large urban centres. Annes and Redlin (2012) suggest that, although cities can be liberating because many rural gay men can explore and experience alternative sexualities, they are also disciplinary in presenting a hegemonic 'effeminate' and 'superficial' gay identity model which does not satisfy rural gay men. Therefore, even though the city is a key space to develop rural gay men's identities, it is not an end-point in their lives and they engage 'in movement from city to country and, often, back again' (67) to find a balance with their gay masculine identity.

In the case of Brazil, Marcelo Teixeira (2015) asserts that large cities such as Rio and São Paulo *are imposed* as the only alternatives for gay people from rural areas or small and middle-sized cities. This has homogenising effects over local gay subcultures which reproduce more valorised metronormative gay lifestyles and embodiments, making invisible their own particularities. The works of scholars such as Néstor Perlongher (2008 [1987]), James Green (1999), and Richard Parker (1999) in São Paulo and Rio describe the influence these cities have on the internal gay migratory flows and in the construction of gay subjectivities in Brazil. The anonymity and sense of freedom achieved in big cities are crucial in the development of gay identities (Langarita and Salguero 2017). However, Miskolci (2014), cited in Teixeira (2015), remarks that digital technologies (for example, gay geolocation apps) are changing the rural/urban binary because rural and small cities have the opportunity to establish homoerotic encounters as never before, reconfiguring and widening the commercial circuits for the gay consumers.

Although much empirical work is needed to analyse Halberstam's critiques of metronormativity in Brazilian queer mobility circuits, most of these accounts refer—again—to the experiences of gays and lesbians. Even though more effeminate, self-identified, gay males can be severely punished for their 'transgression' to heteronormativity, they still have the ability to 'pass' with relatively more 'success' than do trans women who embody a feminine appearance. Yet, many small cities and rural regions in Brazil do not respect gender diversity, and transphobia is large enough to make Brazil the country where more trans people are killed in the world (TGEU, Transgender Europe 2017). During my ethnographic work, big cities were perceived by the participants as much safer to become *travestis* than in their places of origin. This is described next.

The Origins

None of the 13 inhabitants of the *casarão* was born in the city of Rio de Janeiro. Only two came from cities in the State of Rio de Janeiro, while the rest were born in small and middle cities of the States of Pará (from the North region), Paraíba, Ceará, Alagoas, Rio Grande do Norte, and Bahia (from the Northeast region), Minas Gerais and Espírito Santo (from the Southeast region). The only participants who were born in the city of Rio were Reyna, Alessandra, Lina, Bibi, Cristina, and Tony, that is, the *travestis* of the so-called first generation. Of the interviewees in Spain, only two came from Rio de Janeiro, although one was originally from Minas Gerais and the other from Porto Alegre (the South region). The rest were from São Paulo and its surroundings.

The Gay Group of Bahia (GGB 2016) describes how the North and Northeast regions of the country concentrate the highest rates of killings of LGBTI people in Brazil, while the less violent are the South and Southeast regions. This does not mean that in the States of Rio de Janeiro and São Paulo, which belong to the Southeast regions, there are not homophobic, lesbophobic, and transphobic attacks against LGBTI people. However, the violence registered in the North and Northeast areas are even more striking. According to the International Policy Centre for Inclusive Growth (IPC-IG) (2016), although the poverty rates fell in Brazil between 2004 and 2013, the main profiles of poverty remain the same: rural areas and the North and Northeast are the poorest regions of the country. Northeast is also considered the most underdeveloped region of Brazil (Williams 2014) and presents the higher rate of illiteracy (16.2%) in 2015, followed by the North region (9.1%) (IBGE, Brazilian Institute of Geography and Statistics 2016).

There are significant findings if we intersect the places of origin of the participants with their socioeconomic status and age. On the one hand, all the participants from the city of Rio de Janeiro not only exceeded 50 years of age but were in a more stable social position and economically more wealthy. The vast majority had earned a lot of money in Europe as sex workers. Lina, Bibi, and Cristina considered themselves 'beloved and respected' artists who were lip-synching to famous singers in some theatre shows in Rio, Reyna—although she continued working both as an outdoor sex worker and artistic performer—was a powerful and admired *madrinha* in Rio and Europe, Alessandra was an influential *mãe,* and Tony, who never self-identified as a *travesti* but lived as one, had cross-dressed and been a sex worker in the best years for *travesti* prostitution in Paris. At the time of interview, Tony was working as a social agent in a project of the City Council of Rio among the *travesti* population. In general, all of them had at least one apartment of their own, came from middle-class families, and were able to attend school as 'men' because only during the 1970s did the Brazilian military government allow them—and not without persecution and violence—to dress up and expose their incipient feminine transformations in public spaces.

On the other hand, and as the fieldwork advanced, most of the younger *travestis* I met moved to Rio from other regions (the majority from the Northeast). They had little or almost no schooling, had experienced poverty in childhood, and were rejected by their families. Whether they ran away or were thrown out of their homes at an early age, they had to begin experiencing (even as *gayzinhos*) their first encounters with the world of prostitution, an activity that allowed them to survive and earn money. For example, Samanta remembered that 'my family threw me out of the house, at the age of 14 I assumed myself as gay in front of my family and most of my family did not accept me, they kicked me out of the house' (personal interview, 8 September 2008, Rio de Janeiro). Samanta also recounted that she had enjoyed no childhood and that it was 'robbed' from her. Samanta's parents died when she was 4 years old and she was raised by her uncle and aunt. It was her uncle and her own brothers who continually humiliated and mistreated her and ended up throwing her out of the home. They used to give her a single plate of food a day, remarking that she did not deserve it. Just when, at age of 19, she began a new life in Rio she received her first birthday cake (Field notes, 23 July 2008). Finally, she became aware of the hypocrisy of society. Her uncle, who always humiliated her as a *bicha*, liked penetrating her best friend Natalia, still a *gayzinho*. When I asked Natalia, who also lived in Rio, if she had agreed to have sex with Samanta's uncle, she answered 'yes,' she had even liked it because he had a big penis, which had given her great pleasure.

Keila's narrative was slightly different. She was the only one of the participants—of the younger generations—who began to study at university, although she abandoned it shortly after. She came from a city in the State of Rio de Janeiro and, even though she had a good relationship with her parents, she told me that:

> K: My brothers do not accept me.
> J: What do they do to not accept you?
> K: They do not talk to me, they threaten me with death. (Keila, personal interview, 23 May 2008, Rio de Janeiro)

This situation meant that Keila could never visit her parents when one of her brothers was in the house. The stories seemed to repeat themselves. Their places of origin are associated with oppression, hatred, violence, and poverty, and although many of them have been able to reconstruct their relationships with the families once they have assumed their lives as *travestis*, the money they often provide them with is presented as a new mediator of the relationship. 'Your family only loves you when you have money,' Samanta asserted (Field notes, 28 May 2008). I met Samanta's brother, one day in the *casarão*, who had travelled to Rio to ask her for money. She left him waiting all day in a room, and at nightfall, Samanta told him that she had nothing to give him. Money had then provided Samanta with the opportunity of a small liberating revenge.

As was further explained, in Chap. 4, once identified as *gayzinhos*, they can begin their first 'production' processes: sporadic cross-dressing, subtle make-up, longer hair. Taking hormones becomes an attractive option for those who can begin to slightly modify their teenage bodies. These first

178   J. Vartabedian

performances of femininity are practised in secret to avoid social and familiar disapproval. According to 'expert' *travestis*, their first attempts at performing femininity were quite 'grotesque' and 'rudimentary' because, as Karina recognises, 'when we start, we are quite *caricatas*' (Field notes, 17 June 2008). In their jargon, *caricata* means a 'clown' person, and it is also related to the exaggerated and amusing way in which gay or heterosexual men dress up as women in carnivals, without the desire to faithfully copy them: they want to be 'caricatures' of women (Corrêa 2009). Some *travestis*, if they are not thrown out of their homes before, wait to reach adulthood before deciding to start the process of transformation. However, it is usually necessary to leave the home completely if they wish to assume their *travesti* identities and to start living *as* women. This happened to Priscilla who recounted that she left her home to respect her parents since 'when I got to 18 it was when I really started, the career itself, life started … at 18, after I left the house of my parents' (personal interview, 22 May 2008, Rio de Janeiro).

While I was in Rio, I noticed that many *travestis* who lived in the *casarão* (controlled by Reyna), or in one of the apartments belonging to Alessandra, and worked in the streets of Lapa, had come from the city of Natal, the capital of the Northeastern State of Rio Grande do Norte. Reyna and Alessandra had 'secretaries' who lived in Rio but came from the Northeast who, at the same time, had other contacts in different cities of the Northeast region. These contacts were the ones who accessed the young and 'future' *travestis* to be 'invited' to travel to Rio. This 'invitation,' which followed the same system that will be described for those travelling to Europe, involved lending them money for the plane ticket while they were forced to make an economic and moral commitment with the *mãe/madrinha* who 'financed' the trip. The 'future' *travestis* thus had direct access to Rio, a place where they got to live in one of the houses of the *mãe/madrinha* and work in the prostitution venues authorised for it.[3] In this way, they received the protection needed to live and work in Rio while they were taught to modify their bodies and become more feminine. In return, the young *travestis* were inserted into a spiral of continuous debt and commitments. In addition, the 'secretaries' who brought them to Rio got a commission for each new *travesti* incorporated into the system.

To make the trip even more attractive, the 'future' *travestis* were told that, in Rio, they would earn a lot of money, have more work, and get beautiful bodies. The great majority, who arrived in the city 'dry,' that is as they say, without silicones, knew that, in Rio, they would benefit from the resources and networks available to beautify themselves—that were concealed in their places of origin. Therefore, Rio was presented as a city full of possibilities for the young *travestis* who wanted to start a new life. However, many times, the reality they found did not fit their expectations. Although they felt safer and freer in Rio to begin their gender transitions, it could be also very hard: becoming a 'successful' *travesti* took time, dedication, and much effort, and was not always achieved with the immediacy that many newcomers expected. Moreover, they had to face competition and a harsh social, hierarchical system in which many of them felt lonely and under great pressure to pay off their debts. Lucy—a participant located outside the Northeast/Rio *travesti* route—described how the so-called secretaries were people who 'deceived and lied' to those who were contacted in Natal because 'they are incited to be "pumped up" so they are contracting more and more debts once they arrive in Rio' (Field notes, 7 September 2008). Moreover, one of the participants of the 'first generation' referred to the younger *travesti* sex workers as 'slaves, now they are working for someone, are taken, the person pays their tickets, they live in prostitution, and they exploit them. Very few get rid of the mafia' (Martine, personal interview, 5 August 2008, Rio de Janeiro).

In Rio de Janeiro: The Main School

The city of Rio de Janeiro is the capital of the State of Rio de Janeiro, located in Southeastern Brazil, and it was the main political centre of the country until Brasilia was created in 1960. After São Paulo, it is the second most populated city and also occupies the second position as leader of the economy of the country. Recognised internationally for its cultural icons and landscapes, it is the destination that has more tourists from all over Latin America. This *cidade maravilhosa* as it is recognised worldwide is, therefore, a great financial, cultural, tourist, and fashionable reference for Brazil.

180   J. Vartabedian

In Brazil, the *interior* refers to rural areas or cities that are not the capital of each state or its surroundings. Rather than thinking about a single axis coast/interior that divides the country, there are many *interiors* that are usually represented by stereotypical and negative images related to remoteness, backwardness, the popular, or tradition. In this way, it is perceived—by the participants who are originally from the city of Rio de Janeiro—that not only those new generations of *travestis* who come from the North and Northeast 'escape' from intolerant and prejudice contexts, but also that those coming from the *interior* of São Paulo or Rio de Janeiro find in this city great freedom. In fact, *travesti* migrations are not exclusively an 'escape'; rather they are also a way of finding themselves and deciding to face with all its consequences the full experience of their gender identities. Parker (1999), in his work on homoerotic practices and gay culture in Brazil, describes the tight association between *travesti* sex workers and big cities in the country. One of his participants, João, synthesises this idea:

> There isn't really any kind of space for the *travestis* in small towns. There may be effeminate *bichas*, but not *travestis*. *Travestis* only exist in the city —and the bigger the city the better ... So the effeminate *bichas* from the interior go to the city and become *travestis* —they enter into the underworld (*submundo*) of the *travestis* and transform themselves into *travestis*. And the *travestis* from smaller cities try to get to big cities like Rio. It is a whole kind of circuit of movement with a kind of hierarchy of places that are considered better than others. (Parker 1999, 193, emphasis in original)

Taking into account this hierarchy of space, Rio is an important place to *produce travestis*' bodies. I use this verb to connote that, in these large cities, highly valued bodies are created in the *travesti* subculture. Considering the popular practice of injection of industrial silicone ('pumping') described in Chap. 4, *travestis* recognise the *bombadeira* as a sculptor of bodies; they themselves often use the expression 'Alessandra made my body.' Generally, the bodies created in Rio or São Paulo are more admired than those produced by a possibly inexperienced and unsolicited *bombadeira* in a small city in the interior of a State. Although the 'famous' *bom-*

badeiras cannot guarantee the 'perfection' of the bodies created, and can also make some lethal 'mistakes,' they are highly sought after and many of them have proven experience in the 'business.'

There is no single body pattern when thinking about how they get to Rio. There are people who only take hormones once in Rio and some *travestis* arrive already 'pumped up' (commonly, by having previously lived in other cities). Their arrival in Rio frequently promotes new body modifications, as most of them arrive 'dry' and the injections of silicone are often immediately demanded. As Roberta asserts: 'Then in Rio de Janeiro I injected four litres of silicone with the *bombadeira* from here, I put prostheses for breasts, I made the nose, I filled [with liquid silicone] the face' (personal interview, 7 August 2008, Rio de Janeiro). Although 'pumped up,' the process of beautification never ends, and they certainly perceive Rio as the place that offers innumerable aesthetic possibilities for those who seek to feminise (more) their bodies. Like in every school, their teachers are more expert and experienced *travestis*, *mães*, *madrinhas*, and *bombadeiras*. This city, therefore, presents new bodily practices to modify their bodies: the 'pumping' of silicone and, for those who want to and can go further, cosmetic surgeries. The latter can be carried out once they travel to Europe. Even though they often prefer to perform them in Brazil because of their cheaper costs and the greater confidence they have in the Brazilian surgeons who also have an international reputation as 'one of the best in the world,' Europe is still associated with a more 'sophisticated' standard of beauty. Therefore, in order to become a 'successful' and 'beautiful' *travesti*, they have to transit through different body and space itineraries that seem to be quite well delineated in the *travesti* subculture. Graciele, the family doctor of the *travestis* in Lapa, clearly states:

> They are becoming more beautiful here in Rio, they learn how to be beautiful here in Rio; the way they talk is different, the way they act is different. Rio has other demands and here they have more facility to have a surgery, to inject silicone. Then, normally, they arrive much uglier than they leave, they arrive even much more masculine. It's funny that more beard to shave, the tinier breasts they have. Here they are transforming even their gesture: they arrive tougher, and then they are refining themselves. It's funny to see

182   J. Vartabedian

that transformation. Then when they start to look more beautiful, then they go to Europe. (Personal interview, 19 August 2008, Rio de Janeiro)

Dr Graciele reflects thus on the influence that Rio has on *travestis'* bodily changes. She implicitly establishes some dichotomies, also reinforced through the narratives of the participants, which describe *travestis'* process of transformations: yesterday/today, ugliness/beauty, masculinity/femininity, toughness/refinement. The past is associated with ugliness, with a yet non-feminine and tough *'travesti'* who is (still) not legible. Beauty, then, seems to transform and introduce them into a new life while they become intelligible subjects, according to *travesti's* aesthetic patterns. In this way, some *travestis made in Rio*—those who feel 'beautiful,' 'feminine,' and 'refined'—have much more chances for the following scale: Europe. In short, Rio is the great school in which to become a *travesti*, it is presented as a territory full of possibilities for those who wish to transit into this universe. As Samanta emphasises: 'Rio de Janeiro for me is everything, Rio de Janeiro is a mother, was a mother for me. It was here that I found myself, I discovered myself, and I began to value myself' (personal interview, 8 September 2008, Rio de Janeiro). Next, I focus on how *travesti* sex work is organised in the streets of Rio in order to analyse the ways paid sexual practices that involve *travestis* and clients are structured in the city.

The Territories of Sex Work in Rio

During my research in Rio de Janeiro, street prostitution remained the main modality of work. Considering that the street is also the space of circulation of desire (Perlongher 2008 [1987]), I analyse how a spatial hierarchy is established in the territories of *travesti* sex work when articulating a series of physical, sexual, and social elements that are negotiated between *travestis* and clients (Benedetti 2005; Parker 1999). As described in Chap. 3, my participation in the 'Program to combat child sexual exploitation' of the City Council of Rio de Janeiro allowed me to enter different *travesti* prostitution venues in the city while delivering condoms and lubricants to the sex workers. I examine their main—but not the only ones—prostitution venues, located in some neighbourhoods in different key areas (zones) of the city: (a) City Centre: Lapa (where the *casa-*

rão was located) and Glória,[4] (b) North Zone: São Cristóvão, (c) South Zone: Copacabana, and (d) West Zone: Barra da Tijuca. Most of these venues are those I could access alongside the project of the City Council.

Firstly, it is relevant to remember that the sale of sex is not illegal in Brazil and—contrary to other abolitionist countries such as Sweden—the purchase of sex is not criminalised either. However, there are many regulations that criminalise different activities related to prostitution, with the purpose of avoiding 'sexual exploitation.' Ultimately, these public politics end up persecuting sex workers, removing them from public spaces, and leaving them more vulnerable. When analysing Rio de Janeiro's state politics towards female (non-trans) sex work, Blanchette et al. (2017) assert that it exists as a mix of 'unregulated regulation' with prohibitionism that constantly intervenes over the sex work in the city. The police, with great 'discretionary power,' 'cleans up' the streets to push 'prostitution out of regions ear-marked for rapid urban development in function of Rio's mega-sporting events' and gentrification plans (Blanchette et al. 2017, 55). Although outside the temporal limits of my research, it is worth noting that the police conducted many more raids and closed many female prostitution venues during the 2014 World Cup and the 2016 Olympic Games in an attempt to change 'Rio's prostitution-friendly reputation.' In other words, the government's zoning ordinances, police harassment, and domain law aim to trap street-based prostitution and 'channel it into areas where it will not intermix with tourism and middle-class life' (Blanchette and Silva 2011, 141). The geographies of desire are, therefore, moving and changing continuously. Furthermore, the increasing influence of the Internet on selling sex has reconfigured the use of the space in recent years: to avoid police persecution, sex workers prefer to work in enclosed places in order to feel more secure (Silva and Blanchette 2011). In this way, it is not my aim to present a 'faithful' picture of the *travesti* prostitution venues in Rio (nor in Barcelona). Rather, I present the participants' ways of understanding the space when the fieldwork of this research was done.

The City Centre

This is a key commercial area in the city but also the traditional place where that section of the population considered as very 'marginal' used to live, such as sex workers, drug traffickers, and itinerants who are also linked to the historical bohemian Rio de Janeiro nightlife (Parker 1999). Lapa stands out as an important centre of the *carioca* cultural activity. In the 1950s, Lapa was well known for the *carioca* bohemian night-life—its famous cabarets and restaurants were frequented by artists, politicians, and intellectuals. In recent years, after surviving a period of devaluation and decadence in the area, Lapa has returned to assert itself as one of the centres of cultural and tourist life of the city. It has maintained its original architecture, and many of the buildings from the early part of the last century, so characteristic of the neighbourhood, have been restored. While I was in Rio, there were bars offering live shows, very old and poorly preserved houses (as in the *casarão*), different types of shops, expensive restaurants, and run-down hotels to facilitate paid sexual encounters—as this is one of the recognised *travesti* prostitution venues in the city. All these combined make Lapa an important tourist centre with a vivid nightlife.

In Lapa, *travestis* distanced themselves territorially from the female (non-trans) sex workers who also worked in this area. As shown in Map 7.1, *travestis* were located along the start of an avenue, Avenida Mem de Sá, and its opposite and perpendicular streets, the so-called Rua Riachuelo, Rua Lavradio, Rua Gomes Freire. The intense traffic among Avenida Mem de Sá made it almost impossible to negotiate with the clients in their cars, although the other, less affluent, streets would allow it. However, most of the clients usually moved on foot and were taken to some of the cheap hotels in the area once the negotiation was established.[5] Just in front of the *caserão,* there was a hotel where the participants went frequently, in fact, many of them stood in front of the hotel's door to attract the attention of passers-by and clients.

The clients were usually low-to-middle class male workers who returned home after their workday. Also, although to a lesser extent, they worked with foreign tourists who approached this attractive neighbourhood.

Trans Migrations: Brazilian *Travestis'* Spatial... 185

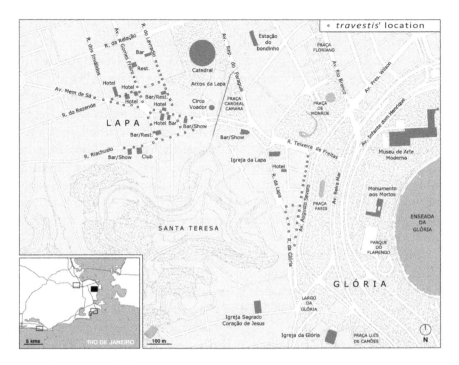

Map 7.1 Lapa and Glória

According to the *travestis* who worked here, the sexual services requested varied between the client's desires to penetrate (*comer*) and be penetrated (*dar*), with a greater preponderance towards the latter sexual activity. Using the currency exchange rate at the period of fieldwork, *travestis*' fees ranged roughly from £7–10 for fellatio, to £14–18 for a 'complete' service (fellatio and penetration). The price of the hotel was paid separately by the clients and for half an hour they had to pay, approximately, £3.50 for a very basic place. Finally, the *travestis* presented very different bodies to their clients: there were those who had only taken hormones, others had already been 'pumped up,' and the most admired ones, such as Samanta and Priscila, who had undergone cosmetic surgery (on breasts and noses). In any case, most of them presented a 'feminine' appearance, taking care of the combination of revealing dresses and their use of make-up.

Very close to Lapa, in the neighbourhood of Glória, there is another area where the *travestis* worked along the Avenida Augusto Severo (see Map 7.1). Unlike Lapa, this is not a place for cultural and leisure activities. On the contrary, its commercial zone is active only during the day and its main tourist attractions are its churches and some monuments of great historical value. Glória lost much of its access to the sea from the moment the Parque do Flamengo was built, levelling the terrain that belonged to the sea. Consequently, the area bordering the neighbourhood in the direction to the sea is composed of parks. Avenida Augusto Severo is then right at the limit where this big green zone begins and has little traffic because it is only one of the many parallel roads that allow the connection between the North and the South Zones of the city.

The main difference with the *travesti* sex work in Lapa was that the clients in Glória could contact them in the cars, and if a client wanted a more 'modest' service, that is, without paying the price of the hotel, there was the possibility of finding a quiet corner to park the car or perform a fellatio, or even a 'complete' service in the park in front of the street. If the territory of Lapa was controlled exclusively by Reyna and Alessandra, in Avenida Augusto Severo, there were other *mães* controlling the space, as previously agreed among them. Finally, although I did not notice significant aesthetic differences between the *travestis*, there was a belief among some participants in the *casarão* and the social educators of the team of the project in the City Council that those who worked here were 'prettier' than those in Lapa (or so they judged).

The North Zone

This is composed of numerous neighbourhoods very different from each other: from very highly valued residential areas to those where a very low-income population live. The main industrial areas of Rio grew here, a fact that configured a territory where the factories were mixed with the shacks of the migrant workers arriving in the city. The São Cristóvão neighbourhood is a historic area of the city. Very close to the Maracaná Stadium is the Quinta da Boa Vista, a very large public park where the Palace is located—which was the residence of the imperial family (in the nineteenth

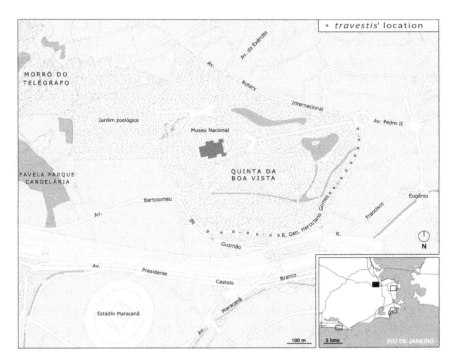

Map 7.2 São Cristóvão

century)—the National Museum (administered by the Federal University of Rio de Janeiro), and the zoo. Bordering the southeast sector of the park, and a few metres from the railway station, is the Rua General Herculano Gomes, which was the main street from which *gayzinhos/travestis* worked (see Map 7.2).

The first day I visited the surroundings of the Quinta da Boa Vista, I was advised by the team of the City Council that this area was more 'marginal.' They told me that the *gayzinhos/travestis* generally stole the clients and were more 'aggressive.' According to one of the social educators: 'you will realise this yourself from the way they arrive to get the condoms' (Field notes, 6 June 2008). Most of the *gayzinhos/travestis* were very young. The team suspected that many of them were minors, although they all said that they were 18 years old, as they knew that revealing their real age would create problems for them: legally, they would no longer be considered sex workers but 'exploited' people. However, this area with little urban population, remote and hidden among lush vegetation, was hardly controlled by the police, and the presence of minors was 'tolerated.'[6]

These young *gayzinhos/travestis* were very thin, without breasts, and with very short hair (very few used wigs). It seemed that they did not begin to feminise their bodies. At most, some had just started to take hormones. They dressed very simply, with tight denim shorts, tops, and flip-flops. Next to them, the territory was also shared with much older *travestis*, with a lot of silicone in their bodies (face, breasts, buttocks), and dressed provocatively in few clothes. In fact, they often showed and pulled their breasts out of their bras and also displayed much of their buttocks. It was inevitable to compare their bodies with those of the *gayzinhos/travestis*. Older bodies were further 'deteriorated' and embodied the hard life they had led, the abuse of liquid silicones, and the self-cuts to protect themselves from the arbitrary arrests during more repressive years in the past. Contrarily, the curveless and silicone-free bodies of the youngest offered a frequently cheaper aesthetic alternative to fulfil the clients' desires. *Travestis* who worked in other areas considered the *gayzinhos/travestis* working here 'uglier,' with no chances to work anywhere. The prices of services were the lowest of all the venues, since the vast majority of clients belonged to the working-class: they could charge £3.50 for fellatio and £7 for a 'complete' service. The clients who contacted them when walking were taken into the trees to consummate the sexual services. For those who went by car (many taxi drivers), it was also cheaper to remain in the same vehicle: the service did not usually extend to more than ten minutes.[7] Finally, all the Quinta da Boa Vista clients preferred to penetrate the *gayzinhos/travestis*.

The South Zone

This is the most prosperous area of Rio and that most frequented by national and transnational tourists. It has the highest average income in the city, as well as the highest average literacy rate. It has grown geographically from older districts such as Catete and Flamengo to more modern creations (early twentieth century) such as Copacabana, Ipanema, and Leblon. This expansion arose when the middle and upper classes sought open spaces along the coast, free from the 'annoying presence of the poor' (Parker 1999,

128). Copacabana is the first large neighbourhood built by the sea, and perhaps it is the most famous neighbourhood of the city. Between the decades of the 1930s and the 1950s, Copacabana was linked to different events and artistic movements that made it an indisputable cultural and tourist reference point. However, despite its opulence and glamour, since the 1970s, its slow decline began, as its fame attracted a significant number of residents of different social backgrounds, which—together with real estate speculation—created an overcrowded space. Ipanema and Leblon replaced Copacabana as the most fashionable areas in the South Zone.

Copacabana also became an important centre for both the heterosexual sex market (Blanchette and Silva 2004, 2011) and gay life, inside and outside of commercial sex. It was in Copacabana where I had the opportunity to start my fieldwork in Rio. There, I met, in front of the emblematic Hotel Copacabana Palace, Reyna. Working in a beach bar called 'Rainbow,' on the main gay beach of Copacabana, Reyna took part in one of the shows of *transformistas* and *travestis* that was organised on the promenade of the beach every Sunday night. On that beach, Reyna was treated with absolute devotion and respect and her influence went beyond the limits of the territory of Lapa.

Copacabana was an important workplace for the *travestis*. They were located along the Avenida Atlântica—a great avenue of double hand bordering the beach (see Map 7.3)—specifically, in the streets that surround the Praça do Lido (between the Avenida Prado Júnior and Rua Duvivier). If one observes the extension of the Avenida Atlântica, it is clear that they were located within a very short stretch. Nevertheless, it was one of the traditional *travesti* prostitution venues and, in addition, it had a series of bars, clubs, and restaurants that made it an area that was changing. Up to the end of 2009, there was another venue to the south of the Avenida Atlântica which stood near the intersection of the Rua Miguel Lemos, where the famous 'Help' nightclub was and which closed its doors later that year. This nightclub went from being an exclusive place for the upper-class young people from Rio to become the main place where foreign tourists could contact female (non-trans) sex workers who offered their services there. Taking advantage of the great influx of tourists and natives, the *travestis* found this another profitable place to find clients.

The white, middle-class clients frequently negotiated with the *travestis* from their cars, and, if they were tourists staying in the numerous hotels

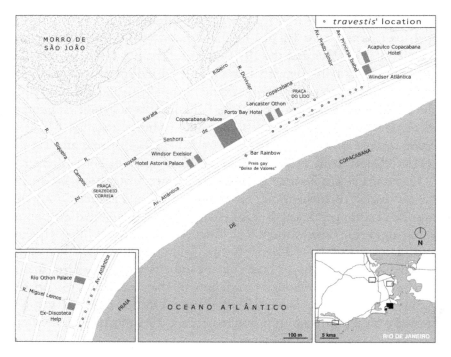

Map 7.3 Copacabana

in the area, they went on foot to contact them. The prices were more or less the same as in Lapa and Glória, although the 'complete' did not go down from £18. According to the *travestis,* the vast majority of their clients preferred to be penetrated. Finally, *travestis* working in this area were 'all made up,' that is, they had injected at least litres of silicone to feminise their bodies. There was a belief among the *travestis* who worked in the different prostitution venues of the city that the *travestis* who felt the most beautiful were those working in an area of a higher socioeconomic level in the city. As Natalia clearly stated: 'Those of Copacabana are believed to be better than those of Augusto Severo, these are better than those in the City Centre and those of the Quinta da Boa Vista. It all depends on where each one is' (Field notes, 6 August 2008). The next area to describe represents one more step in this hierarchy they created of the spaces in Rio.

The West Zone

This is the largest area in Rio. A massif divides the area into two parts: the northern part is composed of the old districts of the Rio suburb, concentrates numerous industries, and has a population that comes from the low and lower-middle class (an area with similar characteristics to those found in the popular part of the North Zone), and the southern part, which is located between the massif and the sea, presents a different history and socioeconomic organisation as it is an area of permanent growth characterised by its residential areas, its new real estate developments, and high standard of living. Jacarepaguá and Barra da Tijuca are two of the most emblematic neighbourhoods of the West Zone. Although we visited the two districts with the project of the City Council, I focus on Barra da Tijuca because it is one of the fastest growing areas that attracts, not only the richest families in the city, but also the *travestis*.

The *travestis* were situated on the avenue that runs along the coast, but they were mainly concentrated in the Praça São Perpétuo (popularly known as Praça do "Ó") (see Map 7.4). This square—small, family-run, and with little vegetation—has no commercial and tourist activity, just a couple of restaurants and a hotel that became famous after a scandal involving the Brazilian football player Ronaldo (see endnote 4 in Chap. 5). Nevertheless, it was chosen by *travestis* because it is the gateway to the most exclusive area of the neighbourhood. Almost all clients travelled in luxury cars and those who walked by were tourists who frequently came or went to one of the five-star hotels along the coast. For example, the Sheraton Hotel is approximately a ten-minute walk from the Praça São Perpétuo. The *travestis* who worked here came almost exclusively from the northern part of the same West Zone. They usually brought their heels, make-up, and a few clothes in a bag, and they would get ready there, behind some trees or parked cars. Their bodily aesthetic appearances looked very 'feminine': hormones, liquid silicones, and breast augmentation (cosmetic surgery) were the most common practices they had employed to beautify themselves. They recognised that they had to regulate their hormone consumption because clients liked them to keep their penises erect, as most of them wanted to be penetrated. Among the

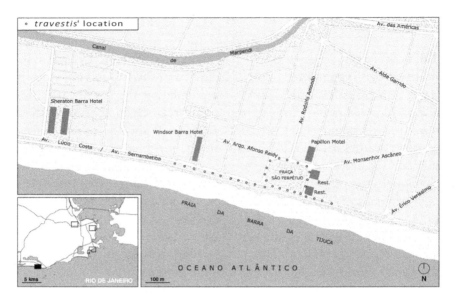

Map 7.4 Barra da Tijuca

participants, it was prestigious to work here, as the clients had more money and could pay more, although the minimum price was the same as in Copacabana (£18). As it was one of the most famous venues in the sex market in Rio, it was very difficult that a *travesti* working in the discredited Quinta da Boa Vista would suddenly decide to move and start working in Barra da Tijuca. This possible territorial relocation required knowing the codes that were inscribed in that space. In Barra da Tijuca only those *travestis* who had constructed a very 'feminine' body could work in a satisfactory manner, be respected by their peers, and be accepted by one of the *mães* of the area who, ultimately, would decide who worked there or not.

In short, this portrayal—although not exhaustive—allows us to geographically situate *travestis*' main perceptions of the space and street-based sex work organisation while this research was done in Rio. These territories, far from being neutral physical spaces, were laden with significance. For the *travestis* who felt themselves the most 'beautiful' and 'feminine' ones, as they believed, working in Barra da Tijuca would bring them more prestige than in Lapa, and they would also earn more money. The poorest clients with the desire to *comer* young *gayzinhos,* or even older *travestis,* would find their place on the streets of Quinta da Boa Vista. In the same way, those middle-upper social class clients would discreetly negotiate, from their cars, the sexual services (generally, to be penetrated) of (by) a more 'exclusive' *travesti* in Copacabana or Barra da Tijuca. In this way, the *travestis* and their clients appropriated a series of meanings linked to the territories to configure the geographies of *travesti* sex work in Rio. At the same time, this territoriality was intimately connected with different identity markers that were analysed in relation to *travestis'* bodies (beautiful, feminine; ugly, not feminine, old), the socioeconomic level of the clients (low, middle-upper class) and the sexual services offered (*comer, dar*). These references were, as a result, relationally inscribed into the territories (Perlongher 2008 [1987]). However, the process of *travestis'* identity constructions did not end in this *cidade maravilhosa.* The *travestis* who could expand their personal and job perspectives could find in Europe the great scale to, presumably, become 'successful' *travestis.* It is time to travel again.

Transnational Migrations: The Charm of Being 'European'

Europe is not simply another scale among the many territories that *travestis* can transit to transform their bodies, feel safer, or improve their lives. Their transnational migrations to Europe, since the 1970s, constitute an event of decisive influence in *travestis'* main narratives and experiences. Europe has not only allowed the 'first generations' to begin to beautify themselves *as* women, but it has also enabled a significant number of *travestis* to earn lots of money and—although some social, political, and economic constraints have caused profits to fall more recently—the trip to Europe continues to be considered an activity that gives prestige and empowers the *travestis* who, with 'success,' have been able to take a step forward in the career of becoming *travestis.*

The Pioneers

At the end of the 1960s, Daloá was the first Brazilian to arrive in Paris and work as a dancer in the exclusive cabaret houses *Chez Madame Arthur* and *Le Carrousel*, both belonging to Monsieur Marcel, where the famous European transsexual artists such as Coccinelle and Bambi also worked (Foerster 2014). Then, at the beginning of the 1970s, other *travestis* arrived in Paris, such as the Brazilian popular actress Regina and Valéria.[8] In fact, at that time, Daloá and her successors' bodies did not resemble the ones of the contemporary *travestis*. They arrived in Paris as *transformista* artists. In Brazil, not only were body transformation techniques not yet developed, but the *'travestis'* were also forbidden from being exhibited *as* women 24 hours a day in public places, as explained in Chap. 3. During the military dictatorship, cross-dressing was only tolerated in the theatres and during the carnival. Up to the 1970s, those who were encouraged to go into the streets with a feminine appearance were harshly repressed (Figari 2009). Therefore, in a setting of such prohibition, it was very difficult to modify their bodies and the techniques to do it were not yet well developed.

In the case of the first Brazilians who arrived in Paris, the shows of transsexuals and *transformistas* were booming in the major European cities. In these scenarios, the artists sang live, danced, and unfolded their 'feminine charms' in front of a selected public marvelling at the possibility that these beautiful artists had been 'men.' When I asked Regina if the women also worked in *Le Carrousel* she answered categorically: 'No, women never entered, women never. Whether operated women [transsexuals] or *travestis*. They just had to have breasts' (personal interview, 15 August 2008, Rio de Janeiro). Brazilians like Regina and Valéria first took hormones in Europe to begin to have breasts and feminise their bodies, as the admired European transsexuals had done before (Foerster 2014).

In Barcelona, this modality of show was also very famous, despite the Franco dictatorship, and notable places were *Barcelona de Noche* or *Gambrinus*. According to the memoirs of Pierrot, actor and showman of the main shows in Barcelona, 'in the 1970s the success of trans people in the show was so spectacular that no room lost the opportunity to have in its cast "the challenge to the most overflowed imagination"'

(Pierrot 2006, 155). One of the first Brazilians to arrive in Spain was Lorena Capelli. She was one of the few who came to Europe already dressed *as* a woman because her father was part of the diplomatic corps and obtained an official document authorising her to go through the streets of Brazil with a 'feminine' appearance. However, compared to Paris, the city of Barcelona was not the main destination for Brazilian *travestis*. Most of them arrived there once the 'golden age' of Paris began to decline in the mid-1980s.

All the older participants recognised that the success that these pioneers had in Paris was surprising. According to them, they felt admired and respected by European men as never before. Concurrently, thanks to hormones, they also felt more 'beautiful,' and when they returned to Brazil, they generated a great media impact as well as expectation among the rest of the *travestis*. Referring to Regina's trip to Europe, Cristina told me: 'she left Brazil and already wore a wig, was more a *transformista*. When she returned from Paris, then everyone looked at that woman sitting there who went to see a show, sitting there a blond woman, flamboyant, super chic. My God, is it possible? It's Regina!' (personal interview, 12 September 2008, Rio de Janeiro).

Thus, the artistic and corporeal experiences of people like Regina and Valéria did not go unnoticed. As Regina described, the *travestis* started to arrive in Paris once they knew about the others' success but most of them could not enter *Chez Madame Arthur* and *Le Carrousel*. However, there were a few exceptions, such as Eloína who also made the first incursions into the streets of Paris as a sex worker. It was soon discovered that this business earned a lot of money and when Eloína came back to Brazil for holidays, she strategically displayed her jewels, dresses, new style, and femininity. The success that the first *travestis* had in Paris was such that they began (especially, Eloína) to spread among the rest of Brazilians who, in that city, would earn a lot of money. An alternative Brazilian gay journal of those days (*Lampião da Esquina*) interviewed Eloína, 'that mulatta, is one of the best known Brazilian *travestis*, resident eight years ago in Paris and who comes to Rio every year during the holidays and can be found in fashionable places' (Bastos 1980, 3). In the article, she explained how she modified her body in France (hormones, silicone, and breast prosthesis) and that she had already bought her second apartment in Rio and was planning to open a boutique in the neighbourhood of Ipanema. As Tony, who also went to Paris to work as sex worker, expressed to me, 'Paris was the hen of golden eggs' (personal interview, 15 September 2008, Rio de Janeiro).

Therefore, from the late-1970s, a large number of Brazilians began travelling to Paris to work exclusively in the field of commercial sex. Trevisan (2007 [1986]) points out that there were charter flights arranged to transport *travestis* specifically to Paris: the so-called flights of beauty (Vale 2005). James Green (1999, 252) recounts that the growth of the market was such that 'Brazil began to export *travestis* to Europe.' Hutta and Balzer (2013, 88) mentioned there was 'a kind of exodus of Brazilian *travestis*' and up to 500 of them were living in Paris. Vale's (2005) research with Brazilian *travestis* in France shows that, as a result of their power and dominance in the field of prostitution, in the 1980s, the word *brésilien* became synonymous with *travesti*. Moreover, different interviewees said that the arrival in Paris of this contingent of *travestis* was not unnoticed:

> The Brazilian *travestis* … were victorious, victorious. And they continue to be. Anywhere in the world when it comes to prostitution, as soon as a Brazilian woman or a *travesti* arrive, they will be always in the first place. (Tony, personal interview, 15 September 2008, Rio de Janeiro)

> They became famous because they have invaded Europe, the way of being… (Lina, personal interview, 6 August 2008, Rio de Janeiro)

> It was a Brazilian invasion. But it was a counterculture … they imposed a way of behaving, the Brazilian *travestis* changed the *travestis* of the world: the Venezuelans, Colombians, French … they changed their way of acting, costuming and behaving according to the Brazilians. (Pedro, personal interview, 13 September 2008, Rio de Janeiro)

Some participants identified the arrival of Brazilians into Europe by using the word 'invasion.' Pedro was an entrepreneur who owned a club/cabaret that promoted shows and beauty pageants for *travestis* in Rio, in the 1970s, during the period of censorship and repression. Through the experiences and confidences of his *travestis*' friends travelling to Europe, Pedro became a privileged witness to their transnational migrations. He told me that, from Rio, every week, three *travestis* went to Paris. They worked between nine and ten months a year and then they returned to Brazil with no less than £30,000 in their possession. Pedro even remembered one of them who returned with £80,000, which at the time was equivalent to three or four apartments. They also arrived with kilos of gold because, as he explained, *travestis* knew how to relate to the 'Arab thieves' who provided it to them. Pedro thus analysed *travestis'* migrations to Paris as an 'invasion,' recognising how they quickly appropriated the weak local trans sex market and occupied its main prostitution venues in the Bois de Boulogne. In addition, for the first time, they felt respected. As some of them remembered, while in France they were called 'mademoiselle,' whereas in Brazil they encountered violence and even death. It is possible, therefore, to understand the attraction that France generated in a significant number of Brazilian *travestis* eager to prosper and obtain financial security while still young (Garcia and Lehman 2011).

The rise of this 'golden age' in Paris arrived then between 1978 and 1980, the year in which Elisa was murdered. As discussed in Chap. 4, Elisa was a very influential and powerful Brazilian *travesti* in Paris who controlled both the prostitution business and the distribution and application of liquid silicone. Silicone 'pumping' made by Brazilians began in Paris and Elisa was the great precursor. The murder of the 'Pigalle Queen,' at the hands of Claudia, marked the beginning of the decline of the most fruitful years of Brazilian *travesti* in Europe. It started a period that some of my interviewees considered 'marginal' because, without the effective control of Elisa, many rivalries, envy, scandals, and threats surfaced among the *travestis* themselves. At the same time, the pressure from the French authorities grew: between 1980 and 1984, expulsions were multiplied because of irregularities in their visas. From the second half of the 1980s, other destinations were being chosen in Europe. During the 1990s and, relatively speaking, until today, travel to Italy became the great goal of the new generations of *travestis* (Teixeira 2008, 2011). Countries such as Spain, Germany, Switzerland, and the Netherlands were incorporated from 2000, and migrations to Spain intensified after the second half of the 2000s (Patrício 2008; Pelúcio 2011; Silva and Ornat 2014).

The Importance of Europe

Although *travestis'* migratory routes are permanently reconfigured and the political and economic conditions of the destination countries change, the motivations for reaching Europe have remained practically the same over the years. The 'charm' of Paris continued to attract new generations of *travestis* who kept on associating this city (and Europe) with a distinctive and glamorous lifestyle. One night in Barcelona, in the Camp Nou area where the largest number of *travesti* sex workers was concentrated, one Brazilian greeted another one while asking her where she had been since she had not seen her for a long time, this *travesti* answered: 'I came from Paris' (Field notes, 26 October 2010). I would have flatly accepted this remark if, on the same night, I had not heard another *travesti* saying the same thing in an ironic way since, in fact, neither of them had been in Paris. This city still remained in the *travesti* imaginary closely linked to its prestigious 'golden' era. However, this splendour was finished.

Although less 'charming' than Paris, many other cities and countries in Europe have provided great social and economic advantages to the *travestis* since the mid-1980s. Some studies (Kulick 1998; Silva 1993) have also emphasised how Europe represents a social ascent in the *travesti* subculture. Their economic achievements (especially for those who could then buy houses in Brazil) were displayed as real 'trophies' that allowed them to recognise the 'successful' *travestis*. At the same time, body care, new aesthetic surgeries, imported brands of clothes, expensive perfumes, and jewels reflected the prestige and glamour achieved by their stays in Europe. Europe presented the possibility of accessing other cultures and languages, gaining new experiences, feeling respected and desired by 'real' men, and, very importantly, avoiding the great discrimination associated with Brazil (Silva and Ornat 2014). Francisca, who worked in Barcelona, described why she left Brazil:

> Many *travestis* decide to go to Europe and leave Brazil. Why? Not because there is money here, people think it's because of money, no! It's because of the mistreatment [in Brazil]. We have no right to enter a restaurant and be seen as a human being. We, in Brazil, are seen by the car, by the brand of

the clothes that you are wearing, we are not seen as a human being … Here in Europe, the *travesti* is treated like a normal human being. Here men give more value to the *travesti*. (Francisca, personal interview, 30 July 2009, Barcelona)

The search for 'normality' then, as it was expressed by Francisca, became an important reason to stay in Europe. All the participants who still lived, or had lived, in Europe, agreed that they never felt as free and respected as when in Europe. However, not everyone wanted to leave Brazil permanently. Many *travestis* were only interested in spending few years in Europe to earn enough money to get a good life for themselves and, often, to be the economic support of their families in Brazil.

Travelling to Europe required the existence of a solid network to guarantee the displacement. In a more complex way than those going to Rio, the *mães/madrinhas* also 'financed' the trip to Europe with a pre-established sum of money (during my stay in Rio, the 'loans' ranged from £10,000 to £13,000) which included the passport, flight ticket, some cash to enter the country, accommodation for the first weeks, purchase of the venue where they would work, and the 'protection' that the names of the *mães/madrinhas* provided at the destination. As Reyna said: 'Because I do not only give the flight ticket or the prostitution venue, but I am giving my own passport, my name. Reyna M. is known and respected throughout Europe' (Field notes, 19 August 2008). The gains *mães/madrinhas* got for these loans were substantial; approximately two-thirds of the funding for the trip. However, *mães/madrinhas* did not see themselves as 'exploitative' or pimps, but rather as 'agents' who enabled *travestis* to enter and remain in another country. Despite this unequal relationship in which the debtors were often intimidated and threatened to return their debt as soon as possible, very few *travestis* considered that they were involved in a network where they were 'exploited' and 'trafficked.' On the contrary, they understood this agreement as a form of 'help,' that is, this social network was commonly used as the (only) way many *travestis* had to migrate (Patrício 2008; Piscitelli 2008; Teixeira 2008). In sum, *travesti* transnational migrations to Europe were a great business and a source of prestige for all the people involved in these transactions. According to a Brazilian *travesti* activist in Rio, almost two decades ago, a *travesti* had prestige if she exhibited her voluminous body: the more silicone the better. Nowadays, the *mães/madrinhas* were recognised figures because the 'prestige is measured through the power and networks created in relation to the migrations to Europe' (Field notes, 10 June 2008). Therefore, the more *travestis* taken to Europe, the more respected she would be.

Regarding the meaning that these trips had for the *travestis*, Europe represented an important promotion on a material, symbolic, and corporeal level. Those who travelled to Europe were called 'Europeans' among the group. The 'Europeans' were identified by their 'beauty,' 'refinement,' and 'sophistication,' that is, they embodied a series of ideals that when they returned to Brazil—temporarily or permanently—were positively valued. However, being 'European' had to be related to the 'success' of a migratory project. *Travestis* who lived in Europe believed that it was wrong to imagine, from Brazil, that their lives were much better. As Marcia related from Barcelona: 'In Brazil everyone thinks that here we eat caviar' (personal interview, 31 July 2009). On the contrary, life in Europe could be very hard. European economic recession, local policies that restricted and prohibited outdoor sex work, the fear of deportation, loneliness, and the access to heavier drugs such as heroin were some of the difficulties they found once in Europe. The 'failures' of the *travestis* in Europe, then, were less acknowledged (or well hidden, to avoid embarrassment) from Brazil (Garcia and Lehman 2011; Silva and Ornat 2014). Nevertheless, Europe continued fascinating new generations of *travestis* who did not give up travelling into these territories that conferred prestige. However, not all the *travestis* could travel to Europe. Aizura (2014, 141) refers to Berlant's (2011) category of 'cruel optimism' to denote this dream and desire of a better life that rarely materialises in many trans lives.

Travestis also believed that being 'European' meant being more 'beautiful.' One of the signs of the 'success' of *travestis* in Europe was observed through their bodies. It was assumed that those who returned from Europe felt more 'beautiful.' Generally, once in Europe, they had more resources and access to surgical and aesthetic procedures to feminise their bodies. However, not all the cosmetic surgeries were carried out in Europe. Many *travestis* preferred to come back to Brazil and undergo cosmetic surgery with national surgeons during their holidays. Most of the 'Europeans' I met both in Rio and Barcelona had 'completed' their (though endless) process of feminisation. However, there were some exceptions. For example, Regina, Tony, Cristina, and Bibi (from the 'first generation') never 'pumped up' or had undergone any cosmetic surgery during their stays in Europe. Hormones were their main way of feminisation. Bibi told me that Europe exposed them to a context where there was a great competition and, consequently, the pressures to feel more 'beautiful' were greater. She was interviewed in Rio but had lived 25 years in Barcelona. Although she barely changed her body, she said:

> Those who went to Europe were better, right?, with plastic surgeries, with a series of things. And those who remained did not do so many things, they stayed here in a quieter and limited life, they did not try to perfect themselves so much, they were comfortable, they did not have so much vanity. (Bibi, personal interview, 12 September 2008, Rio de Janeiro)

Bibi herself stated that, 'my personality surpasses everything, body and everything.' Her strong self-esteem kept her then 'dry,' with no silicone or implants in her body.

The close relationship between beauty and Europe can also be explained through the history of the 'discovery' of Paris by the first 'travestis' who started to modify their bodies once in France. That is, they arrived in Paris as *transformistas* and returned to Brazil as 'beautiful' and 'feminine' *travestis*. Pedro remembered that 'Regina, Valéria, Eloína … all went to take the hormones in Paris, all of them went as men, they could not embark as a woman, until 1976 they all embarked as men' (personal interview, 13 September 2008, Rio de Janeiro). During this period, use of the industrial liquid silicone began in Paris and was widely disseminated. Desirous of experiencing the 'wonderful' effects of this substance, most of the bodies built by this generation sought very voluptuous shapes. They were bodies that did not go unnoticed and, even today, are called 'Paris bodies.' As if a registered trademark, these bodies are still alive in the imagination of the newer generations, although the 'naturalness' of the youngest seems to be imposed as an aesthetic value among the *travestis*.

In short, it was in Paris, and across Europe, that the bodies of the *travestis* began to take shape and they could reaffirm their identities as they felt like 'beautiful' *travestis*, becoming admired and intelligible subjects. In this way, Europe was still considered as a destination associated with beauty among the participants. By this, I do not mean that there are no *travestis* feeling 'beautiful' who have never left Brazil. The younger generations who began taking hormones very soon, achieved favourable aesthetic results, according to the beauty ideals of the group. However, even more valued are those who, with 'success,' have lived at least a season in Europe and have been able to embody the 'glamour' and 'refinement' associated with it. Liposuction, breast implants, rhinoplasty, laser depilation, or face filling applications were some of the most requested practices related to some phase of their trips to Europe. For the *travestis* then, whether on a symbolic or material level, the 'Europeans' were always 'beautiful.' Next, we move on to explore how, once in Barcelona, the main *travestis'* prostitution venues were organised in that city.

The Territories of Sex Work in Barcelona

The city of Barcelona is the capital of the province of Barcelona and the autonomous community of Catalonia. After Madrid, it is the second most populous city in Spain. It is located next to the Mediterranean Sea, about 120 km south of the Pyrenees and the border with France. Barcelona is recognised as a 'global city' (Sassen 2005) because of its cultural, financial, and touristic importance in a globalised economic system, it is one of the main ports of the Mediterranean, and an important point of connection between Spain and France. Spain has the fifth largest economy in the European Union and its economic growth since 2000 has attracted mainly Brazilian immigration (Masanet et al. 2012).

Spain, like Brazil, adheres to the abolitionist system in which sex work is not officially regulated (but it is not illegal either), that is, the state does not pursue or prohibit prostitution as long as it is voluntary, and only intervenes in cases of pimping. However, despite this declared abolitionism, there is a de facto regulation that is implemented, above all, through persecution and repressive interventions by the police. A high percentage of female (trans and non-trans) and male sex workers in Spain are immigrants. According to TAMPEP (2009), between 80% and 90% of the sex workers in Spain are foreign nationals. One of the first difficulties immigrants encounter when beginning their migratory projects is the entry to Europe. Under the guise of 'regulating migratory flows,' European states hinder legal migration and pursue illegal migrants, increasingly strengthening border controls (Anderson 2017). However, this tightening of migration policies does not prevent the arrival of non-EU people but transforms the means of doing so. The more restrictions to enter European territory that exist, the more people will use the support of different types of networks that will enable migration, either by advancing the money for the trip, by providing contacts at the place of destination, or facilitating the obtaining of visas.

Once on Spanish territory, and when the three-month tourist visa is over,[9] many people are in an irregular administrative situation (popularly known as being 'without papers'). According to the Aliens Act, this situation exposes people to the constant threat of deportation and the inability to move freely through the country. The fear of expulsion may become real in the face of frequent identity checks, by the police and protected by law, to which foreigners are subjected. The possibility of changing legal status to access to the rights of citizens is very complicated for many, while obtaining a permit of residence is coupled in most cases with the possession of a work contract. Since sex work is not officially considered a job, those engaged in this activity have no option to regularise their situation. It is, therefore, the very norm of immigration that places many sex workers, as immigrants 'without papers,' in situations of extreme vulnerability and helplessness, forcing them to live in precarious conditions far from the idyllic 'Europe of Rights.'

The visibility of street sex work is an issue of central interest to public authorities. In Barcelona, one of the methods created by the administration to manage this phenomenon, and to contain political, media and neighbourhood pressure, is to deploy a series of police operations to 'clean' the most 'problematic' areas of the city. Large joint raids are organised between the *Guardia Urbana* (the municipal police) and the *Policía Nacional* (national police) for issues of ('illegal') immigration, or the

Mossos d'Esquadra (autonomous police), for anti-drug operations or against trafficking in persons. However, as Fernández Bessa (2010, 148) argues, 'although police action is justified in arresting pimps who can exploit prostitutes, in practice, most of these processes end up with the expulsion of immigrant women who engage in sex work.' In other words, the authorities find, in the Aliens Act, the most effective argument for 'solving,' at least provisionally, the phenomenon of street sex work.

In recent years, Barcelona has been transformed as a result of urban design and real estate policies. It is paradoxical that, at the same time that the qualities of the diversity of its urban culture are exalted, municipal ordinances are issued to control them. It is believed that in order to maintain this highly lucrative model of the city, a series of practices and mechanisms that regulate and restrict the circulation of people considered 'undesirable' for the public space must be implemented. The controversial Ordinance of Measures to Foster and Guarantee the Coexistence in the City of Barcelona (also called the 'Civic Ordinance') of 2006 made the free exercise of street sex work in Barcelona more critical. Ultimately, the Ordinance harasses and punitively fines the sex workers and the clients, as it prohibits both the offering and the request of sexual services in the public space. In 2012 there was a hardening of the Ordinance focused on mainly sanctioning the client, with fines ranging from between £900 and £1375, increasing according to the proximity to schools. The Ordinance is also tough on sex workers and clients discovered having sex in a public space: here, fines can reach £2750.

In what follows, I analyse *travesti* sex workers' use of the space in Barcelona. Fieldwork was undertaken before the tightening of the Ordinance. Consequently, when describing the prostitution venues, it must be considered that they may now be in a constant process of reconfiguration, since the regulations of the public administrations are also designing the geographies of sex work in the city (Hubbard et al. 2008). Specifically, these regulations contribute to increasingly fewer people having the opportunity to work in the streets, and the sex workers therefore engage in alternative strategies to face this already declared prohibitionism.

The Streets

Les Corts District

Les Corts, as it is written in Catalan, is the main area of *travesti* prostitution in Barcelona and is where almost all the Brazilians can be found. It is located in the southwest sector of the city and is one of its entrance points when accessing the Avinguda Diagonal. In the residential La Maternitat i Sant Ramon neighbourhood, there are three major facilities: the stadium of Barcelona Football Club (Camp Nou), the historic cemetery of Les Corts, and the Maternity Hospital Complex. Specifically, *travestis* were situated between the metro station called Zona Universitaria, in the direction of Avinguda Diagonal, and the Camp Nou (called the Camp Nou area). In an almost triangular space, there are located several faculties, higher technical schools, and the park of Bederrida, where a large open air car park is currently located (see Map 7.5). Outside the hours of study, its streets are practically deserted, that is in the evenings and early morning. It is, therefore, a quiet place, with a flow of cars in the avenues that surround the area, and is located next to one of the main male concentration places of the city (the Camp Nou).

Among the *travestis* who work in the streets, disputes to obtain the best prostitution venues are part of their lived experiences, and have a long tradition (Vale 2005). One morning, I was invited by the NGO, *Àmbit Dona*, to participate in a workshop for trans people who were constructing their own website. There were six participants: one Spanish and the rest Ecuadorians and Peruvians. As soon as I introduced myself and explained the subject of my research, three or four of them immediately began to complain about the Brazilian *travestis*: 'Brazilians are very violent, bad, very bad. They take you out of the area with knives, they burn you with fire. They are a bad race' (Field notes, 19 October 2011). This possibly exaggerated comment reveals the tensions that arise in a highly competitive milieu where the bonds of solidarity seem to be weak and the will to understand or to integrate with 'others' is almost non-existent. Added to this is the language barrier, placing the Brazilians in a linguistically more isolated position than the rest of the Spanish speakers. Spaces

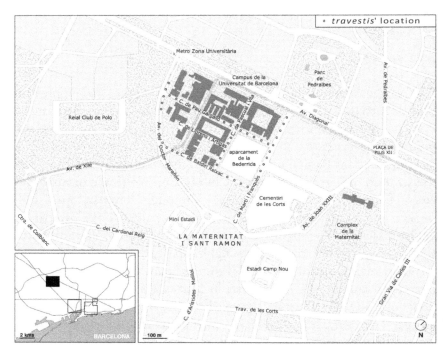

Map 7.5 Les Corts

are hierarchical and ordered to determine who can and who cannot be in a certain place. The Camp Nou area is clearly organised according to nationalities, as these are the catalysts of rivalries (Fernández Dávila and Morales 2011). For example, Ecuadorians and Brazilians do not mix in the same street.

During my fieldwork research, the Brazilians were the most numerous and noisy group at the Camp Nou. They drank and danced to the music from their mobile phones while, performing their 'Brazilianness,' catching the attention of clients and passers-by in the area. Most of the clients used their cars to negotiate the services that were going to be performed later in those cars, once they were parked in a quiet place. Also, clients on motorcycle, bicycle, or on foot came up here to engage in what was agreed, in a wooded area. The prices ranged from £18 for fellatio, to between £27.50/£36.50 for the 'complete' service. Finally, most of their clients sought to be penetrated. They were then aware—as a *travesti* stressed—that in the Camp Nou, 'whoever is better endowed works more' (Field notes, 26 October 2010).

Ciutat Vella District

The Ciutat Vella (Old Town) District includes the entire historical city centre, which includes different neighbourhoods. The Raval and the Gòtic are divided by Les Rambles, an emblematic promenade extending from the Plaça de Catalunya (the heart of the city centre) to the old port. Les Rambles' promenade is characterised by its press, flower and bird kiosks, various cafes and restaurants with their terraces available until late at night, street markets, and artists (many living statues) and painters who sell their works to tourists and bystanders.

Female (non-trans) sex workers were located near the most central part of Les Rambles, in between the Teatre Liceu (theatre) and the Boqueria market. This is one of the gateways to the Raval where, in the so-called Chinatown, one of the main female (non-trans) prostitution venues in the city was established (Medeiros 2002). As can be seen in Map 7.6, *travestis* were situated in the direction of the port, near the Santa Mònica Arts centre, although some *travestis* could be found a little way up the street, nearer the Teatre Liceu. Compared to the Camp Nou, this used to be a very 'weak' *travesti* prostitution venue in Barcelona with almost no Brazilians and with many older *travestis*/transsexuals, most of them Spanish. According to the NGO Stop SIDA (Fernández Dávila and Morales 2011), only between four and eight *travestis* were identified as working in this area, usually between midnight and 5 am in the morning to avoid police persecution, although some of them did 'have papers.' Most of them were from Colombia, Ecuador, Peru, and Spain. There was a belief—shared among the *travestis* themselves—that those working here 'survived' the harsh conditions of the sex market in the city, robbing the clients who moved by walking or in their cars. This information was confirmed by Stop SIDA, which recognised that it is in the district of Ciutat Vella where more situations of violence between sex workers and clients have been reported.

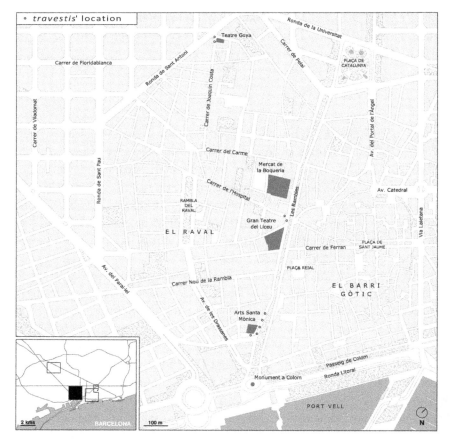

Map 7.6 Ciutat Vella

Finally, there is another minority focus in the extreme north of the district, where some *travestis* were located near the Goya Theatre, on the corner of the street Joaquín Costa, almost at the intersection with the Ronda de Sant Antoni. This commercial and residential area used to be an important venue for female (non-trans) sex workers (especially during the day). However, over the years, successive police controls served to significantly reduce the supply of sexual services in that place. Just a few *travestis* are positioned there at dawn.

Sant Martí District

One of the neighbourhoods here is the Vila Olímpica del Poblenou, built for the 1992 Olympic Games as a residence for athletes. Its later transformation into a residential neighbourhood, and the recovery of much of the coastline to create spaces for leisure, have greatly revitalised this area. Limited by the large Parc de la Ciutadella, according to data from Stop SIDA, the five to six *travestis* working in the area were located along the street called Ramon Trias Fargas, towards the Avinguda Icària, where there are different Faculties and Research Centres of the Pompeu Fabra University campus, as well as its library (see Map 7.7). They came from

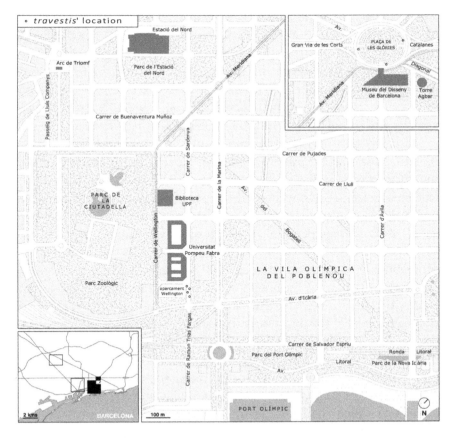

Map 7.7 Sant Martí

Spain, Panama, Colombia, and Ecuador. Going up towards the park of the Estació del Nord (the bus station of the city), along with the streets like Sardenya and Buenaventura Muñoz, female (non-trans) sex workers were positioned. As a whole, this residential area is characterised as being quiet, with numerous parks, wooded areas, and, especially the street chosen by the *travestis*, with a university campus. As in the Camp Nou, the combination of a university area that is deserted at night coupled with the existence of parks and spaces where some sexual services could be easily performed, outlines a territory suitable for street sex work.

In this same district of Sant Martí, towards its north part, is located Plaça de les Glòries, a large square in the process of transformation where the three main axes of the city converge: Avinguda Diagonal, Gran Via de les Corts Catalanes, and Avinguda Meridiana. It is employed as a roundabout of elevated highways. Stop SIDA also registered that the female (non-trans) sex workers were located along the Avinguda Meridiana, reaching the central square of Glòries. There were only a few *travestis*, mostly from Colombia and Ecuador, who worked in the area of the square. The abundant traffic ensured that only late at night drivers of vehicles and motorcycles could stop to negotiate their services.

With the exception of the Camp Nou, I have made very few visits to other territories where *travestis* worked in Barcelona. Some obstacles during my fieldwork in Barcelona are described in Chap. 1, together with the fact that focusing exclusively on the experiences of the Brazilian *travestis* limited some results of this section. At the same time, the constant mobility of the *travesti* population in search of new territories to work, as a consequence of the police persecution towards street sex work, made it more difficult to think about a 'faithful' cartography of the territories of sex work in Barcelona. Although the street has always been chosen as a place where sex workers feel free and autonomous, nowadays, the situation has changed. The oppression that sex workers experience in the public space is not generated—as it is thought from public and media discourses—because of pimps who 'exploit' and 'force' women, mainly, into prostitution,[10] but due to the suffocating situation of being 'without papers' and the subsequent police harassment and persecution. Public policies are then hardened against those engaged in street sex work because it is an 'undesirable' activity for the urban, economic, and touristic purposes of the city.

Considering this scenario, it is easier to understand why the number of Brazilian *travestis* engaged in street sex work is becoming smaller, or if they are still on the streets; many have to complement this modality of work with other ways of offering their sexual services. The vast majority, as immigrant citizens 'without papers,' and sex workers, move—like women—through a double 'illegality' (Teixeira 2008). However, in the case of *travestis*, their gender identity should be considered an 'extra' element of discrimination and stigma. Although, in Europe, social rejection towards trans people does not acquire the tragic dimensions it has in Brazil, and at the same time *travestis* are aware that in Europe they feel more respected and freer, trans people continue to be discriminated against in Spain. A report commissioned by the State Federation of Lesbians, Gays, Transsexuals and Bisexuals (FELGTB) (Domínguez 2011) reveals the economic precariousness of the trans population in Spain, as well as its high unemployment rate and the social rejection to which they are subjected daily (see also Platero 2014). Moreover, the *travestis* sex workers are affected not only by the street sex work's restrictions but also by the effects of the so-called economic crisis which also influences, as they say, the availability of money for their clients. Despite this horizon that may discourage many 'Europeans,' we next analyse how *travestis* strategically employ some practices to secure a place in the increasingly competitive and tough Spanish sex market.

The Flats

The vast majority of *travestis* have been adapting to the restrictions imposed on public spaces in which to work and have chosen closed spaces such as the flats in which to develop their activity. There are two types of flats: the agency ones (managed by a third person) and the self-managed. In the first case, the flats, or clubs, are run by a manager who will charge 50% of their income for housing, food, and advertising of their sexual services if they are resident, that is, if they live and work in the same place. 'Agencies' can be both business-type organisations that work with a significant number of *travestis* and also people who were usually engaged in prostitution and, as tenants or owners of a flat, sub-let rooms to set up this business, creating a more 'family' type of organisation. Sex workers talk about 'doing *praça*' (that is, having a vacancy) when they access these flats for a set time of 21 days, following the same rhythm of the menstrual cycle marked by women sex workers. The stay in the flats can also be established for a longer time, even for years, depending on each one's experiences. But, generally, all the flats reserve a space for those who are 'doing *praça*,' so they can offer more options to their clientele by renewing at least some of their workers.

Travestis' mobility is one of the main strategies they employ to work in the Spanish and European sex market. According to Patrício (2008, 137), 'being mobile is part of the construction and reaffirmation of the identity of the Brazilian *travesti*.' In fact, this whole chapter is a proof of this. Within sex work, mobility is used as a strategy for an economic purpose. The main objective is to avoid the 'burnt-face' effect and to be a 'novelty' for the clients (Rojas et al. 2009). For this reason, they are 'doing *praça*' in different flats to offer their bodies and services to clients in other Spanish and European cities. As a result, they are constantly travelling to the Netherlands, Germany, Switzerland, Austria, the UK, or Denmark. We can see that *travestis'* online advertisements announce that they are a 'Novelty,' or remain 'Until May 5,' or are 'Now in Barcelona' as a way to show the importance of their travels to offer different bodies and experiences to clients.

In the self-managed flats, one or two *travestis* share the renting of a flat to live and work. The type of organisation is not hierarchical, as in the other system. On the contrary, the *travestis* themselves keep the totality of the profits and each one is in charge of managing their own promotion as well as deciding the number of hours they will work. However, renting a flat of their own is not easy and implies a minimum economic stability that not all of them can assume in order to pay the months of deposit usually required when signing the agreement of lease. But, more importantly, the absence of a work contract or a proof of income also limits this option, since this is also usually one of the requirements. As *travestis*, sex workers, and those 'without papers,' the chances of getting a proven salary are almost impossible. In other words, having a self-managed flat is a privilege.

It takes time, money, or a client/*marido* who can 'finance' it. Owning a flat is another indicator of the 'success' of a *travesti* in Europe. As not all the 'Europeans' have the same status and recognition in the Spanish sex market, I introduce the emic term 'top' to designate those 'Europeans' who seem to be one step above the rest (Pelúcio 2009). As discussed, not all the 'Europeans' can be 'successful' and the 'top' *travestis* refer to those who have been able to achieve economic and social well-being and, at the same time, the recognition and admiration of the wider group.

On the one hand, those who still work in the streets consider that, in the flats (managed by a third party), they can never have the freedom found in outdoor prostitution to demand the working conditions that they want. In the streets, they can decide how many hours to work each day and, above all, know that their earnings do not have to be shared with anyone. They prefer to avoid, if possible, the figure of a manager/boss who orders, controls, and limits. On the other hand, as a consequence of the fear of deportation and given the intense police persecution and the greater vulnerability of those who are 'without papers,' the flats can also be spaces where they can feel more secure than in the streets and with less exposure to danger, in a broader sense. Rosanne, who worked both at the Camp Nou and agency flats, recounted in an interview in Barcelona: 'In flats, you feel secure, the fact that there is an environment and if something happens, I think it is easier if you, you feel safer. And on the street no, you enter a car, you go to a hotel and you do not know what is going to happen' (personal interview, 27 August 2009, Barcelona).

The prices charged on the flats are stipulated by the length of stay: £65 half hour and £90 for an hour. 'Top' *travestis* can charge £140 half hour and £180 for the hour. Unlike in Brazil, the *travestis* can offer many diverse services in the flats. Compared to the street work mode, this breadth of services is due to the fact that they have more time and privacy, but it is also a working strategy to attract the increasingly demanding Spanish client. As Pelúcio expresses (2011, 205), *travestis* know that Spaniards want more than 'a woman with a cock.' The Internet has an increasingly relevant role in the *travesti* sex market as the main way to announce and make themselves and the services offered visible. On some of the websites where they advertise in Spain,[11] we can read the great versatility of the services available and the professionalism they display to meet the expectations of all the clients: from beginners to those who like cross-dressing and sadomasochism. As seen in Chap. 6, they have to stand out in this competitive sex market and thus strategically employ their 'Brazilianness' to take advantage of the hypersexualised construction of a racialised nationality (Piscitelli 2011; Silva and Ornat 2014, 2016). In their written texts of presentation, most of them explicitly say they are from Brazil, use very typical Brazilian names, or add a small flag of Brazil next to their names, as is possible on one of the websites. Moreover, while self-presenting themselves as 'brunette of infarction,' 'very hot mulatta,' or 'beautiful brunette with a cinnamon skin, hot as the summer' *travestis* are racialising their bodies and taking advantage of a 'sexualised negritude' (Pelúcio 2008, 12) that (only) has a positive meaning in their transnational contexts and in the field of sex work. We have seen in Chap. 4 that, when in Brazil, they carry out practices to whiten their appearance; in Europe, *travestis* and their clients value the brown/*mulata* identity as an element that gives them prestige in the transnational sex work market (Duque 2011). In this way, 'nationality/raciality is thus used strategically to improve their economic situation, which demonstrates that identities that are normally experienced as oppressive can also be used to overcome other oppressions' (Silva and Ornat 2014, 1082). Therefore, through the images or videos included in their announcements, *travestis* display how 'hot' and 'sexy' *mulatas* can be and openly exhibit their penises, buttocks, and breasts when posing erotically. The detailed description and exposition of their endowment are of great importance, as their 'big' and 'erect' penises are highly appraised by the clients who mostly prefer to be penetrated. In sum, working in flats has become one of the main modalities of sex work in Barcelona. Beyond the 'idyllic' dream of becoming a ('top') 'European,' the Spanish sex market can be tough, and Brazilian *travestis* reproduce a view of themselves as very 'hot' and 'sexy' (*mulatas*). In doing this, they appropriate and make a positive use of these racialised objectifications to stand out as desired sex workers.

The travel comes to an end. Although, in reality, this journey never ends, because the processes that comprise it are constantly being reconfigured and negotiated. However, at least partially, we have accompanied a large part of the corporeal, sexual, and spatial experiences of some Brazilian *travestis*, both in Rio de Janeiro and in Barcelona. While there is not one common journey, many *travesti* sex workers usually transit on similar paths to become what they want to *be*. Yet they do not claim a finalist transition from one gender to another, one to rest safely at 'home.' Rather, their journey is constantly shaped by many borders that delineate *travestis'* identities. We have seen that it is not easy to move as a trans person in public places. Discrimination, prejudice, and violence can structure most of trans people's daily experiences. Trans mobilities are thus acts of survival, which enable them to embody both pleasure and social rejection. Following their most significant migratory displacements, *travestis* showed us that their mobilities also contribute to their becoming intelligible subjects. The spatial and embodied journeys converge to give sense to *travestis'* constant processes of transformation. In this way, I framed this chapter within the particularities of trans migrations to understand that their spatial mobilisations were not exclusively for economic reasons, but to satisfy wider demands at the level of sexuality and gender (to live their sexual practices and gender identities more freely), the corporeal (to feminise and beautify the bodies), and the social (to be more respected by the society and admired by their peers).

In addition, the description of the territories of sex work in both cities allowed us to better comprehend local dynamics related to *travestis'* aesthetic presentations, sexual practices, or clients' socioeconomic status (the latter being more differentiated in Rio). Although street sex work is part of most *travestis'* experiences regarding sex work, in Barcelona, it was more difficult to work in the streets due to regulations and police persecution as sex workers 'without papers.' However, as professional sex workers, Brazilian *travestis* are highly valued by clients who are looking for 'women with something else.' Once in Europe, *travestis* perform strategically their 'Brazilianness' and sexualise their 'brownness' to work more and, ultimately, become 'successful' (and 'top') 'Europeans,' a status also lived and experienced through their bodies: they feel more beautiful and desired, and make profit from it. Concurrently, the history of the first *travestis* who arrived in Europe (Paris) has contributed to the understanding of the great influence Europe has had in the construction of *travestis'* identities. Finally, although Europe is represented as a step forward among the *travestis*, the price they have to pay is also high and the fine line between 'success' and 'failure' is many times too fragile, making the desire for a 'good life' to be just a dream.

Notes

1. When analysing trans women sex workers' experiences in Bogotá, Colombia, Ritterbusch (2016) uses the concept '(im)mobility' to describe their limited mobility to four blocks in the city. She recounts that '(im)mobilities are forcibly imposed as a means of maintaining traditional, heteronormative relations in society and as a means of eliminating deviant gender identities from society or keeping them at a distance' (424). See also Doan (2016).
2. The local expression to name Venezuelan trans (*travesti*) people.
3. In Brazil, sex workers call *pontos* to the places where they can work in the streets. Most of them are controlled by *mães/madrinhas*, and then *travestis* must pay to them in order to be allowed to work there.
4. Although it is very frequent that Glória is considered as belonging to the City Centre, in fact, it jurisdictionally corresponds to the beginning of the South Zone. However, I will follow local perceptions which locate Glória in the City Centre not only because of its extreme proximity to this area, but also because the practices and social representations of the neighbourhood are more similar to the City Centre than to the South Zone (the latter, one of the most bourgeois areas of the city).
5. For the *travestis*, it was important to distinguish the ways in which the clients approached them. The differences were generally evident among the clients who arrived on foot and in cars, that is, *travestis* identified more affluent clients according to their cars.
6. This 'toleration' is very different from what it happens in the tourist and wealthy districts of Copacabana, Ipanema, or Barra da Tijuca, where the child sexual exploitation is, formally, 'combated.' During 2007 and 2008, the Government of the State of Rio de Janeiro launched a series of operations called 'CopaBacana,' 'IpaBacana,' and 'BarraBacana' (in Portuguese, *bacana* means 'fantastic') to make an urban 'cleaning' of Copacabana, Ipanema, and Barra da Tijuca, respectively. They then focused on 'combating' child sexual exploitation, drunk drivers, or street vendors. During the fieldwork, and especially in Barra da Tijuca, I noticed how the police especially intimidated the clients of prostitution (and the *travestis* were very angry about this operation). One of the members of the project of the City Council highlighted the contradictions between the policies of the Government of the State of Rio de Janeiro that, ultimately, sought to end prostitution, and the programmes of the City Council of Rio de Janeiro that delivered condoms among women and *travesti* sex workers (Field notes, 22 August 2008).

7. The nearest hotel was about 5 km, the more expensive option for those who wished to spend the whole night with them.
8. In this section, I will keep the original names of the *travestis* who are publicly known in Brazil, with the exception of my interviewees of whom I prefer to remain anonymous.
9. Generally, the great majority of *travestis* enter the Spanish territory as ('false') tourists. This method, however, does not guarantee entry to the country. Police officers working at airports identify, with a wide margin of discretion, people who are possibly 'false tourists.' Because of the significant presence of Brazilian women and *travestis* in the Spanish sex industry, this type of police intervention focuses mainly on flights coming from countries such as Brazil (López Riopedre 2010).
10. Policies on sex trafficking focus exclusively on abused women and children. Trans people do not need to be 'saved' from an official discourse nor do they often feel exploited (Patrício 2008; Piscitelli 2008; Teixeira 2008).
11. https://www.slumi.com/travestis/espa%C3%B1a, http://www.erosguia.com/, http://www.taiakashemales.com/, http://www.rincontranny.com/portal/

References

Ahmed, Sara, Claudia Castañeda, Anne-Marie Fortier, and Mimi Sheller, eds. 2003. *Uprootings/Regroundings. Questions of Home and Migrations*. Oxford/New York: Berg.

Aizura, Aren. 2006. Of Borders and Homes: The Imaginary Community of (Trans)sexual Citizenship. *Inter-Asia Cultural Studies* 7 (2): 289–309.

———. 2014. Trans Feminine Value, Racialized Others and the Limits of Necropolitics. In *Queer Necropolitics*, ed. Jin Haritaworn, Adi Kuntsman, and Silvia Posocco, 129–147. Abingdon/New York: Routledge.

Alsop, Rachel, Annette Fitzsimons, and Kathleen Lennon. 2002. *Theorizing Gender*. Cambridge: Polity Press.

Anderson, Bridget. 2017. Towards a New Politics of Migration? *Journal Ethnic and Racial Studies* 40 (9): 1527–1537.

Annes, Alexis, and Meredith Redlin. 2012. Coming Out and Coming Back: Rural Gay Migration and the City. *Journal of Rural Studies* 28 (1): 56–68.

Anzaldúa, Gloria. 1987. *Borderlands/La Frontera: The New Mestiza*. San Francisco: Aunt Lute Books.

Bailey, Marlon. 2011. Gender/Racial Realness: Theorizing the Gender System in Ballroom Culture. *Feminist Studies* 37 (2): 365–386.

Bastos, José A. 1980. Eloína dá o serviço: operação, implantes, silicone, etc. *Lampião da Esquina* 2 (21): 3. http://www.grupodignidade.org.br/wp-content/uploads/2015/11/25-LAMPIAO-DA-ESQUINA-EDICAO-21-FEVEREIRO-1980.pdf. Accessed 30 July 2012.

Baydar, Gülsüm. 2012. Sexualised Productions of Space. *Gender, Place and Culture* 19 (6): 699–706.

Bell, David, and Jon Binnie. 2000. *The Sexual Citizen: Queer Politics and Beyond*. Cambridge: Polity Press.

Benedetti, Marcos. 2005. *Toda feita: o corpo e o gênero das travestis*. Rio de Janeiro: Garamond.

Berlant, Lauren. 2011. *Cruel Optimism*. Durham: Duke University Press.

Blanchette, Thaddeus, and Ana P. Silva. 2004. *A mistura clássica: o apelo do Rio de Janeiro como destino para o turismo sexual*. Rio de Janeiro: Leitura Crítica.

———. 2011. Prostitution in Contemporary Rio de Janeiro. In *Policing Pleasure: Sex Work, Policy, and the State in Global Perspective*, ed. Susan Dewey and Patty Kelly, 130–145. New York: New York University Press.

Blanchette, Thaddeus, Gregory Mitchell, and Laura Murray. 2017. Discretionary Policing, or the Lesser Part of Valor: Prostitution, Law Enforcement, and Unregulated Regulation in Rio de Janeiro's Sexual Economy. *Criminal Justice and Law Enforcement* 7 (2): 31–74.

Brown, Michael. 2000. *Closet Space: Geographies of Metaphor from the Body to the Globe*. New York: Routledge.

Brown, Michel. 2012. Gender and Sexuality I: Intersectional Anxieties. *Progress in Human Geography* 36 (4): 541–550.

Browne, Kath. 2004. Genderism and the Bathroom Problem: (Re)materializing Sexed Sites, (Re)creating Sexed Bodies. *Gender, Place and Culture* 11: 331–346.

Cantú, Lionel. 2002. *De Ambiente*. Queer Tourism and the Shifting Boundaries of Mexican Male Sexualities. *GLQ: A Journal of Lesbian and Gay Studies* 8 (1–2): 139–166.

Cantú, Lionel, Nancy Naples, and Salvador Vidal-Ortiz, eds. 2009. *The Sexuality of Migration: Border Crossings and Mexican Immigrant Men*. New York: New York University Press.

Carrillo, Héctor. 2004. Sexual Migration, Cross-Cultural Sexual Encounters, and Sexual Health. *Sexuality Research and Social Policy* 1 (3): 58–70.

Corrêa, Gustavo. 2009. Carmens e drags: reflexões sobre os travestimentos transgenéricos no carnaval carioca. MA dissertation, University of the State of Rio de Janeiro (Brazil).

Cotten, Trystan. 2012. Introduction: Migration and Morphing. In *Transgender Migrations. The Bodies, Borders, and Politics of Transition*, ed. Trystan Cotton, 1–7. New York/London: Routledge.

Cresswell, Tim. 2004. *Place: A Short Introduction*. Oxford: Blackwell.

Doan, Petra. 2009. Safety and Urban Environments. Transgendered Experiences of the City. *Women and Environments International Magazine* 78 (79): 22–25.

———. 2010. The Tyranny of Gendered Spaces – Reflections from Beyond the Gender Dichotomy. *Gender, Place and Culture* 17 (5): 635–654.

———. 2016. You've Come a Long Way, Baby: Unpacking the Metaphor of Transgender Mobility. In *The Routledge Research Companion to Geographies of Sex and Sexualities*, ed. Gavin Brown and Kath Browne, 237–246. Abingdon/New York: Routledge.

Domínguez, Juan F. 2011. *Transexualidad en España: Análisis de la Realidad Social y Factores Psicosociales Asociados*. Malaga: Faculty of Social and Labour Studies, University of Malaga and FELGTB.

Duque, Tiago. 2011. *Montagens e Desmontagens: desejo, estigma e vergonha entre travestis adolescentes*. São Paulo: Annablume.

Fernández Bessa, Cristina. 2010. Movilidad bajo sospecha. El conveniente vínculo entre inmigración y criminalidad en las políticas migratorias de la Unión Europea. *Revista Interdisciplinar da Mobilidade Humana* XVIII (35): 137–154.

Fernández Dávila, Percy, and Adriana Morales. 2011. *Estudio TranSex 2010. Conductas de riesgo y detección de necesidades para la prevención del VIH/ITS en mujeres transexuales trabajadoras sexuales*. Barcelona: Stop SIDA. [Unpublished Technical Report].

Figari, Carlos. 2009. *Eróticas de la disidencia en América Latina: Brasil, siglos XVII al XX*. Buenos Aires: Fundación Centro de Integración, Comunicación, Cultura y Sociedad – CICCUS and CLACSO.

Foerster, Maxime. 2014. On the History of Transsexuals in France. In *Transgender Experience: Place, Ethnicity, and Visibility*, ed. Chantal Zabus and David Coad, 19–30. New York: Routledge.

Fortier, Anne-Marie. 2003. Making Home: Queer Migrations and Motions of Attachment. In *Uprootings/Regroundings. Questions of Home and Migrations*, ed. Sara Ahmed, Claudia Castañeda, Anne-Marie Fortier, and Mimi Sheller, 115–135. Oxford/New York: Berg.

García, Antonio G., and M. Sara Oñate. 2010. De viajes y cuerpos: proyectos migratorios e itinerarios corporales de mujeres transexuales ecuatorianas en Murcia. In *Tránsitos migratorios: Contextos transnacionales y proyectos familiares en las migraciones actuales*, ed. García Antonio, M. Elena Gadea, and Andrés Pedreño, 361–403. Murcia: Universidad de Murcia.

Garcia, Marcos R.V., and Yvette P. Lehman. 2011. Issues Concerning the Informality and Outdoor Sex Work Performed by *Travestis* in São Paulo, Brazil. *Archives of Sexual Behavior* 40: 1211–1221.

Gopinath, Gayatri. 2005. *Impossible Desires: Queer Diasporas and South Asian Public Cultures*. Durham: Duke University Press.

Gorman-Murray, Andrew. 2007. Rethinking Queer Migration Through the Body. *Social and Cultural Geography* 8 (1): 105–121.

———. 2009. Intimate Mobilities: Emotional Embodiment and Queer Migration. *Social and Cultural Geography* 10 (4): 441–460.

Green, James. 1999. *Beyond Carnival: Male Homosexuality in Twentieth-Century Brazil*. Chicago: The University of Chicago Press.

GGB, Gay Group of Bahia. 2016. *Relatório: Assassinatos de LGBT no Brasil*. https://homofobiamata.files.wordpress.com/2017/01/relatc3b3rio-2016-ps.pdf. Accessed 25 July 2017.

Halberstam, Jack. 1998. *Female Masculinity*. Durham: Duke University Press.

———. 2005. *In a Queer Time and Place: Transgender Bodies, Subcultural Lives*. Nova York: New York University Press.

Herring, Scott. 2010. *Another Country: Queer Anti-urbanism*. New York: New York University Press.

Hines, Sally. 2006. What's the Difference? Bringing Particularity to Queer Studies of Transgender. *Journal of Gender Studies* 15 (1): 49–66.

Howe, Cymene, Susanna Zaraysky, and Lois Lorentzen. 2008. Transgender Sex Workers and Sexual Transmigration Between Guadalajara and San Francisco. *Latin American Perspectives* 158 (35/1): 31–50.

Hubbard, Phil, Roger Matthews, and Jane Scoular. 2008. Regulating Sex Work in the EU: Prostitute Women and the New Spaces of Exclusion. *Gender, Place and Culture* 15 (2): 137–152.

Hutta, Jan, and Carsten Balzer. 2013. Identities and Citizenship Under Construction: Historicising the 'T' in LGBT Anti-violence Politics in Brazil. In *Queer Presences and Absences*, ed. Yvette Taylor and Michelle Addison, 69–90. Basingstoke: Palgrave Macmillan.

IBGE, Brazilian Institute of Geography and Statistics. 2016. *Pesquisa nacional por amostra de domicílios: síntese de indicadores 2015*. http://biblioteca.ibge.gov.br/visualizacao/livros/liv98887.pdf. Accessed 25 July 2017.

IPC-IG, International Policy Centre for Inclusive Growth. 2016. *Perfil da pobreza: Norte e Nordeste rurais*. http://www.ipc-undp.org/pub/port/Perfil_da_pobreza_Norte_e_Nordeste_rurais.pdf. Accessed 25 July 2017.

Johnston, Lynda. 2016. Gender and Sexuality I: Genderqueer Geographies? *Progress in Human Geography* 40 (5): 668–678.

Kaplan, Caren. 1996. *Questions of Travel*. Durham: Duke University Press.

Kulick, Don. 1998. *Travesti: Sex, Gender and Culture Among Brazilian Transgendered Prostitutes*. Chicago: University of Chicago Press.

Langarita, Jose A., and M. Alejandra Salguero. 2017. Sexiled in Mexico City: Urban Migrations Motivated by Sexual Orientation. *Bulletin of Latin American Research* 36: 68–81.

Lefebvre, Henri. 1991. *The Production of Space*. Oxford: Blackwell.

Lewis, Vek. 2012. Volviendo visible lo invisible: hacia un marco conceptual de las migraciones internas trans en México. *Cuicuilco* 54: 219–240.

———. 2014. Nuevos Ambientes, ¿Historias Compartidas? Sexuality, Cultural and Sexual Identity and Practices Among Gay-identified Latin American Migrants in Sydney. *Journal of Intercultural Studies* 35 (5): 513–531.

Lewis, Rachel, and Nancy Naples. 2014. Introduction: Queer Migration, Asylum, and Displacement. *Sexualities* 17 (8): 911–918.

López Riopedre, José. 2010. Inmigración colombiana y brasileña y prostitución femenina en la ciudad de Lugo: Historias de vida de mujeres que ejercen la prostitución en pisos de contacto. PhD dissertation, The National Distance Education University (Spain).

Luibhéid, Eithne, and Lionel Cantú, eds. 2005. *Queer Migrations: Sexuality, U.S. Citizenship, and Border Crossings*. Minneapolis/London: University of Minnesota Press.

Manalansan, Martin. 2005. Race, Violence, and Neoliberal Spatial Politics in the Global City. *Social Text* 23 (3–4(84–85)): 141–155.

———. 2006. Queer Intersections: Sexuality and Gender in Migration Studies. *International Migration Review* 40 (1): 224–249.

Masanet, Erika, Rosana Baeninger, and Miguel Mateo. 2012. La inmigración brasileña en España: características, singularidades e influencia de las vinculaciones históricas. *Papeles de población* 18 (71): 87–119. http://www.scielo.org.mx/scielo.php?script=sci_arttext&pid=S1405-74252012000100004&lng=es&tlng=es. Accessed 2 Aug 2017.

Massey, Doreen. 1994. *Space, Place, and Gender*. Minneapolis: University of Minnesota Press.

McDowell, Linda. 1999. *Gender, Identity and Place: Understanding Feminist Geographies*. Minneapolis: University of Minnesota Press.

Medeiros, Regina P. 2002. *Hablan las putas. Sobre prácticas sexuales, preservativos y SIDA en el mundo de la prostitución*. Barcelona: Virus Editorial.

Miskolci, Richard. 2014. Negociando visibilidades: segredo e desejo em relações homoeróticas masculinas criadas por mídias digitais. *Bagoas – Estudos gays, gêneros e sexualidades* 8 (11): 51–78.

Morokvasic, Mirjana. 1984. Birds of Passage Are Also Women. *International Migration Review* 18 (4): 886–907.

Namaste, Viviane. 2006. *Genderbashing*. Sexuality, Gender, and the Regulation of Public Space. In *The Transgender Studies Reader*, ed. Susan Stryker and Stephen Whittle, 584–600. New York: Routledge.

Nash, Catherine. 2010. Trans Geographies, Embodiment and Experience. *Gender, Place and Culture* 17 (5): 579–595. New York: New York University Press.

Padilla, Mark, Sheilla Rodríguez-Madera, Nelson Varas-Díaz, and Alixida Ramos-Pibernus. 2016. Trans-Migrations: Border-Crossing and the Politics of Body Modification Among Puerto Rican Transgender Women. *International Journal of Sexual Health* 28 (4): 261–277.

Parker, Richard. 1999. *Beneath the Equator: Cultures of Desire, Male Homosexuality, and Emerging Gay Communities in Brazil*. New York: Routledge.

Patrício, Maria Cecília. 2008. No truque: transnacionalidade e distinção entre travestis brasileiras. PhD dissertation, Federal University of Pernambuco (Brazil).

Patton, Cindy, and Benigno Sánchez-Eppler, eds. 2000. *Queer Diasporas*. Durham: Duke University Press.

Pelúcio, Larissa. 2008. Travestis brasileiras: singularidades nacionais, desejos transnacionais. Paper Presented at the 26 Brazilian Anthropology Meeting, Porto Seguro, June 1–4.

———. 2009. *Abjeção e Desejo: uma etnografia travesti sobre o modelo preventivo de aids*. São Paulo: Annablume, Fapesp.

———. 2011. 'Amores perros' – sexo, paixão e dinheiro na relação entre espanhóis e travestis brasileiras no mercado transnacional do sexo. In *Gênero, sexo, amor e dinheiro: mobilidades transnacionais envolvendo o Brasil*, ed. Adriana Piscitelli, Glaucia de Oliveira Assis, and José M. Nieto Olivar, 185–224. Campinas: Unicamp/PAGU.

Perlongher, Néstor. 2008 (1987). *O negócio do michê: Prostituição viril em São Paulo*. São Paulo: Editora Fundação Perseu Abramo.

Phizacklea, Annie, ed. 1983. *One Way Ticket: Migration and Female Labour*. London: Routledge and Kegan Paul.

Pierrot. 2006. *Memorias Trans. Transexuales-Travestis-Transformistas*. Barcelona: Morales i Torres Editores.

Piscitelli, Adriana. 2008. Entre as 'máfias' e a 'ajuda': a construção de conhecimento sobre tráfico de pessoas. *Cadernos Pagu* (31): 29–63.

———. 2011. ¿Actuar la brasileñidad? Tránsitos a partir del mercado del sexo. *Etnográfica* 15 (1): 5–29.

Platero, Lucas. 2014. Trans*exualidades. In *Acompañamiento, factores de salud y recursos educativos*. Barcelona: Edicions Bellaterra.

Prosser, Jay. 1998. *Second Skins: The Body Narratives of Transsexuality*. New York: Columbia University Press.

Puar, Jasbir. 2002a. *Queer Tourism: Geographies of Globalization*. Durham: Duke University Press.

———. 2002b. Circuits of Queer Mobility: Tourism, Travel, and Globalization. *GLQ: A Journal of Lesbian and Gay Studies* 8 (1–2): 101–137.

———. 2007. *Terrorist Assemblages: Homonationalism in Queer Times*. Durham: Duke University Press.

Ritterbusch, Amy. 2016. Mobilities at Gunpoint: The Geographies of (Im)mobility of Transgender Sex Workers in Colombia. *Annals of the American Association of Geographers* 106 (2): 422–433.

Rojas, Daniela, Iván Zaro, and Teresa Navazo. 2009. *Trabajadoras transexuales del sexo: el doble estigma*. Madrid: Fundación Triángulo.

Rose, Gillian. 1993. *Feminism and Geography: The Limits of Geographical Knowledge*. Minneapolis: University of Minnesota Press.

———. 1995. Place and Identity: A Sense of Place. In *A Place in the World? Places, Culture and Globalization*, ed. Doreen Massey and Pat Jess, 87–132. Milton Keynes: The Open University.

Sassen, Saskia. 2005. The Global City: Introducing a Concept. *The Brown Journal of World Affairs* 11 (2): 27–43.

Sharpe, Pamela. 2001. Introduction: Gender and the Experience of Migration. In *Women, Gender and Labour Migration*, ed. Pamela Sharpe, 1–14. London: Routledge.

Silva, Hélio. 1993. *Travesti: a invenção do femenino*. Rio de Janeiro: Relume Dumará.

Silva, Joseli M. 2013. Espaço interdito e a experiência urbana travesti. In *Geografias malditas: corpos, sexualidades e espaços*, ed. Joseli Silva, Marcio Ornat, and Alides Chimin Jr, 143–182. Ponta Grossa: Todapalavra.

Silva, Joseli M., and Marcio J. Ornat. 2014. Intersectionality and Transnational Mobility Between Brazil and Spain in *Travesti* Prostitution Networks. *Gender, Place and Culture* 22 (8): 1073–1088.

—. 2016. Sexualities, Tropicalizations and the Transnational Sex Trade: Brazilian Women in Spain. In *The Routledge Research Companion to Geographies of Sex and Sexualities*, ed. Gavin Brown and Kath Browne, 331–340. Abingdon/New York: Routledge.

Silva, Ana P., and Thaddeus Blanchette. 2011. Amor um real por minuto: a prostituição como atividade econômica no Brasil urbano. In *Sexualidade e política na América Latina: histórias, intersecções e paradoxos*, ed. Richard Parker and Sonia Corrêa, 192–233. Rio de Janeiro: Sexual Policy Watch.

TAMPEP. 2009. *Sex Work in Europe: A Mapping of the Prostitution Scene in 25 European Countries*. http://tampep.eu/documents/TAMPEP%202009%20European%20Mapping%20Report.pdf. Accessed 4 May 2015.

Teixeira, Flávia do B. 2008. L'Italia dei Divieti: entre o sonho de ser *européia* e o *babado* da prostituição. *Cadernos Pagu* 31: 275–308.

—. 2011. *Juízo* e *Sorte*: enredando *maridos* e *clientes* nas narrativas sobre o projeto migratório das travestis brasileiras para a Itália. In *Gênero, sexo, amor e dinheiro: mobilidades transnacionais envolvendo o Brasil*, ed. Adriana Piscitelli, Glaucia de Oliveira Assis, and José M. Nieto Olivar, 225–262. Campinas: Unicamp/PAGU.

Teixeira, Marcelo de A. 2015. 'Metronormatividades' nativas: migrações homossexuais e espaços urbanos no Brasil. *Áskesis* 4 (1): 23–38.

TGEU, Transgender Europe. 2017. Trans Day of Remembrance (TDoR) 2017. Trans Murder Monitoring (TMM) Research Project Update. *Transrespect Versus Transphobia Worldwide*, November 20. http://transrespect.org/en/tmm-update-trans-day-remembrance-2017/. Accessed 2 Jan 2018.

Trevisan, João. 2007 (1986). *Devassos no paraíso: a homossexualidade no Brasil, da colônia à atualidade*. Rio de Janeiro: Record.

Vale, Alexandre F. C. 2005. O Vôo da Beleza: travestilidade e devir minoritário. PhD dissertation, Federal University of Ceará (Brazil).

Vogel, Katrin. 2009. The Mother, the Daughter, and the Cow: Venezuelan *Transformistas'* Migration to Europe. *Mobilities* 4 (3): 367–387.

Wang, Sean. 2014. Encountering Metronormativity: Geographies of Queer Visibility in Central New York. *Wagadu: A Journal of Transnational Women's and Gender Studies* 12: 92–124.

Williams, Erica. 2014. Sex Work and Exclusion in the Tourist Districts of Salvador, Brazil. *Gender, Place and Culture* 21 (4): 453–470.

8

Travestis' Paradoxes in the Contemporary World

In 2017, Brazilian visual artist Nayara Leite presented at the University of the Arts in London an installation called The Good Garden—*O Bom Jardim* in Portuguese—the location where *travesti* Dandara dos Santos was brutally tortured and killed by five men in the city of Fortaleza, Northeast Brazil, in February of that year. The crime gained international attention because it was recorded on a mobile phone, and the video was circulated on the Internet. In the video, it was possible to see Dandara 'sitting on the ground, covered in dust and blood, being kicked in the face, beaten with a plank of wood and forced into a wheelbarrow. According to the authorities, she was later taken to a nearby street, shot twice in the face and then bludgeoned; the killing is not shown in the video' (Phillips 2017). The installation piece sought to show the alarming and violent number of trans people's killings in Brazil, the country with the highest trans murder rate in the world (TGEU, Transgender Europe 2017). Artist Leite used both a poster with 136 frames extracted from the video and a wheelbarrow with soil to represent Dandara's death and funeral. The object was filled with 136 photographs of Dandara buried in it. Each photograph had also the name and causes of death of the other 135 trans people who were killed between February 2016 and February 2017 in Brazil (Jorge 2017).

© The Author(s) 2018
J. Vartabedian, *Brazilian* Travesti *Migrations*, Genders and Sexualities
in the Social Sciences, https://doi.org/10.1007/978-3-319-77101-4_8

225

One week after Dandara's murder, on the newsstands all over the world, Brazilian trans model Valentina Sampaio appeared on the cover of the influential French Vogue fashion magazine with the cover line 'Transgender beauty: How they are shaking up the world.' The French Vogue's editor asserted that being a trans person 'is a detail one would prefer not to have to mention,' adding that Valentina was on the cover not only for her beauty 'but because despite herself she embodies an age-old, arduous struggle to be recognized and not be perceived as something Other, a gender exile' (Thomas 2017). Valentina grew up in Aquiraz, a small coastal town very near Fortaleza, Northeast Brazil. She had the support of her parents, studied fashion, and moved to São Paulo to work in a modelling agency, after being discovered by a makeup artist some years before. She also appeared on the cover of Elle Brazil and is currently the ambassador for L'Oréal Paris.

Dandara and Valentina embody one of the many paradoxes we have discussed throughout this book. Although both were born in the same state of the country (Ceará, part of one of the most transphobic regions of Brazil), their lives' circumstances were very different. Dandara was from a low-income class, had only completed primary education, self-identified as *travesti*, and worked as a sex worker in São Paulo and Rio de Janeiro for many years. According to her mother, 'My "son" [as she calls Dandara] lived being humiliated' (Lavor 2017, my emphasis). As described in Chap. 3, Dandara was considered an abject being, somebody outside any intelligibility and who 'deserved' to die. Conversely, Valentina comes from a middle-class family, her parents paid her university fees, always felt a 'woman,' and has no single story of bullying while she was studying because 'everything was very natural' and her schoolmates respected her, as she was seen 'as a little girl' (Lucon 2016). She lives travelling and working as an international model. Although Valentina's trans 'detail,' as the editor of Vogue mentioned, is (still) displayed as a 'successful' example (one of the few that exist in Brazil) of trans people's rights for recognition and equality, her body is 'fostered for living' (Puar 2007, 36). In Chap. 6, the concept 'queer necropolitics' allowed us to understand 'the symbiotic co-presence of life and death' (Haritaworn et al. 2014, 2) in which some (queer) bodies are let live and others *must* die. In this way, Dandara and Valentina reflect the contradictions of a Brazilian heteronormative society which renders some trans bodies more valuable than others while they are intersected by class, race, gender, sexuality, and education, as identitary elements which situate them differently on the side of life or death.

In addition, while Brazil is represented as a 'paradise' of beauty in which Brazilians seem to be more tolerant of sexual and gender diversity, as shown in its Carnival festivities, one LGBTI person is killed every 25 hours in Brazil, and the risk of murder is 14 times greater for trans people (generally, for those identified as *travestis*) compared to gay people (GGB, Gay Group of Bahia 2016). As was examined in Chap. 4, Brazil is transnationally recognised for its beautiful beaches and landscapes, beautiful models such as Gisele Bündchen, Adriana Lima, Lea T, and Valentina Sampaio, and beautiful *mulatas*—the queens of the popular Carnival festivities. Brazil is revealed as one of the most important centres of plastic surgery in the world, and its techniques and surgeons are respected and copied worldwide. In a country where appearance matters as a means of upward mobility, feeling beautiful and in good shape become social mandates that traverse all of the social strata. As the most famous surgeon Ivo Pitanguy declared, everybody should have the 'right to beauty' and poor people also deserve better chances in life. While Brazilian white models are praised all over the world, darker (and poorer) ones remain sexualised. In this way, local and transnational perceptions of Brazilian women's beauty have contributed to the promotion of what Carrier-Moisan (2015) calls a 'tropical paradise' in which, mainly, foreign men imagine the highly eroticised black or *mulata* women are available for any sexual encounter. One participant of the 'first generation' of *travestis* recounted that female Brazilians have men's preference because 'they have the fame for the Carnival, the samba, the women are naked on the promenade. When from abroad people think in Brazil, they think of the Carnival and naked women' (Lina, personal interview, 6 August 2008, Rio de Janeiro). Brazilians' 'success' within the transnational sex market also reinforces this myth based on a colonial project which has exoticised and sexualised *its* women (Piscitelli 2011; Silva and Ornat 2016). Concurrently, the Carnival is thought of as a place where gender roles are reversed and its supposed freedom and permissiveness are widely celebrated. But heterosexual men who temporarily become transvestites rather than reversing gender roles are, in fact, collectively reaffirming their masculinity through a parody or farce, as Figari (2009) explained. Social, racial, sexual, or gender inequalities are not erased during the Carnival and are, indeed, maintained.

In sum, Brazil is imagined as a 'tropical paradise' in which the beauty, tolerance, and freedom of its inhabitants make it a 'dream' country in Latin America. However, Brazilians' daily reality is more complex and crossed by racial, social, and sexual inequalities that do not disappear under the scalpel nor during Carnival. *Travestis* are still far from being accepted and respected in contemporary Brazil. Thus, as Kulick's (1998) ethnography has demystified, *travestis* are not a symbol of the country's gender and sexual diversity, but their killings are the effect of the 'structural violence' (Lewis 2012) of a rigid heteronormative society which considers them illegitimate non-subjects. It may be unusual to talk simultaneously about beauty and death, life and suffering, desire and hate. However, it is in this context of great polarities and paradoxes where Brazilian *travesti* sex workers embody the contradictions of a society which maintains a love and hate relationship with them: they are loved as hypersexualised sex workers but also hated as abject beings. They are desired as 'fascinating' subjects but also perceived as dangerous people, dehumanised, and left outside any neoliberal productivity (Aizura 2014; Edelman 2014). In this book, thus, I wondered how it is to become a *travesti* in a social milieu with so much antagonism. How is it, as Marcia Ochoa questions when referring to the Venezuelan *transformistas*, to be 'able to exist within a space of violence and death, to negotiate its excesses, and to make [their] bod[ies] out of these excesses' (2014, 164). In other words, how is it to become a 'beautiful' and 'feminine' *travesti* in a society which, ultimately, lets them die?

Feeling Beautiful as a Strategy of Survival

In Chap. 4, *travesti* beauty was presented as a *feeling* that exists in its continuous *doing*, that is, beauty is experienced through daily routines and work on their appearance and it is produced through a relational interaction between the individual and the social (Moreno Figueroa 2013). As

Colebrook (2006) has questioned, the point is not if beauty is bad or good, but how the pragmatics of beauty intersects with gender, race, class, and ageing while beauty is being experienced by the subjects. For the *travestis*, as part of a Brazilian culture which valorises beauty, modifying their physical appearance was not thought of as a merely hedonistic or superficial task, but as an empowering practice which situates them—although uncertainly—in the world. The participants recounted that becoming *travestis* was a decision that required—according to most of them—certain body modifications and a will towards feeling like beautiful *travestis*:

> I wanted another life for myself. My dream was to become a *travesti*, to transform myself, to be beautiful and it was my own choice of becoming a *travesti*. Then nature helped me a little, and [laughing] I became the woman I am today ... Most come [to Rio de Janeiro] in search of success, to make a living, to become a *travesti*, to be transformed as the great majority arrive as gay, without experience. So they come in search of transformation. I came here, I was inspired by Reyna [her *madrinha*], I saw that body, that beautiful *travesti* so I was doing little by little. I may not be like her but I'm getting there, I'm fine, I'm well transformed. (Samanta, personal interview, 8 September 2008, Rio de Janeiro)

Samanta made it clear that her decision to become a *travesti* was part of a 'dream,' a long process in which she was inspired by her *madrinha* to learn how to transform herself. In this way, their identities as *travestis* are something that confers 'success,' money, beauty, and, as Priscila expressed, the opportunity to feel desired and praised: 'I admired the woman, when a beautiful woman passed and the boys made compliments to her, you know? I kept looking and watching, thinking "Ah! This is what I want to be," so that men could admire me. I thought that was very glamorous, a beautiful girl passing by and a man giving her a compliment, do you understand? I think it's cool' (Priscila, personal interview, 22 May 2008, Rio de Janeiro). Lina also remembered when she was young that:

> When I transformed myself, I was luckier, not only here, but also in Europe. I had many gifts from rich men, millionaires, I won many jewels, coats, things of beauty, I was beautiful, feminine, blonde ... I felt very beloved, so courted even them [the men] knowing that I was a *travesti*, they

noticed it because I was a young and different woman, was in makeup, with lipstick and was full of glamour while I walked in the street. (Lina, personal interview, 6 August 2008, Rio de Janeiro)

Beauty, thus, becomes a profitable 'treasure' which enables them to stand out and be 'different' women, admired and desired while they take economic advantage of it. As Roberta stressed, people can say, 'Wow! *He*'s a *travesti*, *he*'s a *viado* [fag] but *he*'s beautiful' (personal interview, 7 August 2008, Rio de Janeiro, my emphasis).[1] In this way, beauty allows the *travestis* to show that they are something more than 'fags' and *gayzinhos*. Beauty gives them prestige and situates them favourably within their own social stratum. Also, as we have seen, the gaze of the others (more particularly, men) contributes to their self-reaffirmation as 'beautiful' *travestis*. I agree with Alvaro Jarrín (2017) in that beautification practices are simultaneously empowering and disempowering and that it would be too simplistic to consider that *travestis* have internalised sexism when they modify their bodies *only* for men and according to an exclusively economic rationality as sex workers. In doing that, we would erase 'how actors on the ground experience beauty and embrace it for their own purposes' (Jarrín 2017, 197). Therefore, *travestis* are not *mere* beauty consumers, but beauty has productive effects over their lives as it is a means to become legible subjects and achieve social recognition, mainly among their peers and local admirers. In addition, *travestis*' embodiment itineraries never end. In their search for 'perfection,' most follow different aesthetic practices to reach it. As this is an unattainable ideal, they embark in an endless and expensive process which causes them many sufferings: beauty is also about pain and the risky practices of beautification.

Beauty, thus, is one of the main elements *travestis* have to give sense to their gender identities: while becoming 'beautiful' *travestis*, they are constructing themselves as social subjects who claim certain intelligibility; not gays, nor *viados*, but *travestis*, 'beautiful' *travestis*. One of the first conclusions of this book is that *travestis*' identity formations are closely related to the goal of feeling like beautiful, desired, and admired *travestis*. I understand it as a first strategy of survival to become legible subjects in a social context that dehumanises them. This does not mean that 'beautiful' *travestis* are not killed in Brazil. Although 'beautiful,' as sex workers, as black, *morenas* or working-class, they can be the target of transphobia. However, beauty—at least temporarily, as it is part of an ongoing and endless process of transformation—strengthens their identities as *travestis* and situates them in the world. To remember Samanta's powerful statement, 'I owe nothing to society, I turn my back on society. As a *travesti*, I feel much better, although society wanted me to be gay, as a man. I am brave enough to assume my identity as a *travesti*, to rebel and face society in a skirt … Today as a *travesti*, I walk out onto the street and I feel them [men] looking at me, desiring me when I step close.'

Femininity/Masculinity or When Sexuality Meets Gender

Beauty, as an element that confers power and prestige, is displayed and highly valorised through sex work. Chapter 6 examined the importance of prostitution in *travestis'* narratives as the main economic activity most of them are *allowed* to work within, but sex work is also a space for the construction and learning of femininity and for the reaffirmation of their bodily transformations. Although sex work is also the territory that *travestis* identify most with violence and death, it remains their main professional option and a source of income to invest in their bodies. In this way, beauty and sex work are closely related and constitute *travestis'* gendered experiences. In Chap. 5, we have added the analysis of how *travestis* interact socially and sexually with their clients and *maridos* to understand how gender and sexuality are closely related to give sense to *travestis'* experiences.

The 'active'/'passive' hierarchical model of sexuality is one of the ways to organise, mainly among working-class Brazilians, the notions of masculinity and femininity that structure their sexual interactions. For *travestis*, 'real' men should only penetrate; and those who assume the 'feminine' role, should be penetrated. Thus, the different forms in which the body is used in the sexual encounters are what gives meaning to the ways *travestis*, clients, and *maridos* engage sexually and are located along the binary oppositions macho/fag, strong/weak, or virile/effeminate.

Most of the *travestis* said that it is when they adopt the 'female' role in their sexual intercourses that they are satisfied and can construct and express their femininity. Particularly, the masculine characteristics of their *maridos* are usually enhanced to counteract their own fantasies linked to femininity. However, they also affirmed that they loved penetrating their clients and had much pleasure with it. In other words, although *travestis* move permanently through the limits of masculinity and femininity, they employ a rigid, binary, and hegemonic conception of what is perceived as 'masculine' and 'feminine' while organising their erotic and social interactions. In this ways, *travestis'* gendered and sexual experiences 'discourage' more radical queer assumptions based on trans identities as a symbol of transgression, as discussed in Chap. 2. Although some trans people destabilise more radically the male/female and the hetero/homo binaries, some other experiences—including those of the *travestis'*—cannot be made invisible under the more extreme constructionism of queer theory.

This book has contributed to a critical approach to queer theory and politics when understanding *travesti* sex workers' lived experiences. They can follow normative gender conceptions of what is to be a 'woman' and a 'man,' which provide meaning to their bodies and sexual practices: when feeling desired *as* women, *travestis* are reinforcing their own femininity. However, the fact of not denying (and also enjoying) acting *as* men destabilises—though, generally unintentionally—the formation of a 'coherent' and finalist (trans) identity. It is this chameleon-like ability which makes them 'different' and 'fascinating': they are capable of performing the gender assigned to men and women, without *being* men or women. Reyna, for example, explained that she was not a woman, but a *travesti*, because 'I do not belong to any sex or I'm all at the same time, isn't it? … I know I am a human being and I am Reyna, and it depends on the client's point of view or the one who looks at me, I can be a man or a woman, or I can be both' (personal interview, 6 May 2008, Rio de Janeiro). It is in the intersection of gender and sexuality that *travestis* will transit simultaneously along the margins of femininity and masculinity. Although *travestis'* embodiment journeys cannot be labelled exclusively as 'transgression' or 'submission,' they definitely mobilise and interpellate the structures on which the learnt notions on sex, gender, and sexuality lie.

Travestis' Mobilities

Finally, together with gender and sexuality, *Brazilian Travesti Migrations* has employed space as the third element to understand *travestis'* identity formations. In Chap. 7, we accompanied some of the transits the participants experienced to become and live as *travesti* sex workers. This research proposed that when the *travestis* inhabit new geographical territories, they are simultaneously *producing* themselves as *travestis*. Rio de Janeiro and Barcelona were considered two scales, among others, through which *travestis* moved in order to have better economic chances, as they were inserted within the circuits of sex work, but also to have the opportunity to modify their bodies and find a safer place, to feel more respected, and live their gender identities with greater freedom.

As Brazilian big cities were perceived by the participants as much safer to become *travestis* in than their places of origin, Rio de Janeiro was one of the main 'schools' of most of them who were engaged in prostitution, and was the place that offered them more aesthetic, work, and living possibilities. We have also examined some of the territories of sex work in Rio de Janeiro and Barcelona to consider *travestis'* ways of understanding space. These territories were not neutral and were subjected to police persecution and public regulations that limit and criminalise street prostitution, as its visibility is seen as a civic 'problem.' Sex workers are then displaced from public space, leaving them exposed to more vulnerability and reducing their chances to work in the streets, the space par excellence of *travesti* prostitution. Nevertheless, mainly in Barcelona, *travestis*—as sex workers and immigrants 'without papers'—find different strategies to stand out and have 'success' in their transnational mobilisations. Europe, originally Paris, was and is of great importance according to the *travestis'* narratives of all the generations, as it was there where they felt for the first time admired, more respected, and beautiful. Europe is a synonym of prestige and a 'dream,' and those 'Europeans' who live there and obtain the material, social, and symbolic goods necessary to feel like 'successful' *travestis*, are admired within the group. *Travestis'* mobilities are then one of their main strategies used to have better chances in the Spanish and European sex market once they employ the modality of work in flats and promote themselves through the Internet. They also perform their 'Brazilianness' to take advantage of the hypersexualised construction of their racialised nationality and benefit from their 'uniqueness' in transnational settings, where they are highly valued. According to Martine, one of the participants, 'even there are some [*travestis*] who speak Spanish and they advertise themselves on the website as Brazilian people to make more money. And there are Portuguese who say they are Brazilians' (personal interview, 5 August 2008, Rio de Janeiro). Although trans people face discrimination in Spain, within the local sex market, presenting oneself as Brazilian is a positive feature that materialises one of the many paradoxes which shape *travestis'* experiences: they have an economic value as sex workers but are simultaneously rejected as abject 'others' in the wider society.

In other words, trans (*travesti*) migrations can be thought of as acts of survival (Doan 2016) which show us *travestis'* agency as sexualised and gendered subjects to change and improve their lives. In crossing the spatial borders (within and outside Brazil) to find more advantageous economic scenarios to work in as sex workers, *travestis* also become legible subjects, as most of them modify and feminise their bodies to become and feel like beautiful *travestis* and, thus, more empowered to face—paradoxically—the structural and institutionalised violence of living *as travestis*. In this way, while surviving through their engagement with different practices such as those of beautification and mobilisation, *travestis* have the greatest revenge against a heteronormative society which proclaims that their 'non-domesticised' bodies, as *travesti* sex workers, *must* be left to die.

This was an embodied ethnography in which the body becomes central to understanding *travestis'* identity formations. *Travestis'* negotiations of gender and sexuality through their (trans)national displacements were grounded in their bodies. In this way, I questioned queer's tendency towards the disembodiment of identities (Salamon 2010) to focus on the materiality of the bodies as a springboard to examine the social practices and discourses which constitute Brazilian *travestis'* embodied and spatial experiences. Therefore, the bodies that suffer, enjoy, are transformed, injured, or bleed were appreciated to explore the *doing* of *travestis'* daily routines—not only regarding beauty—but also in their social and sexual interactions. In addition, acknowledging that in the process of 'becoming' *travestis* are both destabilising existing power relations and reinforcing them, my aim was to avoid the risk of assuming queerness as the 'norm' from where *all* trans experiences are read as inherently 'transgressive.' Also, in an attempt to evade the 'global metropole' hegemony on trans knowledge (Connell 2012; Noble 2011), I presented Latin American and Spanish research as an alternative to decentre trans experiences coming, mainly, from an English-speaking, white, and middle-class milieu. My goal was to contribute to creating bridges of knowledge between Portuguese/Spanish and Anglo-Saxon discussions on these issues and, more importantly, provide (another) space from which the participants' experiences can be acknowledged to avoid prejudice and discrimination. Coming back to Dandara and Valentina, and although their differences abound, they embodied the paradoxes of a (Brazilian) society that intertwines desire, beauty, and money, but also violence, criminalisation, and death. It may be utopian, but I wish a day in which no new Dandaras or Valentinas appear on the news and that books like this one do not have to be written. We are all human beings and must simply be treated as such.

Note

1. In Brazil, the word '*travesti*' is used with a masculine pronoun. Only trans activists, scholars, and people with less prejudices and more respectful towards *travestis*' female presentations and social names will use the feminine pronoun. Some *travestis* also keep the masculine form.

References

Aizura, Aren. 2014. Trans Feminine Value, Racialized Others and the Limits of Necropolitics. In *Queer Necropolitics*, ed. Jin Haritaworn, Adi Kuntsman, and Silvia Posocco, 129–147. Abingdon/New York: Routledge.

Carrier-Moisan, Marie-Eve. 2015. 'Putting Femininity to Work': Negotiating Hypersexuality and Respectability in Sex Tourism, Brazil. *Sexualities* 18 (4): 499–518.

Colebrook, Claire. 2006. Introduction. *Feminist Theory* 7 (2): 131–142.

Connell, Raewyn. 2012. Transsexual Women and Feminist Thought: Toward New Understandings and New Politics. *Signs: Journal of Women in Culture and Society* 37 (4): 857–881.

Doan, Petra. 2016. You've Come a Long Way, Baby: Unpacking the Metaphor of Transgender Mobility. In *The Routledge Research Companion to Geographies of Sex and Sexualities*, ed. Gavin Brown and Kath Browne, 237–246. Abingdon/New York: Routledge.

Edelman, Elijah A. 2014. 'Walking While Transgender.' Necropolitical Regulations of Trans Feminine Bodies of Colour in the Nation's Capital. In *Queer Necropolitics*, ed. Jin Haritaworn, Adi Kuntsman, and Silvia Posocco, 172–190. Abingdon/New York: Routledge.

Figari, Carlos. 2009. *Eróticas de la disidencia en América Latina: Brasil, siglos XVII al XX*. Buenos Aires: Fundación Centro de Integración, Comunicación, Cultura y Sociedad – CICCUS and CLACSO.

Figueroa, Mónica Moreno. 2013. Displaced Looks: The Lived Experience of Beauty and Racism. *Feminist Theory* 14 (2): 137–151.

GGB, Gay Group of Bahia. 2016. *Relatório: Assassinatos de LGBT no Brasil*. https://homofobiamata.files.wordpress.com/2017/01/relatc3b3rio-2016-ps.pdf. Accessed 25 July 2017.

Haritaworn, Jin, Adi Kuntsman, and Silvia Posocco. 2014. Introduction. In *Queer Necropolitics*, ed. Jin Haritaworn, Adi Kuntsman, and Silvia Posocco, 1–27. Abingdon/New York: Routledge.

Jarrín, Alvaro. 2017. *The Biopolitics of Beauty: Cosmetic Citizenship and Affective Capital in Brazil*. Oakland: University of California Press.

Jorge, Thaís. 2017. Arte e violência: travesti Dandara dos Santos é tema de trabalho em Universidade de Londres. *Globo Notícias*. http://g1.globo.com/ceara/noticia/arte-e-violencia-travesti-dandara-dos-santos-e-tema-de-trabalho-em-universidade-de-londres.ghtml. Accessed 28 Aug 2017.

Kulick, Don. 1998. *Travesti: Sex, Gender and Culture among Brazilian Transgendered Prostitutes*. Chicago: University of Chicago Press.

Lavor, Thays. 2017. 'Meu filho vivia sendo humilhado': caso Dandara expõe tragédia de viver e morrer travesti no Brasil. *BBC*. http://www.bbc.com/portuguese/brasil-39227148. Accessed 28 Aug 2017.

Lewis, Vek. 2012. Volviendo visible lo invisible: hacia un marco conceptual de las migraciones internas trans en México. *Cuicuilco* 54: 219–240.

Lucon, Neto. 2016. 'Nenhuma cirurgia vai me fazer mais ou menos mulher,' diz a modelo trans Valentina Sampaio. *Nlucon*. http://www.nlucon.com/2016/11/nenhuma-cirurgia-vai-me-fazer-mais-ou.html. Accessed 28 Aug 2017.

Noble, Bobby. 2011. 'My Own Set of Keys': Mediations on Transgender, Scholarship, Belonging. *Feminist Studies* 37 (2): 254–269.

Ochoa, Marcia. 2014. *Queen for a Day: Transformistas, Beauty Queens, and the Performance of Femininity in Venezuela*. Durham/London: Duke University Press.

Phillips, Dom. 2017. Torture and Killing of Transgender Woman Stun Brazil. *New York Times*, March 8. https://www.nytimes.com/2017/03/08/world/americas/brazil-transgender-killing-video.html?_r=0. Accessed 1 June 2017.

Piscitelli, Adriana. 2011. ¿Actuar la brasileñidad? Tránsitos a partir del mercado del sexo. *Etnográfica* 15 (1): 5–29.

Puar, Jasbir. 2007. *Terrorist Assemblages: Homonationalism in Queer Times*. Durham: Duke University Press.

Salamon, Gayle. 2010. *Assuming a Body. Transgender and Rhetorics of Materiality*. New York: Columbia University Press.

Silva, Joseli M., and Marcio J. Ornat. 2016. Sexualities, Tropicalizations and the Transnational Sex Trade: Brazilian Women in Spain. In *The Routledge Research Companion to Geographies of Sex and Sexualities*, ed. Gavin Brown and Kath Browne, 331–340. Abingdon/New York: Routledge.

TGEU, Transgender Europe. 2017. Trans Day of Remembrance (TDoR) 2017. Trans Murder Monitoring (TMM) Research Project Update. *Transrespect versus Transphobia Worldwide*, November 20. http://transrespect.org/en/tmm-update-trans-day-remembrance-2017/. Accessed 2 Jan 2018.

Thomas, Dana. 2017. French Vogue's March Cover Features a Transgender Model. *The New York Times*. https://www.nytimes.com/2017/03/01/fashion/paris-fashion-week-french-vogue-transgender-model.html. Accessed 28 Aug 2017.

Glossary

Bicha fag, fairy.

Bombadeira person who injects liquid silicone into *travestis'* bodies.

Caricata a clown and a ridiculous person.

Carioca adjective form of Rio de Janeiro.

Casarão an old house in the neighbourhood of Lapa where most of the *travesti* sex workers I met in Rio de Janeiro lived.

Comer to penetrate.

Dar to be penetrated.

Dar close to exhibit oneself while snubbing other *travestis*.

Gayzinho young and effeminate gay.

Homen client or *marido* of a *travesti* who embodies socially and sexually the roles attributed to men.

Madrinha/afilhada literally, godmother/goddaughter; this is a way of structuring *travestis'* social, symbolic, and economic relationships.

Mãe/filha literally, mother/daughter; this is a way of structuring *travestis'* social, symbolic, and economic relationships. Sometimes, a *mãe* is more powerful than a *madrinha*.

Maricona an emic term that refers to a client who is considered a 'fagot,' that is, is interested in being penetrated.

Maridos an emic category that names *travestis'* partners, regardless of the duration of the relationship or the existence of any formal link.

© The Author(s) 2018
J. Vartabedian, *Brazilian* Travesti *Migrations*, Genders and Sexualities
in the Social Sciences, https://doi.org/10.1007/978-3-319-77101-4

240 Glossary

Mestiçagem racial miscegenation.

Michês male sex workers.

Montagem *travestis'* 'production,' that is, when they begin to make-up and to dress-up with women's clothes only occasionally for some leisurely events.

Morena or mulata mixed race woman.

Praça vacancy for prostitution in closed spaces (flats or clubs).

Programa commercial sexual transaction.

Pumped up to be injected with industrial and liquid silicone.

Transformista female impersonator who is on stage. He is usually a self-identified gay man.

Truque an emic category that refers to the techniques employed by the group to deceive something in order to improve their appearance.

Viado fag.

Index[1]

A
Abject', being, 7, 15, 50, 72, 98, 155, 226, 228, 234
Àmbit Dona, 1, 205

B
Barbosa, Luana, 51
Barcelona, 2, 8–10, 12, 194, 202–204
  Camp Nou, 11, 198, 205–207, 210, 213
  Ciutat Vella, 207, 208
  Les Corts, 205
  prostitution venues, 11, 16, 204, 205, 210
  Sant Martí, 209, 210
Beauty, 73, 101, 102, 104, 229, 230
  and ageing, 151, 152
  and agency/empowerment, 69, 70, 101–103, 182, 195, 229
  and agency/structure, 70
  and body fascism, 71
  doing, 70, 83, 228
  feeling, 7, 15, 70, 83, 103, 228
  and glamour, 74, 202
  and health, 97–101
  and male gaze, 68, 103, 230
  and modernity, 71, 72
  and morality, 102
  natural/artificial, 73–74, 88, 96
  and oppression, 68, 69
  and race, 78, 79
  right to, 93, 227
  and trans, 14, 71
  trans beauty pageants, 71, 72, 105n12
  and whiteness, 75, 78, 214

---

[1] Note: Page numbers followed by 'n' refer to notes.

© The Author(s) 2018
J. Vartabedian, *Brazilian* Travesti *Migrations*, Genders and Sexualities in the Social Sciences, https://doi.org/10.1007/978-3-319-77101-4

242 Index

Bicha, 87, 103, 118–120, 126, 131, 132, 149, 156n5, 177, 180
Body
  and the material, 36, 38, 234
  natural, 82, 97
  and space, 163
Bombadeira, 89, 90, 92, 144, 180
Boneca, 96, 105n12
Brazil, 2, 5, 6, 8
  and beauty industry, 80
  and Black Movement, 80
  and cosmetic surgery, 15, 78, 92, 93, 227
  mulata, 77–79, 81, 153, 227
  North/Northeast regions, 12, 50, 175, 178, 180, 225, 226
  and political collectives, 5
  and race, 15, 76, 77, 80
  and racial democracy, 77–79
  and social mobility, 67, 81–83
  trans murders, 50, 175, 225, 227
Brazilian military dictatorship, 5, 12, 46, 47, 176, 194
Brazilianness, 15, 153–155, 206, 214, 215, 234
Breast implants, 58, 84, 91, 92, 94, 105n11, 152, 191, 202
Bündchen, Gisele, 75, 78, 227
Butler, Judith, 27, 28, 30, 37, 115, 140
Buttocks, 53, 79, 90, 91, 94, 150, 152, 188, 214

C

Caricata, 178
Carioca, 10, 12, 184
Carnival, 5, 45–47, 78, 227

Casarão, 9, 56, 57, 59, 60, 75, 99, 105n14, 128, 129, 143, 144, 148, 167, 175, 177, 178, 182, 184
Chez Madame Arthur, 194, 195
Civic Ordinance (Barcelona), 204
Close, Roberta, 49
Cosmetic surgery, 15, 53, 92–94, 150, 181, 185, 200, 201

D

Depression, 100, 101
Dos Santos, Dandara, 50, 225, 226, 235
Drugs, 47, 97, 101, 102, 124, 142, 200

E

Eloína, 195
Erection, 87, 88, 149, 191, 214
Ethnocentrism, 28
  See also Global metropole
Ethnography
  embodied, 7, 36, 234
  multi-sited, 1, 8
Europe (meaning of), 193–198, 200, 202, 215, 233
European, 200, 202, 211, 215, 233
Exuberant, bodies, 150, 151

F

Fag, 50, 87, 118, 124–127, 130, 230
Femininity
  and body modification, 53, 73, 83–85

and embodiment, 1, 2, 73, 83, 104, 192
and masculinity, 34, 122, 132, 232
and performing, 2, 35, 178

G

Gayzinhos, 53, 54, 60, 84, 176, 177
Gender
  identity disorder, 98, 100
  and performativity, 7, 27
  and sexuality, 15, 114, 115, 232
  and space, 164–166
Global metropole, 6, 32, 235
Globalisation, 139, 164, 170

H

Hair, 53, 74, 76, 77, 79, 86, 95, 96
Hairdressing, 12, 142, 144
Halberstam, Jack, 169, 173, 174
Help, 56, 124, 125, 199
Heteronormativity, 2, 127, 132, 143, 146, 165, 166, 175, 227
Heterosexualisation of desire, 119, 120, 132
Hijras, 24, 25
Hines, Sally, 29, 38, 168
HIV/AIDS, 4, 5, 47, 48, 100, 101
Home, metaphor of, 15, 168, 169
Homen, 118, 123, 126
Hormones, 58, 86–88, 123, 149, 185, 188, 191, 194, 195, 201
  tits, 58
Hypersexualisation, 141, 153, 155, 214

K

Kathoeys, 24, 25, 71, 72
Kulick, Don, 25, 120, 127, 129, 131, 228

L

Laqueur, Thomas, 26, 27
Latin America, 1, 3, 16n1, 235
Le Carrousel, 49, 142, 147, 194, 195
Lea, T., 49, 227
Legibility, 103, 173, 230
Leitī, 72
Lesbians, 50, 51
Lesbophobia, 51
Loneliness, 152, 200

M

Mães and madrinhas, 12, 17n10, 54–56, 123, 144, 167, 178, 199, 200
Male/female, 7, 14, 25, 26, 28, 29, 34, 35, 38, 91, 232
Maricona, 123, 124, 126, 132
Masculinity, hegemonic, 50, 51, 123, 127
Materiality, 37, 38
Mestiçagem/miscegenation, 76–80
Metronormativity, 174
Michês, 126
Misogyny, 51
Money, 11, 54–56, 58, 92, 95, 96, 99, 102, 121, 122, 124, 126–130, 139, 141, 142, 149, 150, 155, 171, 172, 176–178, 193, 195, 199, 229, 234, 235
Monroe, Marilyn, 75

244 Index

Montagem, 53, 84
Muxes, 24, 25

N

Nadles, 23, 25
Natalia, 58, 59, 177, 190
Necropolitics, see Queer
  necropolitics
Normative spaces, 15, 165, 166
Nose, 71, 79, 84, 94, 96, 181, 185

P

Pain, 31, 60, 83, 88, 91, 104, 122, 230
Paris, 5, 194–198, 201, 202
Passing, 30, 50, 51, 71, 87, 166, 175
Pelúcio, Larissa, 35, 53, 76, 97, 122,
  125, 131, 133n2
Perlongher, Néstor, 126, 134n6, 174
Photography, 13, 59–62
Pitanguy, Ivo, 93, 227
Positionality, 9
  and privileges, 13, 57
Post-coloniality, 169
Program to combat child sexual
  exploitation, 10, 182
Projeto Damas, 9, 10
Prosser, Jay, 168
Prostitution, *see* Sex work
Pumping', of silicone, 85, 88–92, 97,
  105n9, 150, 180, 181, 185, 201
  history of, 89, 197

Q

Queer diaspora, 164, 171
Queer migrations, 15, 170, 171

Queer necropolitics, 15, 140, 143, 226
Queer theory, 6, 14, 22, 28, 29, 38
  and radical deconstruction, 7, 29,
    30, 39, 232
  critiques to, 29, 31, 32, 232

R

Real men, 50, 119, 122, 124,
  129–131, 198, 231
Researcher's body, 8, 36, 57–59
Reyna, 12, 54–56, 75, 176, 178, 189
Rhinoplasty, 80, 90, 105n13, 202
Rio de Janeiro, 8, 9, 12, 175, 176,
  179, 184
  Associação de Travestis e
    Liberados, 48
  Barra da Tijuca, 133n4, 183,
    191–193, 216n6
  Copacabana, 183, 189, 190, 192,
    193, 216n6
  Glória, 183, 186, 190, 216n4
  Lapa, 9, 12, 55, 99, 144, 167,
    178, 181, 184, 186, 189, 190,
    193 (*see also Casarão*)
  prostitution venues, 10, 16, 182,
    183, 192
  São Cristóvão, 183, 186, 187
  school, 54, 181, 182, 233
Rogéria, 49
Rubin, Gayle, 28, 115

S

Safety, city, 15, 175, 180, 233
Sampaio, Valentina, 226, 235
Sanitary citizenship, 98
Scandal, 133n4

Sedgwick, Eve, 28, 115
Sex industry, 139, 145, 150, 153, 154, 156n2
Sex reassignment surgery, 3, 5, 35, 97
Sex work, 2, 15, 16n1, 47, 140–142, 144, 146, 147, 155, 231
  and body modification, 15, 149–150, 152, 231
  and death, 148, 155, 231
  and femininity, 15, 146, 231
  and flats, 211–214
  and immigration, 11, 139, 172, 203, 210, 212
  and pleasure, 148
  and race, 153, 214, 215
  and streets, 167, 205, 210, 215
  and the Internet, 213
  in Brazil, 183
  in Spain, 202, 203
Sex/gender, 14, 21–23, 27, 31, 32, 34, 38
Sexual migrations, 15, 170, 171
Sexualities
  active/passive, 15, 116–120, 126, 131, 231
  masculinity and femininity, 15, 116–118, 120, 129
Shame, 131
Spain, 2, 4
  and travestí, 4
  and political collectives, 4
  and trans, 4, 211
Stigma, 6, 16n1, 51, 142, 144, 146, 147, 152, 171, 172, 211
Stop SIDA, 11, 207, 209, 210
Survival, strategy of, 8, 16, 171, 215, 230, 234
Survivors, 48, 142, 151

Teixeira, Flávia, 124, 125
Third gender, 22–26
T-lovers, 122
Towle, Evan, and Lynn Morgan, 24, 25
Trans
  category, 6
  men, 50, 51
  migrations, 8, 15, 171–173, 215, 234
  and transgression, 7, 14, 28, 35, 235
  subculture, 13
Transformistas, 5, 12, 47, 147, 194, 201
Transformistas (Venezuela), 72, 172, 228
Transgender, 2, 4, 6, 33
Transgression/submission, 31, 32, 36, 230, 232
Transnational migrations/displacements, 12, 14, 163, 164, 173, 193, 196, 199, 234
Transphobia, 34, 50, 51, 142, 156, 175, 227, 231
Transsexual/transsexuality, 3, 4, 6, 12
  and depathologisation, 4
Transvestite, 2, 3
  and cross-dressing, 2, 27, 30
  drag, subversion, 30
Transvestites' Balls, 46
Travestis, 73
  and beauty (*see* Beauty)
  becoming, 14, 15, 52, 84, 104, 169, 229, 234
  bodily resistance, 48, 188
  category, 3, 6, 47

246   **Index**

Travestis (cont.)
  and clients, 15, 121–126, 132,
    152, 184–186, 188, 189, 192,
    193, 207, 212, 213, 231
  and displacement/mobility, 7, 15,
    53, 163, 169, 171, 173, 180,
    199, 212, 215, 233
  and embodiment, 7, 8, 14, 15, 32,
    39, 181, 185, 188, 191, 200, 202
  and empowerment, 7, 33, 103,
    128, 132, 155, 196, 234
  and failure, 95, 200, 215
  first generation of, 12, 141–143,
    175, 193
  hated/loved, 52, 148, 228
  and heteronormativity, 35, 36
  and heterosexuality, 14, 119
  hierarchy, 12, 14, 54, 55
  and humanity denied, 7, 14, 50,
    140, 143, 198, 228, 230
  and intelligibility, 7, 8, 14, 15,
    182, 202, 215, 230
  and *maridos*, 15, 127–132, 148, 231
  and public space, 166, 167, 215

  successful, 74, 95, 96, 102,
    181, 193, 198, 200, 213,
    215, 229, 233
Tropicalisation, 153, 227
Two-sex model, 26, 27
Two-spirits, 24, 25

U

Ugliness, 35, 60, 77, 79, 93,
    96, 97, 103, 149, 182,
    188, 193

V

Violence, 5, 29, 34, 45, 46, 48, 50,
    51, 55, 60, 89, 127, 140, 143,
    148, 155, 166, 167, 171, 173,
    175–177, 197, 207, 215, 228,
    231, 234, 235

X

Xaniths, 24, 25

CPSIA information can be obtained
at www.ICGtesting.com
Printed in the USA
LVHW07*1705290518
578630LV00003B/2/P